COUNTRY HERITAGE SERIES

Birds

of the British Countryside

W.J. Gordon

ILLUSTRATED BY

G. Willis
and R.E. Holding

OMEGA BOOKS

Plate XXXIII. 384-398

INTRODUCTION.

———◦◇◦———

THE object of this book is to enable anyone to recognise and readily distinguish the birds on the British list; and this it does by a system of elimination somewhat similar to that adopted in " Our Country's Flowers."

To the beginner it is assuredly of the first importance that he should know the name of the thing with which he is dealing. Until he knows that, he is unable to ascertain what is already known about it, for the existing books invariably assume that he possesses this preliminary knowledge. And when he knows more of his subject a handy method of separating family from family, genus from genus, and species from species, by a few prominent characteristics, must have its advantages, if only in the saving of labour and time.

Although our book necessarily touches on the general subject, its examples are strictly limited to our country's avifauna, concerning which an awkward question presents itself, which may fitly be answered in this introduction.

What is a British bird? Strictly speaking, there is but one British bird, and that is the one the state of whose health is invariably chronicled in the newspapers on or about the 12th of August. The Red Grouse is the only bird peculiar to this island, and found native nowhere else. The rest of the birds we see around us are mostly characteristic of the whole Palæarctic region, stretching right away to Japan, while some go as far south as the Victoria Nyanza, and further to the Transvaal, and others even breed as far to the north as Grinnell Land, within eight degrees of the Pole.

Of this miscellaneous troop of residents and visitors, regular and irregular, there are nearly four hundred; but among the visitors are a large sprinkling of "casuals," included on very doubtful pretences. Englishmen are often accused of a desire to paint the world red; the average British ornithologist would apparently like to paint all the birds red, provided his name appeared on the label. Really one shudders at the audacity with which the Flamingo, for instance, is claimed as British, although there is an excuse for so claiming him; but when we find Bulwer's Petrel duly naturalised on the strength of a solitary specimen found floating dead in a Yorkshire river, we feel that we are quite near enough to the unreasonable.

There are at least a hundred and fifty species gathered under the home flag, owing to their having been killed in this country in much the same way as if we were to shoot the Chinese Ambassador and claim him as British because he died on British ground. But would he have come in a "wild" state? Perhaps not; but neither did all the birds that figure in the British list.

It is very difficult to draw the line; though, at first sight, the only true ground of admission would seem to be a birth qualification. If a bird can be shown to breed here, out of captivity, some at least of his kind can be assumed to be of British nationality. If, however, we were to adopt this qualification, we should only have the birds whose names appear in the outer margin in our third chapter, and many of our familiar friends would be lost to us. But we need hardly trouble ourselves further in this matter, although we could not well pass it unnoticed. This is a book of identification, not of classification; and it is obvious that our only course is to adopt the full authorised list, and show how the species can be distinguished from each other; and when we have done that, we can remark on the fewness of appearances which has enabled so many of the rarer birds to lengthen and complicate our task.

In our first chapter are the names, both popular and technical, which have been used throughout; in the second is a long list of the common and rarer local names, with references to the numbers under which the birds are described, although, to save mere repetition, these names may not again be mentioned. In the next chapter is the systematic list, so that with the first part of the book, and the plates, a bird whose name is known can be at once identified. The plates contain a figure in colour of a male in full plumage of every species in the three lists, and in a few instances the female is also given. In the fourth chapter the families are sorted out so as to leave the Passerine birds for special treatment; and in the fifth the key to this sorting is given in the table to which the specimen it is desired to name should be referred. The sixth and seventh chapters are on a similar principle: in the one the Passerines are sorted out, and examples given of identification, and in the other the key to this arrangement is given in tabular form. In the eighth chapter the families are grouped into the orders, old and new, although the orders are not necessary in our plan of identification. In the ninth chapter the families are arranged alphabetically, and with this index the specimen should be compared to confirm the diagnosis obtained from the previous keys. When the family is known, reference should be made to the next chapter in which is the analysis into genera; and when the genus is known, the index of species should be consulted in which the genera are in turn analysed, and brief notes given as to plumage, flight, song, and nest. In the twelfth chapter the dimensions of each bird are worked out so as to help in its identification by measurement; and in the last chapter is a tabular arrangement for the identification of the eggs. In short, we have endeavoured to get at the bird's identification in many ways, and have relied on combination for success.

W. J. G.

CONTENTS.

DIAGRAMS.

CHAPTER I.

THE NAMES OF THE BIRDS,

————◆◇◆————

HEREUNDER are the names which our country's birds bear in this book. They have many other names, both popular and technical, and some of them have even shared several of these names amongst them ; in fact, the synonymy of ornithology is so peculiarly rich and bewildering, that the only way of avoiding confusion would seem to be this, of beginning with definitions in the manner of Euclid, that there may be no mistake as to what we are talking about.

The numbers refer to the coloured plates, and are the numbers used throughout.

Alpine Accentor, 46
Accentor collaris.
Auk, Great, 374
Alca impennis.
Auk, Little, 378
Mergulus alle.
Avocet, 304
Recurvirostra avocetta.

Bee-eater, 154
Merops apiaster.
Bee-eater, Blue-tailed,
155
Merops philippinus.
Bittern, 210
Botaurus stellaris.
Bittern, American, 211
Botaurus lentiginosus.
Bittern, Little, 208
Ardetta minuta.
Blackbird, 9
Merula merula.
Blackcap, 26
Sylvia atricapilla.
Bluethroat, Red-spotted,
20
Cyanecula suecica.
Bluethroat, White-spot-
ted, 19
Cyanecula wolfi.

Brambling, 96
Fringilla montifringilla.
Bullfinch, 102
Pyrrhula europæa.
Bunting, Black-headed,
109
Emberiza melanocephala.
Bunting, Cirl, 112
Emberiza cirlus.
Bunting, Corn, 110
Emberiza miliaria.
Bunting, Lapland, 117
Calcarius lapponicus.
Bunting, Little, 115
Emberiza pusilla.
Bunting, Ortolan, 113
Emberiza hortulana.
Bunting, Reed, 116
Emberiza schœniclus.
Bunting, Rustic, 114
Emberiza rustica.
Bunting, Snow, 118
Plectrophanes nivalis.
Bunting, Yellow, 111
Emberiza citrinella.
Bustard, Great, 287
Otis tarda.
Bustard, Little, 288
Otis tetrax.

Bustard, Macqueen's, 289
Otis macqueeni.
Buzzard, 176
Buteo vulgaris.
Buzzard, Honey, 188
Pernis apivorus.
Buzzard, Rough-legged,
177
Archibuteo lagopus.

Canary, Wild, 90
Serinus canarius.
Capercaillie, 269
Tetrao urogallus.
Chaffinch, 95
Fringilla cælebs.
Chiffchaff, 33
Phylloscopus rufus.
Chough, 122
Pyrrhocorax graculus.
Chough, Alpine, 123
Pyrrhocorax alpinus.
Coot, 284
Fulica atra.
Cormorant, 199
Phalacrocorax carbo.
Courser, Cream-coloured,
292
Cursorius gallicus.

CHAPTER II.

LOCAL AND POPULAR NAMES.

————◆◇————

THE references in this list are not to the pages, but to the figures on the coloured plates. It will be seen that many of the names given in the preceding chapter are unfortunately borne locally by very different species, and more instances of this might have been included, as well as more names; but the list as it is seemed to contain all that was note-worthy, and to be quite lengthy enough.

CHAPTER III.

THE COLOURED PLATES.

———◆◇◆———

THE following is a complete list of the birds figured in our coloured plates. The species are arranged in ornithological order, so as to show the system of grouping adopted as being most convenient for the purposes of identification. The names of those birds not yet on record as breeding in this country appear with a wider margin than the rest. The dimensions of all will be found given in tabular form in the twelfth chapter; the eggs are tabulated in the thirteenth chapter.

PASSERIDÆ.

Turdinæ.

Plate I.

1. TURDUS VISCIVORUS—Missel Thrush.
   Dimensions, Jj; *Eggs,* Hj.
2. TURDUS MUSICUS—Song Thrush.
   Dimensions, Hi; *Eggs,* Gg.
3. TURDUS ILIACUS—Redwing.
   Dimensions, Gq; *Eggs,* Fj.
4. TURDUS PILARIS—Fieldfare.
   Dimensions, Jc; *Eggs,* Hn.
5. TURDUS MIGRATORIUS—American Robin.
   Dimensions, Io.
6. TURDUS ATRIGULARIS—Black-throated Thrush.
   Dimensions, Jl; *Eggs,* Gs.
7. GEOCICHLA VARIA—White's Thrush.
   Dimensions, Kk; *Eggs,* Hb.
8. GEOCICHLA SIBIRICA—Siberian Thrush.
   Dimensions, Hq.
9. MERULA MERULA—Blackbird.
   Dimensions, Im; *Eggs,* Gl.
10. MERULA TORQUATA—Ring Ouzel.
    Dimensions, Jk; *Eggs,* Gt.
11. MONTICOLA SAXATILIS—Rock Thrush.
    Dimensions, Gs; *Eggs,* Ga.

Plate II.

12. SAXICOLA ŒNANTHE—Wheatear.
    Dimensions, Ef; *Eggs,* Dk.
13. SAXICOLA STAPAZINA—Black-throated Wheatear.
    Dimensions, Cj; *Eggs,* Dl.
14. SAXICOLA DESERTI—Desert Wheatear.
    Dimensions, Dl; *Eggs,* Br.
15. PRATINCOLA RUBETRA—Whinchat.
    Dimensions, Bb; *Eggs,* Bq.
16. PRATINCOLA RUBICOLA—Stonechat.
    Dimensions, Bi; *Eggs,* Ch.
17. RUTICILLA PHŒNICURUS—Redstart.
    Dimensions, Cg; *Eggs,* Bs.
18. RUTICILLA TITYS—Black Redstart.
    Dimensions, Cs; *Eggs,* Di.

PLATE IV.—*continued*.

Parinæ.

50. ACREDULA CAUDATA—White-headed Long-tailed Tit.
     Dimensions, Bo ; *Eggs*, AF.
51. ACREDULA ROSEA—British Long-tailed Tit.
     Dimensions, Bn ; *Eggs*, AC.
52. PARUS MAJOR—Great Tit.
     Dimensions, Bm ; *Eggs*, BK.
53. PARUS ATER—Continental Coal Tit.
     Dimensions, Ae ; *Eggs*, BC.
54. PARUS BRITANNICUS—British Coal Tit.
     Dimensions, Af ; *Eggs*, BB.
55. PARUS PALUSTRIS—Marsh Tit.
     Dimensions, Aj ; *Eggs*, AJ.
56. PARUS CŒRULEUS—Blue Tit.
     Dimensions, Ai ; *Eggs*, AE.
57. PARUS CRISTATUS—Crested Tit.
     Dimensions, Ag ; *Eggs*, AQ.

Sittinæ.

58. SITTA CÆSIA—Nuthatch.
     Dimensions, Ch ; *Eggs*, Co.

Troglodytinæ.

59. TROGLODYTES PARVULUS—Wren.
     Dimensions, Ab ; *Eggs*, BI.

Motacillinæ.

Plate V.

60. MOTACILLA ALBA—White Wagtail.
     Dimensions, Fq ; *Eggs*, DH.
61. MOTACILLA LUGUBRIS—Pied Wagtail.
     Dimensions, Ga ; *Eggs*, DU.
62. MOTACILLA MELANOPE—Grey Wagtail.
     Dimensions, Gm ; *Eggs*, CF.
63. MOTACILLA FLAVA—Blue-headed Yellow Wagtail.
     Dimensions, Dj ; *Eggs*, CN.
64. MOTACILLA VIRIDIS—Grey-headed Yellow Wagtail.
     Dimensions, Dt ; *Eggs*, CI.
65. MOTACILLA RAII—Yellow Wagtail.
     Dimensions, Ei ; *Eggs*, CI.
66. ANTHUS PRATENSIS—Meadow Pipit.
     Dimensions, Da ; *Eggs*, DM.
67. ANTHUS TRIVIALIS—Tree Pipit.
     Dimensions, Dk ; *Eggs*, EB.
68. ANTHUS CAMPESTRIS—Tawny Pipit.
     Dimensions, Ff; *Eggs*, EN.
69. ANTHUS RICHARDI—Richard's Pipit.
     Dimensions, Gc ; *Eggs*, EH.
70. ANTHUS SPIPOLETTA—Water Pipit.
     Dimensions, Ek ; *Eggs*, EE.
71. ANTHUS OBSCURUS—Rock Pipit.
     Dimensions, Ee ; *Eggs*, EF.

Oriolinæ.

72. ORIOLUS GALBULA—Golden Oriole.
     Dimensions, Ib ; *Eggs*, HC.

Laniinæ.

Plate VI.

73. LANIUS EXCUBITOR—Great Grey Shrike.
     Dimensions, Ig ; *Eggs*, GH.
74. LANIUS MINOR—Lesser Grey Shrike.
     Dimensions, Hh ; *Eggs*, FM.
75. LANIUS COLLURIO—Red-backed Shrike.
     Dimensions, Gb ; *Eggs*, EO.
76. LANIUS POMERANUS—Woodchat.
     Dimensions, Fg ; *Eggs*, ET.

Ampelinæ.

77. AMPELIS GARRULUS—Waxwing.
     Dimensions, Gh ; *Eggs*, FL.

PLATE X.—*continued.*

Plate I. 1-11

Plate II 12-26.

Plate III. 27-44

Plate IV. 45-59.

Plate V 60-72

Plate VI. 73-86.

Plate VII. 87·101.

Plate VIII. 102-118.

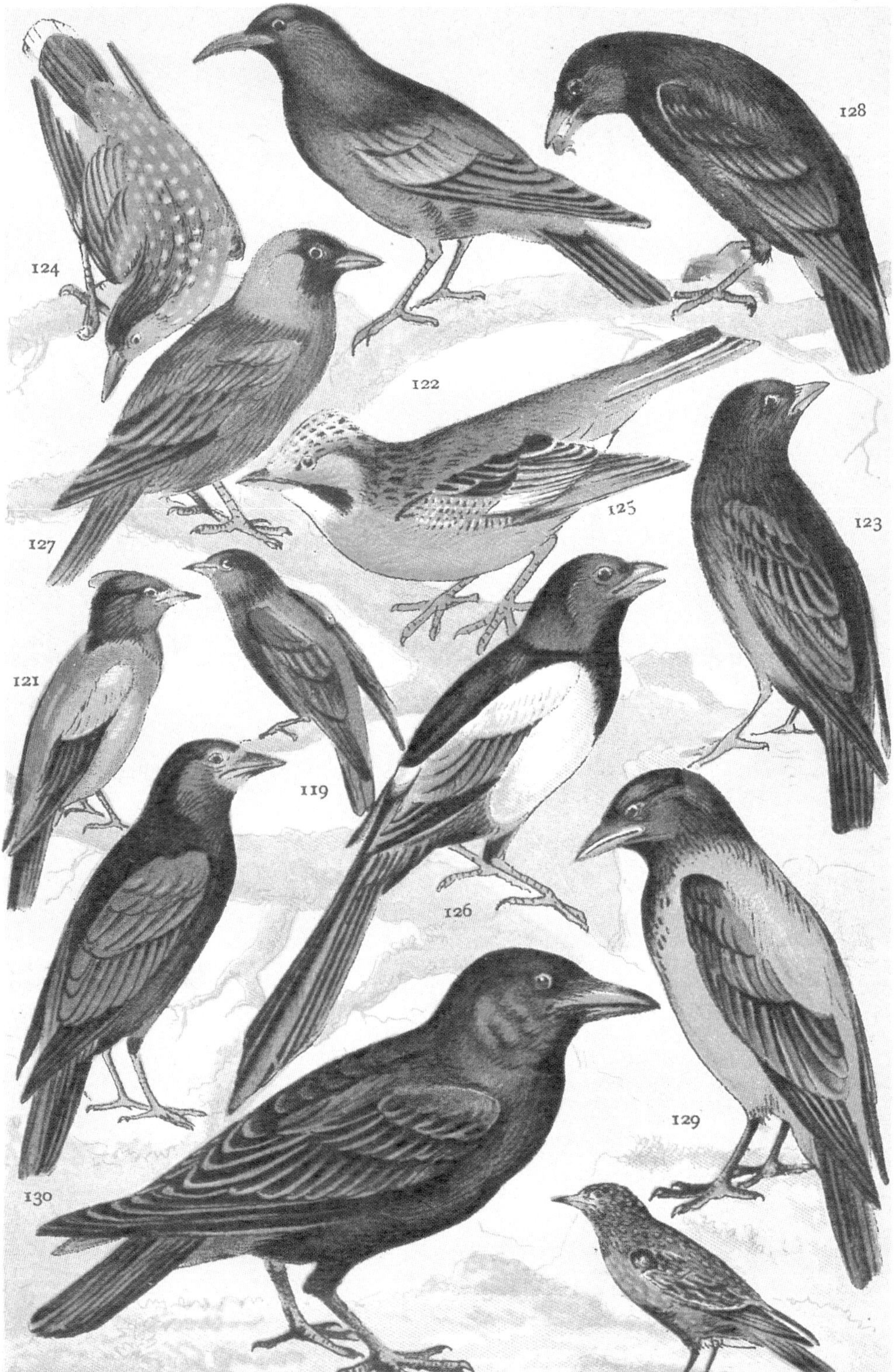
124
122
128
127
125
123
121
119
126
129
130
131
120

Plate X   132-143.

Plate XI. 144-152.

Plate XII. 153-160.

Plate XIII. 161-170.

Plate **XIV.** 171-178.

Plate XV. 179-187.

Plate XVI. 188-198.

Plate XVII. 199-207.

Plate XVIII. 208-216.

Plate XX. 227-234.

Plate XXI. 235-248

Plate XXII. 249-262.

Plate XXIII. 263-272a.

Plate XXIV. 273-284.

Plate XXV. 285-291.

Plate XXVI. 292-303.

Plate XXVII. 304-316.

Plate XXVIII. 317-328.

Plate XXIX 329-340.

335

334

333

332

329

330

337

331

336

338

339

340

Plate XXX. 341-353

Plate XXXI. 354-368.

Plate XXXII. 369-383.

26 COLOURED PLATES.

CHAPTER IV.

SORTATION.

W HAT is the name of the bird we have brought in with us from our walk ? Probably it has many names, both local and technical ; but its local name is useless to us, to begin with, for such names are not systematic, and give no clue to classification. What we have to do, then, is to identify the bird, to discover the species under which it has been described, and in that way arrive at the plain English name by which it is generally known in our district.

Now, individuals are grouped by naturalists into species, species into genera, genera into families, families into orders, and orders into a class or classes. In this case we do not know the species, but we know the class. Here is unmistakably one of the class *Aves*, or birds ; and that is all we can say about it in the present stage of our progress from the general to the particular.

The *Aves* consist of certain orders, but these it will be convenient to leave for a while. These orders are made up of families, and as there are only 35 families in the scheme we have adopted, we can at once begin to sort them out by using whatever characteristic is readiest and handiest for identification, even though it may only hold good for such of their representatives as are found in our list.

To begin with, there is one well-defined group of birds which are easily distinguishable. These are the so-called " Birds of Prey," the *Aëtomorphæ* of Huxley, the *Raptores* of the older classifi-cations. There is no mistaking the long, strong, cruel claws, and the sharp-curving bill of such birds as these ; and, for the purposes of identification, though not for classification — which is a very different thing—it will be found as simple a way as any to work on two main divisions, the first including the birds of prey, and the second all the rest. Retaining, then, the old name of Raptores, which has the advantage of being familiar, we have :—

1. Raptores.
2. Non-Raptores.

It fortunately happens that the first is represented by only three families in the British list. These are :—

1. The Owls.
2. The Vultures.
3. The Eagles, Hawks, Falcons, &c., &c.

or, to use the technical names, the *Strigidæ, Vulturidæ*, and *Falconidæ*.

In the Owls the head is large, the eyes are in front, and the face is round, although in some the "facial disk," as it is called, is not as complete as in others. Many of the Owls, too, have bristles· on the feet instead of feathers ; but surely we are safe in assuming that anyone likely to take an interest in birds will know an Owl when he sees one ; and a lengthy description of the Strigidæ would here be waste of space. The bird we are seeking to identify is certainly not an Owl.

Then, if it be a bird of prey at all, it must belong to either the Vulturidæ or the Falconidæ. The chances are very much against its being a Vulture, for the very good reason that only three Vultures have been shot on British ground within the memory of man. Vultures are but British birds by courtesy, like a good many others. It is interesting to know that our country has been visited by representatives of that singularly uninteresting family ; and that is about all that need be said. The Vultures have bald or downy crowns ; and, consequently, if your bird of prey has feathers on its crown, you may rest assured that it is not one of the Vulturidæ.

We are thus left with the Falconidæ, comprising the true Falcons who capture their prey in the air, the Hawks who capture it on or near the ground, the Harriers, Kites, and Buzzards, who capture it on the ground, and that bird by itself, the Osprey, which captures it from the water. Our bird, however, is not a bird of prey at all ; its claws and beak and the absence of the "cere," or bare skin at the base of the beak, show that clearly enough. It is not an Owl, it is not a Vulture, and it is not a Falcon in any sense of the word.

We have got rid of the Raptores by their claws and beak ; in the identification of the rest it will be found that we can go a very long way on their feet. The feet will not take us all the way, but we shall considerably lighten our load by using them as long as they last. Now, the normal number of a bird's toes is four—three in front and one behind—but in a large number of cases the hind toe is small, and in others it has become obsolete. We can thus start our second group with two main divisions :—

    1.   Three toes.
    2.   Four toes.

Let us take the three-toed birds first. These we can sort at once into those that are web-footed, and those that are not ; but as it will be found that the web extends farther along the toes in some than in others, we can further set up four minor divisions :—

    1.   United as far as the claws.
    2.   United as far as the second joint.
    3.   United at base.
    4.   Divided throughout.

If the bird's foot be found to consist of three toes only, and these toes be webbed up to the claws, it will be assignable to one of four families, and to three of these in respect of only one representative, so that in that case we can tell at once, not only what is its family, but what are its genus and species. If its wings are fin-like and its tail rudimentary, it will be one of the *Alcidæ*, an Auk, a Guillemot, a Puffin, or a Razorbill. If its wings are not fin-like and its tail is of ordinary proportions, it may be either a Wilson's Petrel, Pallas's Sand Grouse, or a Kittiwake Gull. The Petrel you will know by its very long legs ; it is the longest legged Petrel in the British list, and our only representative of the genus *Oceanites*, which is the only genus of the *Procellariidæ* having only three toes. It is not a common bird, but it is unmistakable. Pallas's Sand Grouse is also a rarity, an occasional straggler from the depths of Tartary, that caused quite a sensation amongst sportsmen by its first appearance here some thirty years ago. It is the only species on our list of the one genus *Syrrhaptes*, which is, in its turn, the only representative we have of the family *Pteroclidæ*. It is separable from the rest of this three-toed group by its long wings and its wedge-shaped tail, which has 16 feathers in it.

As the Petrels have one three-toed representative, so have the Gulls, that being the Kittiwake. Occasionally we may find a Kittiwake with the hind toes rudimentary and not obsolete ; but in that case we shall pick him up again among the rest of the Gulls, from whom he is generally distinguishable in the way we have stated. If he has only the three toes he is not likely to be mistaken for a Petrel, a Sand Grouse, or a Guillemot ; he is a true Sea Gull, white and silver grey ; his tail is not wedge-shaped ; and he has very long wings, the flight feathers in which generally number 31.

But, it may be asked, what are the flight feathers of a bird ? Let us strip a wing and study it a little. Here is one, a Rook's, freely treated so as to be clear.

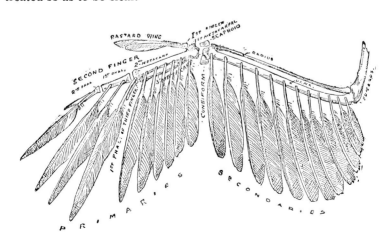

It will be seen at once that the wing answers to the man's arm from the elbow downwards. Only so much of the humerus—called the "funnybone," from the pun on humorous, which has become classical—is left in the drawing as to show its position. Joined on to it at the elbow are the radius and ulna, just as in the human arm, leading on to what represents our wrist and hand. At the joint are the scaphoid and cuneiform bones; and leading on from them is the well-developed second metacarpal, with a rudimentary first metacarpal on one side of it, and a more easily recognisable third metacarpal on the other; to the first metacarpal all that exists of the first finger is attached; to the second metacarpal hang the joints of the second finger; while the third metacarpal has the only representative of the three joints of the third finger. On the first finger, answering to our pollex, or thumb, grows the "bastard wing;" on the other fingers and metacarpals, up to the wrist joint, come the "primary" feathers; and on the ulna come the "secondary" feathers, often called the "cubitals."

The most important point to be noticed at this stage is that the flight feathers, or "remiges" as they are generally called—from the Latin *remex*, an oarsman—are divided into primaries and secondaries at the carpal joint, just where the cuneiform comes, and that the secondaries fit into little pits along the ulna, while the primaries are distributed over the hand and fingers, or, to speak more technically, over the lower metacarpals and the phalanges of the lower digits. The secondaries vary a good deal, but the typical number of primaries is 11; of these six are on the metacarpals; one, the "addigital," is on the third digit; two, the "mid-digitals," are on the first phalanx of the second digit; and two, the "pre-digitals," are on the next phalanx of that digit; the outer of the pre-digitals being the "remicle," which is always rudimentary and sometimes obsolete.

And now, having cleared the ground a little, let us resume. We have seen that our bird does not belong to the *Strigidæ*, or *Vulturidæ*, or *Falconidæ*, or *Alcidæ*, or *Pteroclidæ*, and we have thus definitely identified five families out of thirty-five, and have also discovered that our specimen belongs to neither of the genera of two other families, which can be separated out by their having only three toes, and those united as far as the claws.

Our next group consisted of the three-toed birds with the web extending only as far as the second joint. There is only one family

answering this description, and that is the *Œdicnemidæ*, which has in our list but one genus, *Œdicnemus*, and that with only one species. We are thus able to identify the Stone Curlew by its foot alone.

Our third group with three toes has its toes united at the base, or practically anywhere below the second joint; and our fourth has the toes entirely free, without any webs at all. We can make as short work of the fourth as we did of the second. There is only one family in the list with three toes unconnected by a membrane, and that is the *Turnicidæ*, represented by the one genus *Turnix*, and that by its one species, known as the Andalusian Bush Quail, or Hemipode, which is only admitted as a Britisher under protest.

We have only one three-toed group left. To it belong the Bustards, the *Otididæ*, which have their toes edged with a membrane ; the

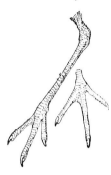

Sanderling, which is the one representative of the genus *Calidris*, the only genus of the Scolopacidæ which has but three toes ; and last and chiefly the whole family of Plovers, or *Charadriidæ*, with the exception of the Grey Plover, the Turnstone, and the Lapwing. From the Plovers the Sanderling is at once distinguishable by its having its bill as long as its head, and having it dilated at the point ; while the Plover's bill is not dilated at the point, and is always either longer or shorter than the head. And thus by taking out the birds of prey and the birds with three toes we have got rid of eight families out of thirty-five, and claimed eight genera out of four more.

But before we consider the four-toed class, which comprises the bulk of the birds, British and otherwise, it would be as well to produce our example, which it would not have done to have brought forward before, inasmuch as it is only too plain that he is not a bird of prey, and that he has more than three toes.

Here he is, mapped out as far as it is necessary for him to be at present, and it would be as well to identify his "districts." Here are his

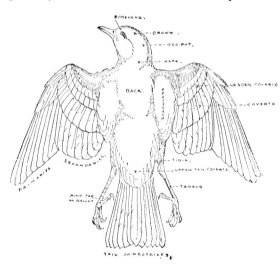

"primaries" and his "secondaries," and, at the upper angle, the "alula" or "bastard wing" we have already spoken of. On the top of the "remiges," or flight feathers, come the "wing coverts," and over them come the "lesser coverts." Between the wing and the back come the shoulder feathers, or "scapulars," and at the base of the back come the "upper tail coverts," from beneath which run the "rectrices," or tail feathers. Above the back is the neck with the "nape," which bears the "nuchal" feathers, the "occiput," or poll, the "crown," already spoken of as being bare in the Vulturidæ, and the "forehead," just above the beak and in front of the eyes.

But let us turn him over. Here we see that the "lore" is between the eye and the beak, and that the "chin" is just underneath the

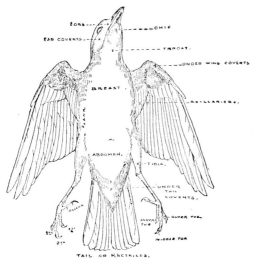

beak, leading on to the "throat," which in turn leads on to the "breast." Below this is the lower breast, bordered by the "flanks," and then comes the abdomen, ending with the "under tail coverts," from under which come the tail feathers, whose upper side we have already seen. Again we have the primaries and secondaries, with the conspicuous break between them, leading up to the carpal joint, the "under wing coverts" being along the top; and on what answer to our armpits are the bird's "axillaries" we shall find so useful in identification when we have to deal with genera and species. The legs will be seen to correspond to human legs, much in the same way as the wings did to arms. The "femur," or thigh bone, is short and is well up; and the knee, with its "patella," comes above where the wing crosses in the sketch. Below it is the "tibia," which has the fibula as part of it, and then comes what is often called the bird's knee, but which you can at once see, from the way it bends inwards, must be its ankle, and which is really in its upper portion the tibiotarsus; from the knee to the foot runs what is known in the bird books as the "tarsus," though it is really the tarso-metatarsus; but the point is of no practical importance in our present endeavour. Below the tarsus come the toes; the hallux, answering to our great toe, at the back; then the inner toe, coming from between the legs outwards; then the middle toe; and the fourth or outer toe. The fifth toe is missing in the birds; when there are but three toes it is the representative of our great toe which has gone; when there are but two toes, as with the Ostrich, it is the second and third that remain. The normal number of phalanges or toe joints is 14, two being in the hind toe, three in the inner toe, four in the middle toe, and five in the outer toe. As we go on we shall find that these numbers vary. But enough of this for a time; we are now strong enough in terms to begin our attack on the four-toed birds.

And we cannot begin better than by eliminating the *Pelecanidæ*, which have not only four well developed toes, but have these toes all webbed together up to the claws, being "totipalmate," as it is called. That one distinction separates the Cormorant, Shag, and Gannet, the only representatives we have of the group, from every other family in the British list.

We can form another group of the birds which have the three front toes webbed together and the fourth webbed on to the tarsus. Under this heading would come the *Colymbidæ*, or Divers; and one representative of the Laridæ, the Ivory Gull, which is our only species of the genus *Pagophila*. There is no difficulty in distinguishing the Gull from a Diver, for he is an entirely white bird, and he has long wings, while the Divers have short wings, and he has a decurved bill, while their bill is compressed or higher than it is broad.

We have now to deal with the birds that have the hind toe free. We can divide these into four groups:

1.—Those that have the three toes united as far as the claws.

2.—Those that have the three toes united as far as the second joint.

3.—Those that have the two united as far as the second joint and two as far as the first.

4.—Those that have the three united near the base.

To the first group there belong—

Phœnicopteridæ.	Laridæ (all that are left).
Ibididæ.	Procellariidæ (all that are left).
Anatidæ.	

The *Phœnicopteridæ* have one representative. He is the Flamingo. His webs are cut into a good deal, but still his feet are undoubtedly webbed to the claws. And really it does not matter. No one is likely to mistake our sample bird for a Flamingo, and the sooner he goes the better. In the *Ibididæ* we have another case of "sole representative in this district." This is the Ibis, with long, slender, down-curved bill; not the Scarlet Ibis, but the "Glossy," or bronzy one, a very unlikely bird to meet with in the fenland now, and

recognisable at once as soon as seen. We have now but three families left, and these are of real importance. To say nothing of the occasionally lobed hind toe, and the extra lobe in some cases on the front of the foot, the Anatidæ, comprising the Ducks, Geese, and Swans, are separable from the rest by their bill, which is either toothed, as in *Mergus*, or else lamellate. The Gulls have their bill neither toothed nor lamellate, and in that respect resemble the Petrels; but then the Petrels have a nail at the end of their bill, which the Gulls have not; and the nostrils of a Petrel are in a tube, while those of a Gull have no such arrangement. The three main families of the "palmate" division are thus marked off with ease, and we can resume the main line with our second group, that including the birds which have three of their four toes webbed as far as the second joint. There are not many such birds. The Spoonbill is

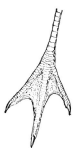

one. He is the sole representative on our list of the *Plataleidæ*, and with him we bid farewell to another family. His spatulate bill distinguishes him from every other bird. The Scolopacidæ are represented in this group of ours by one species only, and that also, curiously enough, is recognisable at once by its bill, which is long and narrow, and curving upwards. There is no trouble in identifying either the Spoonbill and the Avocet, although the latter's web may, exceptionally, stretch a little beyond the second joint. To this group the only other birds that belong are the *Parinæ*, or Tits, a sub-family of the Passeridæ; but it will be sufficient for the moment to have mentioned them. We will leave the Passeridæ as the loose ends of our fabric, and pick them up and deal with them by themselves in due course.

Our next group includes the birds which have two of their feet united as far as the second joint, and two united as far as the first. To this group we can assign but two families — the Kingfishers and the Bee-eaters, otherwise *Alcedinidæ* and *Meropidæ*. There is no difficulty in separating these. The Kingfishers have short tails, the Bee-eaters have long tails; the Kingfishers have a ridged beak, the Bee-eaters have no ridge; and, if it be necessary to go into details, the Kingfishers have 22 remiges while the Bee-eaters have 23.

We are left with the last group in which three toes are united, and in this case the web extends only a little beyond the base. The

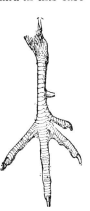

most familiar example of this kind of foot is found among the *Phasianidæ*, which family is made up of most of the game birds—the Pheasants, Partridges, Grouse, Quail, and Ptarmigan. Let our representative foot be that of a Pheasant, which is recognisable by its spur. The Phasianidæ have short legs and short bills, and a curious peculiarity of their's is that the eleventh remex—that is, flight feather—is always shorter than any of the others. The short legs and short bill sufficiently distinguish the Phasianidæ from the *Ciconiidæ*, another member of this group. The Ciconiidæ consist merely of the two Storks, the black one and the white one, neither of which is a Briton by birth or a frequent visitor. With these come three more families—the *Caprimulgidæ*, the *Charadriidæ* in respect of the three genera already excepted, and the *Scolopacidæ*, in respect of the Black-winged Stilt, the Woodcock, the Red-breasted Snipe, the Broad-billed Sandpiper, the Buff-breasted Sandpiper, and the Curlews and Whimbrel, all of which we will sort out by-and-bye.

To the Caprimulgidæ belong the Nightjars, whose gaping bill at

once marks them off from the rest of the group. Another characteristic mark of the Nightjars is the foot, which has the phalanges of the toes as 2, 3, 4, 3, instead of 2, 3, 4, 5, as usual; in another way they are recognisable from the other families with whom we have brought them, by their having only 10 tail feathers; and finally their curious comb-like middle claw will betray them anywhere even if their bill did not. There is, therefore, no difficulty in separating the Ciconiidæ, the Phasianidæ, and the Caprimulgidæ; nor is there any with regard to the remainder of the Charadriidæ in this division. They consist of three genera only, each containing but one species. The Grey Plover is known at once by his white tail broadly barred with black and brown, the Lapwing is at once detected by his long crest, as the Turnstone is by his orange legs.

We have only one group left in which the feet are united by membranes. To it belong the whole of four families and certain representatives of the Scolopacidæ and Passeridæ, the two families in which the feet give us so much trouble because the foot is no basis of classification. These four are :—

> Ardeidæ (the Herons).
> Gruidæ (the Cranes).
> Glareolidæ (the Pratincole).
> Upupidæ (the Hoopoe).

Here we can pick out the Hoopoe at once; his erectile crest distinguishes him. And the Pratincole need not linger in the list; his short bill, short legs, forked tail, and long wings are sufficiently distinctive. With regard to the Cranes and Herons we can divide them on their middle claw, which is smooth in the Cranes and pectinate in the Herons ; but the long pendent secondary feathers of the Cranes at once mark them off from the Herons, even if their shorter beak did not. The genera of the Scolopacidæ are at once recognisable by their long thin bills ; and when we come to deal with the Scolopacidæ as a family by itself, we shall have no difficulty in sorting out *Totanus, Machetes, Bartramia,* and *Limosa;* and the few Passerines that come into the group we can leave as we did before till the final settlement.

It will be remarked that we have completed every family we have yet mentioned except the Scolopacidæ and Passeridæ, which we agreed to treat exceptionally; and that we have now dealt with all the families in which the feet are united, and including the birds of prey, have eliminated from our thirty-five families :—

Strigidæ.	Phœnicopteridæ.
Vulturidæ.	Ibididæ.
Falconidæ.	Anatidæ.
Alcidæ.	Plataleidæ.
Laridæ.	Alcedinidæ.
Pteroclidæ.	Meropidæ.
Procellariidæ.	Ciconiidæ.
Œdicnemidæ.	Phasianidæ.
Otididæ.	Caprimulgidæ.
Charadriidæ.	Ardeidæ.
Turnicidæ.	Gruidæ.
Pelecanidæ.	Glareolidæ.
Colymbidæ.	Upupidæ.

And we have left in for further treatment certain species of Scolopacidæ and Passeridæ. We have not said much of our sample bird as yet, for it is evident from his portrait that his feet are not webbed at all, and consequently we have been dealing with groups to which he could not possibly belong.

Neither can he belong to our next group in which the feet are webbed to each other in peculiar lobes. The best example of a lobed foot is that of a Grebe. It is so unlike anything else that the *Podicipepidæ* are as easy of recognition as the Pelecanidæ.

This broad flat foot is the paddle by which the bird propels itself when under water; for, unlike the Alcidæ, the Podicipepidæ do not use their wings in their sub-aqueous explorings. There are no representatives of either of these families that dive as men dive; the Auks really fly under water, the Grebes really swim, keeping at any depth, and working in and out among the sub-merged plants as expertly as a Duck does among the leaves that rise above the surface. In both families the legs are placed so far back that the bird stands upright like a Penguin.

There are only three families in which lobed feet are found, and it is only in the Podicipepidæ that the peculiarity is common to every species. Among the *Rallidæ* there are two genera, each with a single species, which have lobed feet. These are the Coot and the Moorhen, the former of which has the lobes in broad scallops, a foot so remarkable that it cannot be mistaken for that of any other bird on the British list. The Coot has two marks which make his recognition the easiest of tasks. If you do not know him by his broadly lobed foot, you will know him by the white shield on his forehead, which a facetious naturalist has described as being as useful as a brass plate.

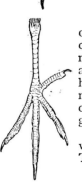

The other representative of the Rallidæ, and the last of the birds with lobed feet, is the Moorhen. In this case they are not so well marked as in the others, but narrow as they may be they are clearly distinguishable, and not likely to be mistaken for the membranes we have previously noted. And they are unlike the narrowly denticulate lobes of *Phalaropus*, which is the only genus of the Scolopacidæ that comes into this group.

We have now to deal with the four-toed birds which have their feet entirely divided from the base. These naturally fall into three groups :—

    1. Having four toes in front.
    2. Having two toes in front and two behind.
    3. Having three toes in front.

And to the last—the "three fingers and a thumb" brigade—belong our most familiar birds, including our example.

But first for the others. There is only one family having its four toes in front. This is the *Cypselidæ* in respect of the one genus, *Cypselus*, of which the only representatives are the Swifts. There are two Swifts in the list, one of which, the Alpine one, is never known to breed here, and is a very infrequent visitor ; so that, practically, we have only one bird with four toes in front. The Cypselidæ have, however, another genus, Acanthyllis, in which three toes are in front, in the ordinary way ; but we shall have that exception to deal with presently.

Some birds have two toes in front and two behind. Amongst us, this "zygodactyle" group is represented by the Woodpeckers and Cuckoos. The distinction, like most of those we have been giving, only holds good for the birds on the British list, for some of the foreign Woodpeckers have only three toes. The Cuckoos belong to the *Cuculidæ*, and the Woodpeckers to the *Picidæ ;* and, while the Cuculidæ can be at once recognised by their long graduated tail, the Picidæ are as readily recognisable by their long wedge-shaped bill and long extensile and bristly tongue.

We have now reached the last of our divisions as regards the feet. The families remaining to be dealt with are only half a dozen in number. They are :—

Cypselidæ, in respect of the one genus *Acanthyllis*.
Coraciidæ, which has only one representative, the Roller.
Columbidæ, the Pigeons.
Rallidæ, in respect of the genera *Crex* and *Rallus*.
Scolopacidæ, in respect of the genera *Tringa* and *Gallinago*.
Passeridæ, in respect of all its genera as yet unmentioned.

To one of these groups our bird belongs. It does not belong to the first, for that consists only of the one genus and one species, the Needle-tailed Swift, only two specimens of which have ever been heard of here, and which is known at once by its having its tail feathers ending in sharp spines. It does not belong to the next, for that also has only one representative, the Roller, which is a brightly coloured bird, not unlike a Parrot in Oxford and Cambridge blues, whereas ours is mere brown and grey. It does not belong to the third, for it is not a Pigeon ; its bill is not deflected, nor does it thin in the middle, and swell towards the point ; nor has it its nostrils in a soft skin at the-base of the bill. It is not a Crake, for its beak is neither short nor stout, nor are its wings rounded, nor its feet large, nor its legs or tail short. It is not a Snipe, nor a Stint, nor a Sandpiper, for that is what the only remaining genera of the Scolopacidæ represent.

And as it is neither assignable to Cypselidæ, nor Coraciidæ, nor Columbidæ, nor Rallidæ, nor Scolopacidæ, the only family that can claim it is the Passeridæ, which is the most important family of birds, not only in Great Britain, but in the world.

Thus far, then, have we gone with the feet. By leaving the Passerines for special treatment and eliminating the birds of prey we have been enabled to sort out all the families in our list. And before we proceed further it will simplify matters to print the plan we have worked to in tabular form.

CHAPTER V.

THE FAMILIES,

———◆◇◆———

RAPTORES, or Birds of Prey; with powerful claws, sharp curving bill, and a cere at the base of the bill.

STRIGIDÆ (Owls)—head large, face round, eyes in front. 161-170.
VULTURIDÆ (Vultures)—crown bald or downy. 171-172.
FALCONIDÆ (Eagles and Hawks)—crown feathered. 173-198.

NON-RAPTORES—
  1. With three toes.
  2. With four toes.
    Three toes—
      1. United as far as the claws.
      2. United as far as the second joint.
      3. United at base.
      4. Divided throughout.
    United as far as the claws—
      ALCIDÆ (Auks, Guillemots, Puffin, and Razorbill)—wings fin-like; tail rudimentary. 373-379.
      LARIDÆ (in respect of most specimens of the genus *Rissa*, the Kittiwake)—wings long, remiges 31; tail not wedge shaped. 367.
      PTEROCLIDÆ (Pallas's Sand Grouse)—wings long; tail wedge shaped and of 16 feathers. 268.
      PROCELLARIIDÆ (in respect of the one genus *Oceanites*, Wilson's Petrel)—legs long. 398.
    United as far as the second joint—
      ŒDICNEMIDÆ (Stone Curlew)—remiges 29. 290.
    United near base—
      OTIDIDÆ (Bustards)—toes edged with membrane. 287-289.
      CHARADRIIDÆ (Plovers, with the exception of the Grey Plover, Turnstone, and Lapwing)—bill longer or shorter than head and not dilated at point. 292-295, 297-300, 303.
      SCOLOPACIDÆ (in respect of the one genus *Calidris*, the Sanderling)—bill as long as head and dilated at point. 324.
    Divided throughout—
      TURNICIDÆ (Andalusian Bush Quail). 277.
    Four toes—
      1. Four united.
      2. Three united; one webbed to tarsus.
      3. Three united; hind toe free.
      4. Two united.
      5. Lobed.
      6. Divided throughout.

Four united—

PELECANIDÆ (Cormorant, Gannet, and Shag)—bill long; tarsus compressed ; third claw pectinate. 199-201.

Three united ; one webbed to tarsus.

COLYMBIDÆ (Divers)—wings short ; bill compressed. 380-383.

LARIDÆ (in respect of the one genus *Pagophila*, the Ivory Gull)—wings long ; bill decurved. 368.

Three united ; hind toe free—

1. As far as the claws.
2. As far as the second joint.
3. Two as far as the second joint and two as far as the first.
4. Near base.

As far as the claws—

PHŒNICOPTERIDÆ (Flamingo)—webs incised ; bill bent half way. 216.

IBIDIDÆ (Ibis)—bill long, slender, and decurved, point rounded; 27 remiges. 215.

ANATIDÆ (Ducks, Geese, and Swans) — bill broad, and lamellate, or toothed. 217-262.

LARIDÆ (Gulls and Terns, except the Kittiwake and Ivory Gull)—bill neither lamellate nor toothed, and without a nail; fourth toe rudimentary. 341-366.

PROCELLARIIDÆ (Petrels and Shearwaters) — nostrils in a tube ; bill unserrate and ending in a nail. 389-398.

As far as the second joint—

PLATALEIDÆ (Spoonbill)—bill spatulate ; 30 remiges. 214.

SCOLOPACIDÆ (in respect of the one genus, *Recurvirostra*, the Avocet)—bill boldly curving upwards. 304.

PASSERIDÆ (in respect of the *Parinæ*)—very small birds, for which see analysis further on.

Two as far as the second joint and two as far as the first—

ALCEDINIDÆ (Kingfishers)—upper mandible ridged ; remiges 22 ; tail short. 151, 152.

MEROPIDÆ (Bee-eaters)—upper mandible not ridged; remiges 23 ; tail long. 154, 155.

Near base—

CICONIIDÆ (Storks)—long bill ; over 30 remiges; long legs. 212, 213.

PHASIANIDÆ (Pheasants, Partridges, Grouse, Quail, and Ptarmigan)—short bill; eleventh remex shortest ; short legs. 269-276.

CAPRIMULGIDÆ (Nightjars)—gaping bill ; 10 tail feathers ; middle toe pectinate ; phalanges 2, 3, 4, 3. 141-143.

CHARADRIIDÆ (in respect of the Grey Plover which has a white tail broadly barred with black and brown, the Lapwing which has a crest, and the Turnstone which has orange legs). 296, 301, 302.

SCOLOPACIDÆ (in respect of the Black-winged Stilt, the Woodcock, the Red-breasted Snipe, the Broad-billed Sandpiper, the Buff-breasted Sandpiper, and the Curlews and Whimbrel. 308, 312, 313, 325, 338-340.

Two united—

ARDEIDÆ (Herons and Bitterns)—bill long and straight ; legs long and straight ; middle claw pectinate. 202-211.

GRUIDÆ (Cranes)—bill moderate ; 33 remiges ; secondaries long and pendent ; legs long, middle claw not pectinate. 285, 286.

GLAREOLIDÆ (Pratincole)—bill short; wings long ; legs short; tail forked. 291.

UPUPIDÆ (Hoopoe)—erectile crest ; remiges 20. 156.

SCOLOPACIDÆ (in respect of the Ruff, Bartram's Sandpiper, the Godwits, and the genus _Totanus_)—long slender bill. 323, 326-337.

PASSERIDÆ (in respect of certain genera as given in the special analysis of that family).

Lobed—

PODICIPEDIDÆ (Grebes)—lobes pennate and entire ; tail rudimentary and downy ; tarsus compressed. 384-388.

RALLIDÆ (in respect of the Coot and Moorhen, the former of which has the lobes broadly scalloped, the latter having them straight and narrow). 284, 283.

SCOLOPACIDÆ (in respect of the genus _Phalaropus_)—lobes narrowly denticulate. 307.

Divided throughout—

   1. Four in front.

   2. Two in front, two behind.

   3. Three in front.

Four in front—

CYPSELIDÆ (in respect of the genus _Cypselus_, the Swift). 138, 139.

Two in front, two behind—

PICIDÆ (Woodpeckers and Wryneck)—long bill ; long extensile and bristled tongue. 144-149.

CUCULIDÆ (Cuckoos)—long graduated tail. 157-160.

Three in front—

CYPSELIDÆ (in respect of the Needletailed Swift)—tail feathers with sharp spines. 140.

CORACIIDÆ (Roller)—bill compressed ; upper mandible decurved at tip ; 23 remiges ; tarsus scutellate in front, reticulate at back. 153.

COLUMBIDÆ (Pigeons) — bill deflected, thinnest in middle, expanding towards point ; nostrils in soft skin at base of bill; feathers without aftershafts ; no down ; second primary longest. 263-267.

RALLIDÆ (Crakes, except the Coot and Moorhen)—short stout beak ; rounded wings ; large feet ; short legs ; short tail. 278-282.

SCOLOPACIDÆ (in respect of the genera _Gallinago_ and _Tringa_)—long slender bill. 309-311, 314-322.

PASSERIDÆ. 1-137.

CHAPTER VI.

EXAMPLES OF IDENTIFICATION.

I N sorting out the British passerine birds we can simplify matters
considerably by beginning with four sub-families which are
represented by only one species each, which species is almost
certain to be recognised immediately.

These are :—

Oriolinæ.	Panurinæ.
Icterinæ.	Ampelinæ.

Is our sample bird a bright-yellow one, like a large canary with
black wings, and a black tipped tail ?   Is it in fact a Golden Oriole ?
No ; it is not.   And as the Golden Oriole is the only species we have
of *Oriolus*, which is our only representative of its sub-family, we can
at once eliminate *Oriolinæ*.

Is it a glossy black bird, with bright scarlet wing coverts ? No. The
only bird like that in the British list is a rare, and probably escaped,
American, known as the Red-winged Starling, which is a species of
Agelæus, and our only representative of its sub-family ; and consequently we need not further trouble ourselves with *Icterinæ*.

Is our bird a little fellow with a rufous tail over three inches long,
and much longer than the rest of his body, and has he in full plumage
a black pointed moustache, which, though obscure at some periods of
the year, is always traceable ? No.   Our bird is quite two inches
longer, his tail is not as long as his body, and he has no moustache at
all.   In short, no one would imagine he was a Bearded Tit ; and with
its sole representative we have done with the *Panurinæ*.

Has he a bold erectile crest like a Cockatoo, and has he red waxy
tips to his secondary feathers or his tail ?   No.   Then he is not a
Waxwing ; and the Waxwing is the only species we have of the
Ampelinæ.

There is another sub-family we can bracket with these, and that is
the *Cinclinæ*, which is represented by only one genus *Cinclus*, which
has two species, one differing from the other only in the greater
blackness of its breast.   These Dippers as they are called, are, however,
so distinct from the rest of our birds, that they are at once recognisable.   Their plumage is blackish brown, dense and fibrous, and,
as befitting the only passerine water birds, they are provided with a
thick undercoat of down, which some people are inclined to describe
as the only true down in the order.   That, however, is open to
discussion.   For our purposes it is enough to know that the foregoing
five sub-families are unmistakable, and that our specimen belongs to
neither of them.

We have 15 sub-families left. These we can sort out on the comparative length of the first primary, which is always narrow among the Passerines. In some of our group this first primary, which must not be mistaken for the remicle, is absent altogether, in others it is just apparent, in others it is almost half as long as the second primary, in others it is more than half as long as the second primary. We can thus, for the purposes of identification, separate the birds we have left into three divisions :—

1. Having the first primary quite half as long as the second.
2. Having the first primary obsolete or minute.
3. Having the first primary less than half as long as the second.

Of the first division we had a capital example in our typical wing on page 31. There are only two Passerine sub-families which have wings like that. One is the *Corvinæ*, comprising the Raven, the Crow, the Jackdaw, Magpie, Jay, and Nutcracker ; and the other is the *Troglodytinæ*, which has as its only representative the well-known Jenny Wren. Now, no one is likely to mistake the diminutive Wren, which is one of the smallest birds we have, for one of the *Corvinæ*. If the size were not enough to prevent the mistake, the long soft

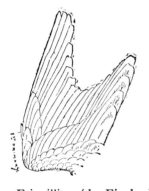

plumage, the erect little tail, and the concave wings, compared to the flat wings of the larger birds, would at once remove all difficulty in recognition.

Our 15 sub-families have thus become 13, and these we can separate into six of one and seven of the other. Let us take the six first. Here is the typical wing of this group. It is that of a Skylark. See how small the first primary is to what it was in the wing of the Rook. In some of the Finches, as we shall see immediately, this feather is absent altogether ; and in none of our six is it a quarter as long as the second. The six are :—

Fringillinæ (the Finches).	Sturninæ (the Starlings).
Emberizinæ (the Buntings).	Hirundininæ (the Swallows).
Motacillinæ (the Wagtails).	Alaudinæ (the Larks).

Let us consider these in order. Does our bird belong to the *Fringillinæ ?* Is he like a Sparrow, *Passer* himself—whence the Passerines etymologically—is he like a Canary ; a Goldfinch ; a Bullfinch ; a Greenfinch ; a Chaffinch ; a Linnet ; a Crossbill ? Has he that peculiar beak, hard, short, and conical ? No. Then he is not one of the Fringillinæ. We need not have looked at his wing in this case ; the beak alone would have been enough.

Is he a Bunting ? But how can you tell a Bunting from a Finch ? Look at the gape line. Look at the head sideways, and see the sharp angle with which the upper mandible shuts on the lower. In the Finches, as in all the sub-families that follow, as you can see by their heads, this line is straight. But there is another distinction between the Finches and the Buntings, and

the one that separates the Buntings out at once. That is, the knobbed palate, that has been made so prominent in our sketch. Open the bird's mouth, and look in the roof of it. The " Bunting knob " is unmistakable. Our bird has no knob, and his gape line is straight. Evidently he is not one of the Emberizinæ.

Is he a Wagtail or a Pipit? Has he a narrow, slender bill, long legs, and a long tail? Certainly not. He is not built lightly enough or gracefully enough for that group. He is not one of the Motacillinæ.

Is he a Starling? Is his plumage shining and metallic in lustre and spotted? If not we can pass the Sturninæ.

Is he a Swallow? Look at his head from above. Is his beak as short and wide as this? Is he a Swallow, a Martin, a Sand Martin? Has he short legs, long wings, and a forked tail? No. Then he is not one of the Hirundininæ.

Is he a Lark? Look at his legs. Is his tarsus plated back and front? No. Then he is not a Lark, and we can clear the track of the Alaudinæ, and try back for our last division.

In this the first primary is about as long as the coverts. Even should there be a difficulty in separating between this and the preceding, it will be found that the characteristics of the sub-families are so clear that the two divisions could very well have been treated as one. At the same time were the thirteen wings before you, you would easily sort out the seven that follow :—

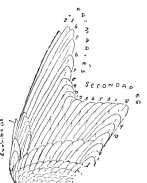

Certhiinæ (the Creepers).
Muscicapinæ (the Flycatchers).
Laniinæ (the Shrikes).
Sittinæ (the Nuthatch).
Parinæ (the Tits).
Accentorinæ (the Accentors).
Turdinæ (the Thrushes and Warblers).

There are only two of the Creepers. One is the Wall Creeper, our sole representative of *Tichodroma*, and of him only two specimens are on record in this country. He is a slaty grey bird, with grey and crimson wings. The other Creeper is the common one, a little fellow, spotted brown above and whitish below, with a long curved slender bill, a rounded tail, with its feathers pointed, and a long curved hind claw. Evidently our bird is not a Creeper ; and we can pass Certhiinæ.

Is he a Flycatcher?   Look at his bill.   Is it broad and flat, with bristles at its base?   Is it such a bill, in fact, as he would catch flies with when he is on the wing?   Are his nostrils partly hidden under the frontal plumes?   Are his toes all free of each other, and the middle one much longer than the rest?   Has he small feet?  Is his wing long and pointed, and with the second primary a trifle shorter than the third, fourth, and fifth, which are longer than any of the others?   If not we can pass on from Muscicapinæ.

Is he a Shrike?   Has he a short bill with a tooth in it, as if he could be a bird of prey on occasion; has he a good deal of soft slaty grey in his plumage; are two of his toes united, the middle toe with the outer?   Has he forward pointing hairs at the base of his bill?   Is his middle toe shorter than his tarsus?   Are his nostrils oval?   Is his third primary longer than the others?  No.   Then he cannot be assigned to the Laniinæ.

Is he a Nuthatch?   Has he a long straight bill like this?   Is he a bluish little fellow, with his two middle tail feathers grey, and pale brown legs with strong and clumsy feet?   No.   Then he is not one of the Sittinæ, for the Nuthatch is our only representative of that sub-family.

Is he a Tit?   Are his three front toes united as far as the second joint, and is his hind claw long?   No.   He is too big for a Tit, even for a Great Tit, and he has no black apron which would distinguish him if he were.

We have only two groups left.   One, the Accentorinæ, has only two representatives, the Hedge Sparrow and the Alpine Accentor, one of which has the throat bluish grey, while the other has it white, with black spots.   He is too large for either of these, even if his bill were strong enough and his wings rounded enough.   That he should be the Alpine bird is unlikely, for only a few stragglers of that species come over here.   That he might be a Hedge Sparrow is more reasonable, but then everyone knows the Hedge Sparrow.   And as we have thus eliminated twelve of our groups, our representative specimen can only belong to the thirteenth and last. He is either a Thrush or a Warbler.

But suppose we have made a mistake?   Then we shall soon find it out, as we should have found it had we allocated him to any of the other families or sub-families; for our scheme is so arranged that if we take the wrong road we shall soon come to "no thoroughfare," and have to return and try somewhere else down the line.   This time, however, we have been right in disregarding the junctions, and following the main line of the plan given in our next chapter.

Our bird, then, is one of the Turdinæ, and we have discovered what he is by separating him from what he is not.   Let us pursue that method.   To what genus of the Turdinæ does he belong?

Open his wing and look at his armpits. Are his axillary feathers chequered? No. Then he is no Geocichla ; he is not a White's Thrush nor a Siberian Thrush, and he would be a rarity if he were. Are his axillaries black? No. Then he is not a Blackbird or a Ring Ouzel. Perhaps they are yellow, and he has an unspotted breast ; if so, his genus is either *Phylloscopus* or *Hypolais;* Phylloscopus if his legs are brown, Hypolais if his legs are blue. But his axillaries are not yellow and his breast is not unspotted. Are his axillaries buff? Has he a buff breast, a reddish brown back, a reddish brown tail ; is he, in short, a Nightingale? No. He is not a Nightingale ; and he is thus unclaimed by five genera.

Now let us try him in another way. Is his chin red ; and is his lower breast white? No. He is not a Robin Redbreast. Is his chin chestnut and his lower breast chestnut? No. He is not a Dartford Warbler. Two more genera are eliminated. The next we might have started with. Has he a bright yellow crest? No. He is not a Gold-crest or a Fire-crest ; and no one would have supposed so from his size.

Perhaps he is a Rufous Warbler? If so his head and back would be chestnut, his breast buff ; his tail rounded and long, and tipped with white ; and he would have been the fourth specimen on record. Evidently he is not *Aëdon*. Has he a white rump, black legs, unnotched bill? Is he a *Saxicola*, in fact? No. He is not a Wheatear. Has he a whitish rump, black legs, a notched bill, and a short square tail ; is he a *Pratincola?* No. He is neither a Stone-chat nor a Whinchat. Has he a bright blue throat? No. He is not a *Cyanecula*. Has he a bluish grey head, a black bill, and a chestnut breast? No. There was only one bird ever seen like that in this country. He is not a *Monticola;* and so far we have tried him in vain for 13 genera, and we have only five to run him down in.

Has he a black throat and a red tail, with black or brown on its two middle feathers ; is he a *Ruticilla?* No. He is not one of the Redstarts. Is his bill without rictal bristles, are his axillaries brown, and is his tail pointed and shorter than the wing? No. That com-bination will not suit him. He is not a *Locustella*. Are his axillaries whitish, is his bill large in proportion to his head, and depressed and broad at the base, and is his tail short and rather round? No. That combination will not do. We cannot get rid of him in *Acrocephalus*. But we have only two left !

How long is he? Over seven inches—over eight really. Then he cannot belong to *Sylvia*, he must belong to *Turdus*. That is one way out of the difficulty, certainly. But suppose he were an under-sized specimen?

Then, if he were assignable to Sylvia, his bill would be faintly notched, and very short and stout, but not broad at the base, his breast would be plain or barred, his wings would be moderate in size, his first primary would be noticeably less than half the length of the second, and his tail would be ashy or brown and white. And as our specimen does not meet these requirements, all we can say is that his genus must be *Turdus*. And if we look on pages 73 and 74, we can try him again through the tabular analysis of the *Turdinæ*.

But to what species of Turdus does he belong? Let us analyse the species and tabulate them, as we shall have to tabulate all the species, and for ready reference arrange them in the alphabetical order of their genera.

Is our bird black with a red breast ? No. He is not *migratorius*, and it would have been a wonder if he were. Has he a black throat and breast ? No. He would have been the third of his kind to be caught in this country if he had. He is not *atrigularis*. Turn him over and look at his axillaries. Are they red ? No. He is not a Redwing. Are they white ? No. He is not a Fieldfare nor a Missel Thrush ; and if he were a Fieldfare he would have a blue rump. What colour are his axillaries ? Pale yellow. That alone will distinguish him. He is olive brown above and whitish below, with a number of triangular brown spots and streaks about him. In fact, he is *T. musicus*, otherwise the common Song Thrush, whom recent classifiers have promoted to the second place on the British list.

And now, with a view to advancing beyond the mere knowledge of the bird's name, let us take the feathers off our Thrush.

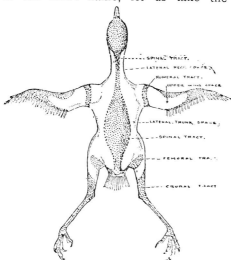

These chiefly consist of the *pennæ*, or contour feathers, which are so-called from their giving the outline of the body. They are exposed to the light. The other feathers, the down feathers, are hidden from the light. In the contour feathers we have a main stem or axis, the *vexillum*, or vane, divided into the solid four-sided shaft or *rachis*, and the hollow, somewhat rounded hollow end, we know as the quill, or *calamus*, which ends in a small aperture through which it receives the vascular pulp. With the sac in which this is embedded are connected the muscles which give the feathers motion. The vane bears the plates, or *barbs*, which are linked together at their free ends by the *barbules*, which are again generally interlinked by *hooklets*. In the Ostrich we have free barbs, and, consequently, loose plumes, but the case is exceptional. In a good many birds each quill has two vanes, one being the shaft, the other the aftershaft, which always springs from the underside ; and, occasionally, shaft and undershaft are almost equal, and a "double feather" is the result.

The down feathers, hidden from the light in adults, are the first feathers of the young bird which are generally replaced by the *pennæ*, and their barbs invariably remain soft and free. In some birds we have a third kind of feather, one with a long shaft and a sort of brush of barbs ; this is a "filoplume." In the Ardeidæ, and in some of the Falconidæ, there is a fourth kind of feather, the summit of which breaks off into fine dust as fast as it is formed. Sometimes these feathers are scattered all over the body, but in many cases they are in well defined positions which are known as "powder down tracts," and these tracts are of considerable use in identifying the Herons, for instance. Just as the powder down is distributed in tracts, so are the contour feathers, except in the case of the Ostriches and their allies, and the Penguins and a few more birds.

That the feathers should be arranged in a definite pattern was to be expected. If the body were feathered evenly it would hamper the bird in its movements. The coat is in fact made to fit, and is cut in such a way as to be workable by the muscles. These "tracts," with their resulting spaces, which were worked out by Nitzsch, are of considerable importance in ornithology, and promise to be of more importance in the future; and

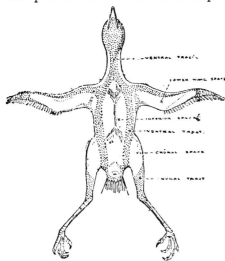

we have, in consequence, given two sketches of our thrush; the first dorsal, the second ventral, with the chief tracts and spaces marked out.

Most birds have a spinal or dorsal tract, a humeral or shoulder tract, a femoral or lumbar tract, and what is known as the inferior tract; some of them have a neck tract; and besides these, are the head tract, the alar or wing tract, the crural or leg tract, and the caudal tract. The spaces are the laterals of the neck, the laterals of the trunk, and the inferior lateral; and besides these, the more or less common spaces are the spinal, the upper wing, the lower wing, the crural, and the head.

The spinal tract is occasionally bordered below with a row of feathers, as in the Woodpeckers. Sometimes it is weak at the nape, as with the Kingfisher. In the Golden Oriole it is widened on the back into an ellipse. In the Crows and Larks it has a space within its boundaries. In the Woodpeckers, including the Wryneck, and in the Swallows it has two lobes. In the Pheasant, the Partridge, and the Quail it is well marked and continuous, and narrow on the neck, but widening from the shoulder blades; while in the Capercaillie it is cleft where it broadens by a longitudinal space from the shoulders upwards. On the other hand, in many birds of prey, it is interrupted at the ends of the shoulder blades, the anterior part becoming wider, and the lower part becoming narrower. And a further variation occurs among the Plovers and Sandpipers, where the hinder part is cleft throughout.

The humeral tract, in the Passerine birds, runs nearly over the middle of the humerus, but in the Pigeons it crosses much nearer the shoulder blade. In the Swifts, Kingfishers, and Hoopoe the femoral tract extends from the extreme end of the ischium to the knee ; but in the Bee-eaters it reaches neither the knee nor the pelvis. The ventral tract is generally unbroken, but in the Cranes and Curlews it has a long branch. In the Passerines, as shown by our Thrush, it is a narrow strip with four branches.

Probably few but cooks and poulterers know to what narrow spaces a bird's feathers are confined ; and fewer still are aware that the pattern of the tracts is an aid in identification. In Nitzsch's " Pterylography" there are a number of maps of feather distribution, to which those taking an interest in the subject should refer ; and in the Central Hall of the Natural History Museum, at South Kensington, will be found our typical Thrush, with a large number of examples of bird structure and plumage—an admirable arrangement which every one should visit, as they should also visit the Bird Museum at Brighton, once Mr. Booth's and now the Corporation's, out on the Dyke Road, a mile from the Jubilee Clock Tower.

But are there no other means of identifying a bird? Yes ; by his flight. But how can you classify flight? It is as difficult as classifying a man's gait, which is just as unmistakable once you know it. In our notes we have endeavoured to give as good an idea of the flight as we could, but we are conscious of the feebleness of our effort. And so with the syllabisations of the song. Attempts have been made to reduce the song to musical form, but those who have tried over such things even on the flute and piccolo and flageolet, know what a burlesque is the result. The nearest approach to it is got by a series of whistles, one for each bird, artificial syringes in fact, for a bird's voice does not come from his larynx but from his syrinx lower down.

Another means of identifying birds is by measurement. That we have done our best to encourage by a table, which is the result of a large number of observations and some two thousand calculations, and which took more time than anything else in our little book. If this is used in addition to the analyses and keys, there will be few failures in identification. The eggs we have dealt with in a similar manner, and we would have added the nests had we been able to discover a workable system of sorting. There are several well-defined types of nests. There is the Sand Martin's nest, for instance, which is a burrow, such as is used by the Kingfisher and others ; there is the Duck's nest made on the ground; there is the floating nest such as is made by the Grebe ; there is the mud nest such as is made by the Thrush and the House Martin ; there is the nest in a tree trunk bored by the Woodpeckers ; there is the flat nest of the Ring Dove, and the Stork ; there is the cave nest of the Rock Dove : there are the woven nests of so many of our small birds, the basket nests of the Crows, the felted nests of the Dippers, the bottle nest of the Tits, and the domed nests of so many other birds ; and then there are, of course, the mere scratch nests of the Phasianidæ, and the no nests at all of the Terns ; and in addition to these are the adapted nests of the Hobby and Peregrine, and the peculiar foundling arrangements of the Cuckoo.

And among these nests we can have another division into those that are built only for the year, and those that are returned to again and again, which are generally built by the birds that pair for life, like the

Swallow, the Raven, the Magpie, the Jackdaw, the Starling, the House Sparrow, the Robin, the Wren, the Ringdove, the Tits, and the Falcons ; the nests for the year being by far the most numerous, and being tenanted by the birds who take a fresh mate annually, such as the Thrush, the Chaffinch, the Whitethroat, the Skylark, the Willow Warbler, and the Snipe, wl o all abandon their nests when the brood is reared, and in some cases migrate about the country; for there is an inland migration as well as a foreign one.

A bird always breeds in the coldest climate he visits, and some birds are migrants in one country and residents in another. The Robin, for instance, is resident here, but migrant in Germany ; and the search for food, warmth, and light will take a bird about an island, just as it will take him across the sea. No bird breeding south of us comes here, except as a straggler ; but a large number of birds breeding in the north visit us for about a month, twice a year, like the Little Stint and Redshank, which linger here on their way to and from more genial climes ; while others, like the Wigeon and Fieldfare, find we are as far south as they care for, and stay the whole of the winter with us. These winter visitants only stay to breed here in rare instances. Those that nest here come in the spring, and some of these come back to their old nests, though the majority merely settle in the same neighbourhood. The same thing holds good regarding the residents that merely migrate about the country ; some will return, year after year, to the old nest, and some will always build afresh. But in most cases, when the nest is returned to, it is improved and enlarged, and we thus have another variety of nest—the one with additions.

But we must not give way to "migration fever" ; let us return to our proper task, having given up flight and song and nest as useless for the main subject, though useful as auxiliaries. Let us take a bird of prey, which, being neither an Owl nor a Vulture, must be one of the Falconidæ. The first question to ask is, if its lores are feathered. The "lore," as we showed in our diagram of the Thrush, on page 34, is the space between the eye and the base of the beak. If the bird has feathered lores, it is a Honey Buzzard, our sole representative of the genus *Pernis*, which is the only bird of the Falcon family in this country that has not its lores bare. If its lores are not feathered, has it a forked tail ? There are only three Falconine genera with forked tails—*Elanus*, of which only one specimen is on record, and that from Ireland ; and *Elanoides*, of which only two specimens have been taken here. It is therefore antecedently improbable that it will be one of these. However, you will know Elanoides at once by his white head and neck, and his long black narrow wings ; and a handsome fellow he is ; and Elanus will give you as little difficulty with his grey head and neck, and his black and white wings. As our bird has neither black nor black and white wings, he must, if he has a forked tail, be a *Milvus*, and of Milvus we have two species on the list—one only seen here once ; the other, *ictinus*, the Kite, which was at one time one of our commonest birds, and even caught his food in Cheapside.

But our specimen has not a forked tail, and therefore he is no Kite. Look at his feet. If his tarsus is feathered to the toes, his genus is *Aquila;* if it is only feathered in front, it is *Archibuteo ;* and if he belongs to either of these genera his fourth primary will be the longest feather in his wing. But as this is not the case, we must continue our search. Is his tarsus " scutellate," that is plated, in front, and " reticulate," that is netted, at the back ; if so, his fifth primary will be the longest, and he will be *Haliaëtus albicilla*, the Sea Eagle, always distinguishable at a glance from Aquila by the featherless tarsus. But there are no reticulations on the back of the tarsus, neither are there on the front ; and we thus get rid of two more genera, in each of which the first primary is longer than the secondaries. One of these is *Falco*, which has breeches, or feathers looking like such, on the legs, and has also a deeply notched bill ; while the other, *Pandion*, has no breeches, and a very faintly notched bill ; in addition to which, Pandion has an outer toe that he can turn backwards as if he were an Owl, and he is the only Falcon that can do this ; " Falconine " had been better said, perhaps, for it seems rather far-fetched to call an Osprey a Falcon. Looking again, we find our bird's tarsus has scutellations both in front and at the back, and examining the wing we find the first primary is very short. He must, consequently, belong to one of three genera. If his fourth primary is the longest, and his first four primaries have a notch in them, he is a *Buteo;* if his third and fourth primaries are the longest, and he has a ruff round his neck, making him look something like an Owl, he is a *Circus;* but if he has the fourth and fifth primaries longest, he is an *Accipiter;* and you can confirm the diagnosis by referring to his wings, which are short compared to the long wings of Circus and Buteo.

But if Accipiter is his genus, what is his species ? There are three Accipiters, one of which is but half the size of the others, so that by measurement he is unmistakable. But leaving measurement alone, we can discover him by his colour. If he were ashy brown above, and whitish below, he would be either *atricapillus* or *palumbarius;* the former of which has only three appearances on record, while the latter is yearly becoming rarer, being no other than the once common Gos Hawk, which in flight can be recognised at once by the vigorous use of the tail in steering, and by the croaking sort of scream. Our bird is greyish blue above, with a white patch on the nape, and he is buffish in ground colour below, the buff being barred with brown ; and lastly, he is a foot long, while the Gos Hawk is nearly two. There is, therefore, every reason to suppose that he is a Sparrow Hawk ; and a Sparrow Hawk, *Accipiter nisus*, he is.

And now, having taken an example from each end of our table, from the Raptores we ruled off at the beginning, to the Passerines we left at the end, on the principle that if a bird did not belong to any of the other families, he must be placed there ; let us have a third and last example from the main brigade—that is, the main brigade of our tabulation, and not in reality, for out of the 10,000 species of birds in the world, more than half are Passerine ; and if we were to count heads instead of species, the preponderance of Passerines would be enormous.

Here is a bird with four toes. Three of them are webbed to the claws, and the hind toe is free from the tarsus, although it has a sort of lobe to it. One look at the broad lamellate bill tells us it is a Duck. The fact is too obvious to be overlooked. Let us turn up at once our analysis of the Anatidæ.

Now, just as we picked out *Pernis* from the Falconidæ by his naked lores, so can we pick out *Cygnus* from the Anatidæ. No one is likely to be in doubt as to what is a Swan; but should he be so, let him look at the lores. Our Duck is not a Swan. Does he belong to the genus *Mergus*? Is he a Merganser? Look at his beak. Is it cut into fine sharp teeth, projecting backwards as if it were a saw? No. Look at a Swan's beak; you will see that the under mandible fits right up into the upper one, and that the sides are apparently grooved. Look at a Goose's beak, and you will see that the leaf-shaped edges look like the edge of a lace collar. Look at a Duck's beak, and you will see the plates as fine as a comb. But a Merganser's beak? It is undoubtedly a saw, and a saw such as is possessed by no other British birds than the four of the *Mergus* genus we know as the Goosander, the Smew, the Hooded Merganser, and the Red-breasted Merganser, *M. serrator.*

Our example is not a Merganser. Is he an Eider? Do the feathers of his forehead come down to form a central tract along his bill? No. Is his bill spatulate, like a spatula? Is he, in fact, a Shoveller? No. Now, we know that he has a lobe on his hind toe. If that were not well developed, or if it were absent, he would belong to one of seven genera. Let us run him through these.

The group can be divided into those having the feet webs notched, and those having them entire. The genera with notched webs are *Dafila* and *Querquedula*, the former with a pointed tail, the latter with a rounded tail. The genera with the unnotched webs can be divided into groups—one with the tarsus reticulate all round, and one with the tarsus of any other pattern. Those with the entirely reticulate tarsi are the Geese, *Anser* and *Bernicla;* Anser with the beak nearly as long as the head, and *Bernicla* with the bill much shorter than the head—a distinction that may not be very great, but is really as great as that adopted by such authors as are not content to treat these two genera as one. There are three genera with the tarsus not completely reticulate; these are *Mareca*, *Tadorna*, and *Anas;* the last with a wedge-shaped tail; the first with a bill much shorter than the head; and the third with a white wing shoulder, and being, in fact, the handsome Sheld Ducks, or Sheldrakes, if you so please.

But our bird had a well-developed hind lobe, and consequently does not belong to this group of seven. It must be one of the five that are left. Look at its axillaries; are they white or brown? White. That is enough. But suppose they were brown. Its genus would then either be *Œdemia*, which are black Ducks with a tumid bill; or *Clangula*, which has the nostrils in the middle of the bill and 16 feathers in the tail; or *Harelda*, which has a tapering bill, and two enormously long middle feathers in a tail which has 14 in all; or *Cosmonetta*, which is the Harlequin Duck, so gaily striped and spotted that he can be picked out at a glance from the whole of the British avifauna. But a Duck with a large lobe on the hind toe and white axillaries must be of the genus *Fuligula.*

But which Fuligula? He has not a black head, and consequently can be neither *cristata* or *marila*. He has not a brown back, and consequently he is neither *nyroca* nor *rufina*. There is only one species left and that fits him exactly:—" head, chestnut; back, grey; wing speculum, grey"; further, his bill is black, blue and black; and finally there is no doubt he is a Pochard. Let us compare his measurements. His reference letters are Od ; the average length of the species is given as 18 in. ; the proportion that his wing should bear to his length is ·47 ; the proportion his tail should bear is ·15 ; the proportion his beak should bear is ·12 ; the proportion his tarsus should bear is ·08. And now for the actual measurements :—length, $17\frac{7}{8}$ inches—we cannot quite stretch to the extra eighth—wing $8\frac{3}{8}$ inches; tail, $2\frac{3}{4}$ inches ; beak, $2\frac{1}{4}$ inches ; tarsus, $1\frac{1}{2}$ inches ; which are surely near enough for all practical purposes.

A word of caution in conclusion. Do not let it be supposed that the accepted classification is dependent on the mere external characters we have chosen as our guides to identify. For the technical descriptions of the different families, genera and species, the student must go elsewhere, and he will then have his work cut out for him in exploring the intricacies of synonymy, and deciding on the authority he will follow in each particular case. And he will probably end by being quite ready for the new classification and the revision of the British list.

CHAPTER VII.

THE PASSERINE SUB-FAMILIES.

T HE sub-families of the Passeridæ are distinguishable as follows,
the remiges being 18 or 19, except where stated :

ORIOLINÆ (Golden Oriole)—bright yellow, with black wings and
tail, remiges often 20. 72.

ICTERINÆ (Red-winged Starling)—glossy black with scarlet wing
coverts. 119.

PANURINÆ (Bearded Tit)—black pointed moustache, long rufous
tail. 49.

AMPELINÆ (Waxwing)—red waxy tips to secondaries ; erectile
crest. 77.

CINCLINÆ (Dippers) — dense fibrous blackish plumage, with
undercoat of down ; white throat ; concave wings ; two toes
united. 47, 48.

These five sub-families are unmistakable, the rest can be divided
into—

1. First primary quite half as long as second.
2. First primary obsolete or minute.
3. First primary less than half as long as second.

First primary quite half as long as second—

TROGLODYTINÆ (Wren)—plumage long and soft ; wings
concave ; two toes united. 59.

CORVINÆ (Raven, Crows, Jackdaw, Jay, and Magpie)—wings
flat ; remiges 19 to 22 ; plumage close and glossy. 122-131.

First primary obsolete or minute—

FRINGILLINÆ (Finches)—bill short and conical ; gape line
straight or arched ; remiges 18. 87-108.

EMBERIZINÆ (Buntings)—bill short and conical ; gape line
angular ; palate knobbed. 109-118.

MOTACILLINÆ (Wagtails and Pipits)—bill narrow and slender ;
legs long ; tail long. 60-71.

STURNINÆ (Starlings)—metallic plumage with spots ; bill
straight and slender. 120, 121.

HIRUNDININÆ (Swallows)—bill wide ; legs short ; wings long ;
tail forked. 81-84.

ALAUDINÆ (Larks)—remiges often 20 ; tarsus scutellate back
and front. 132-137.

First primary less than half as long as second—

CERTHIINÆ (Creepers)—bill long, curved, and slender ; tail rounded ; hind claw long and curved. 85, 86.

MUSCICAPINÆ (Flycatchers)—bill broad, flat and bristled at base. 78-80.

LANIINÆ (Shrikes)—bill short and deeply toothed ; two toes united. 73, 76.

SITTINÆ (Nuthatch)—bill long and straight ; feet large and strong ; two toes united. 58.

PARINÆ (Tits)—three toes united as far as second joint ; hind claw long. 50-57.

ACCENTORINÆ (Accentors)—bill strong and straight ; wings rounded ; tarsus scutellate ; two toes united. 45, 46.

TURDINÆ (Thrushes and Warblers)—see analysis of genera. 1-44.

CHAPTER VIII.

THE ORDERS.

ARRANGED as in the list of coloured plates, our 35 families will be found to group themselves into the following 18 customary ornithological orders.

PASSERES—Passeridæ.

PICARIÆ—Cypselidæ, Caprimulgidæ, Picidæ, Alcedinidæ, Coraciidæ, Meropidæ, Upupidæ, Cuculidæ.

STRIGES—Strigidæ.

ACCIPITRES—Vulturidæ, Falconidæ.

STEGANOPODES—Pelecanidæ.

HERODIONES—Ardeidæ, Ciconiidæ, Plataleidæ, Ibididæ.

ODONTOGLOSSÆ—Phœnicopteridæ.

ANSERES—Anatidæ.

COLUMBÆ—Columbidæ.

PTEROCLETES—Pteroclidæ.

GALLINÆ—Phasianidæ.

HEMIPODII—Turnicidæ.

FULICARIÆ—Rallidæ.

ALECTORIDES—Gruidæ, Otididæ.

LIMICOLÆ—Œdicnemidæ, Glareolidæ, Charadriidæ, Scolopacidæ.

GAVIÆ—Laridæ.

PYGOPODES—Alcidæ, Colymbidæ, Podicipepidæ.

TUBINARES—Procellariidæ.

This, or something on similar lines, is the classification to be found in most of the modern books on birds, the old arrangement into Rapaces, Passeres, Scansores, Gallinaces, Grallæ, and Palmipedes, as given in Stanley, for instance, having long since been abandoned. But it is generally admitted that this classification is merely temporary, and that a new system is inevitable. What this system is to be, except that it will be an anatomical one, is not clear; but it seems probable that it will be based on the arrangement proposed by Huxley in his paper in the "Proceedings" of the Zoological Society for 1867, which arrangement, with a few changes, was that adopted by W. K. Parker in his article on Birds in the Encyclopædia Britannica.

Professor Huxley's paper appears in brief in his "Manual of the Anatomy of Vertebrated Animals." He divides the birds into two great groups :

I. In which the metacarpals are not anchylosed together, and the tail is longer than the body—by the tail being meant that member itself and not the quill feathers it supports.

II. In which the metacarpals are anchylosed together, and the tail is shorter than the body.

To the first group belong the SAURURÆ represented by the Archæopteryx, that curious extinct bird found fossil in the Upper Oolites of Solenhofen, which was about as big as a Rook, which had a long lizard-like tail of twenty separate vertebræ, all distinct from one another and carrying a pair of feathers, one on each side, and which had also two free claws to the wing, &c.

To the second group all the existing birds can, as far as we know, be referred. It can be divided into :

> I.   RATITÆ, having the sternum or breast bone devoid of a keel.
>
> II.   CARINATÆ, having the sternum with a keel.

We need not concern ourselves with the subdivisions of the Ratitæ, as no birds without a keel to their breast bone have been recognised as belonging to our national avifauna, and we doubt if any enthusiast would be bold enough to add one to the British List on the strength of having shot it on British ground.

Familiar as the breast bone may be, on the dinner table and elsewhere, it is perhaps as well to give a sketch in order that there may

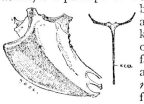

be no mistake. Here is one seen in section and in three-quarter view, in which the keel is duly, though somewhat microscopically, noted. Of the Ratitæ the most familiar example is the Ostrich, which has a breast bone as flat as a raft, raft being *ratis* in Latin and thus being responsible for the derivation.

In the Carinatæ, then, the sternum possesses a keel, and ossifies from a median centre in that keel, as well as from lateral paired centres. The long axes of the adjacent parts of the scapula and coracoid make an acute or a slightly obtuse angle, and are never, even approximately, identical or parallel. The scapula always has a distinct acromion and the coracoid a clavicular process. The vomer is comparatively small, and allows the pterygoids and palatines to articulate directly with the basisphenoidal rostrum.

The Carinatæ, so-called from the Latin *carina*, a keel, are classified according to their palatal bones ; or, to be more precise—we will explain the technical terms immediately we have cleared the way—into :

> I.   Having the vomer broad behind, and interposing between the pterygoids, the palatines, and the basisphenoidal rostrum.
>
> II.   Having the vomer narrow behind ; the pterygoids and palatines articulating largely with the basisphenoidal rostrum.

To the first of these no British birds belong, the type of the group being the Tinamous. Of the second there are three divisions ; and representatives of each of these are to be found in our list. But, to proceed in proper sequence. The group having the vomer narrow behind can be divided into :

> I.   Having the maxillo-palatines free.
>
> II.   Having the maxillo-palatines united.

Dealing first with those having the free maxillo-palatines we find them further classified into :

> I.   Having the vomer pointed in front—Schizognathæ.
>
> II.   Having the vomer truncated in front.

The Schizognathous birds we will tabulate presently, and to save the repetition of some very long words, we will here be satisfied with

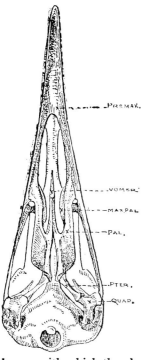

a representative. Here is a "Schizogna-thous" skull, that of the Crane, with the lower half removed so as to show the arrangement of the bones we want. Here *quad.* is the quadrate bone on which the lower jaw works; *pter.* is the pterygoid; *pal.* is the palatine; *max. pal.* is the maxillo-palatine; *premax.* is the premaxillary, and *vomer* is the vomer, the bone which is the key to the classification, and which varies more than almost any other bone in the skull of a bird. It is a small bone, thin as a knife blade and rarely broader, standing on its edge in the very centre of the roof of the bird's mouth, a bone so delicate that it is one of the first to vanish when the student in search of it first prepares a skull. It will be noticed that in the case of the Crane it ends in a point towards the beak, and it so ends in the skulls of Plovers, Gulls, Fowls, and Pigeons, and others. In this group, we may as well quote as paraphrase, "the maxillo-palatines are usually elongated and lamellar; they pass inwards over the anterior processes of the palatine bones, with which they become united, and then bending backwards, along the inner edge of the palatines, leave a broader or a narrower fissure between themselves and the vomer, and do not unite with it or with one another."

But in the skulls of the Passerine birds the vomer is not pointed

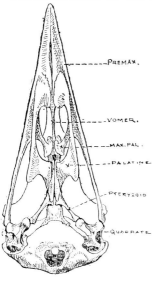

in front. Here, for instance, is the skull of a Raven, one of the Passerines. It is "Ægithognathous," with the maxillo-palatines free, and the vomer unpointed, or rather cut off at a blunt angle. The lettering is as before, but owing to the more open character of the skull the parts are more clearly traceable. Again, the quadrates lead on to the pterygoids which lead on to the palatines, and in the centre of the palatal framework we see the thin edge of the vomer. It will be seen that in this skull, as in that of the Crane, the maxillo-palatines are clearly separate. The vomer in this group is cleft behind, embracing the rostrum of the sphenoid between its forks. "The palatines have postero-external angles. The maxillo-palatines are slender at their origin, and extend inwards and backwards obliquely over the palatines, ending beneath the

E 2

vomer in expanded extremities, which do not become united by bone either with one another or with the vomer. The anterior part of the nasal septum, in front of the vomer, is frequently ossified, and the interval between it and the pre-maxilla filled up with spongy bone ; but no union takes place between this ossification and the vomer."

Dealing next with the group in which the maxillo-palatines are united, we find that a large number of birds have the vomer " either abortive or so small that it disappears from the skeleton. When it exists it is always slender, and tapers to a point anteriorly. The maxillo-palatines are united across the middle line, either directly or by the intermediation of ossifications in the nasal septum." And the posterior ends of the palatines, and the anterior ends of the pterygoids articulate directly with the rostrum, as they do in the Schizognathæ. Under such circumstances the skull is " Desmognathous."

Of such a skull we have an example in that here given of the

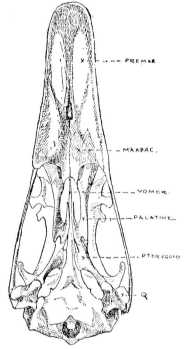

Goose. We need not repeat the references. The differences in the structure of the palate, and consequently of the whole skull are clear enough. This type of skull is represented in the Birds of Prey, the Cuckoos, Kingfishers, Swans and Ducks, Storks and Cormorants, and others. To this group has since been given the name of Saurognathæ, and then it includes the Woodpeckers, the Picidæ, in whom the vomerine halves are permanently distinct and the maxillo-palatines arrested.

But it will perhaps be more satisfactory to give Huxley's grouping in tabular form, so far as it affects the families we have been endeavouring to identify, taking no note of exceptions, for there are exceptions, and leaving the student who takes any interest in the matter to pursue the modifications for himself.

AVES.

1.   SAURURÆ—as the Archæopteryx, only found fossil.
2.   RATITÆ— as the Ostrich, breast bone unkeeled; no British representatives.
3.   CARINATÆ—with keeled breast bone.

CARINATÆ.

1.   *Dromæognathæ*—vomer broad behind.
2.   *Schizognathæ*—vomer narrow behind, pointed in front; maxillo-palatines free.

3. *Ægithognathæ*—vomer narrow behind, truncated in front ;
maxillo-palatines free.

4. *Desmognathæ*—maxillo-palatines united.

DROMÆOGNATHÆ—no British representatives.

SCHIZOGNATHÆ.

Charadriomorphæ—	Œdicnemidæ.
	Glareolidæ.
	Charadriidæ.
	Scolopacidæ.
Cecomorphæ—	Laridæ.
	Alcidæ.
	Colymbidæ.
	Podicipepidæ.
	Procellariidæ.
Geranomorphæ—	Rallidæ.
	Gruidæ.
	Otididæ.
Turnicimorphæ—	Turnicidæ.
Alectoromorphæ—	Phasianidæ.
Pteroclomorphæ—	Pteroclidæ.
Peristeromorphæ—	Columbidæ.

ÆGITHOGNATHÆ.

Cypselomorphæ—	Cypselidæ.
	Caprimulgidæ.
Coracomorphæ—	Passeridæ.
Celeomorphæ—	Picidæ.

DESMOGNATHÆ.

Aetomorphæ—	Strigidæ.
	Vulturidæ.
	Falconidæ.
Coccygomorphæ—	Cuculidæ.
	Alcedinidæ.
	Upupidæ.
	Meropidæ.
	Coraciidæ.
Chenomorphæ—	Anatidæ.
Amphimorphæ—	Phœnicopteridæ.
Pelargomorphæ—	Ardeidæ.
	Ciconiidæ.
	Plataleidæ.
	Ibididæ.
Dysporomorphæ—	Pelecanidæ.

CHAPTER IX

INDEX TO THE FAMILIES AND SUB-FAMILIES.

———◦•◦———

IT is to be understood by the student that the particulars given hereunder are not necessarily those on which the customary ornithological classification is based, but simply such as happen to be most useful for purposes of identification, and that only such points are mentioned as are necessary for distinguishing the families and sub-families from each other with regard to their representatives on the British list.

ACCENTORINÆ—sub-family of Passeridæ (range 5 in. to 7½ in.) —first primary less than half as long as second; bill strong and straight; remiges 19; tarsus scutellate; two toes united. Genus, *Accentor;* the Hedge Sparrow. 45, 46.

ALAUDINÆ—sub-family of Passeridæ (range 5 in. to 7¼ in.)—first primary very small; remiges 19 or 20; tarsus scutellated back and front. Genera, *Alauda* and *Otocorys;* the Larks. 132-137.

ALCEDINIDÆ (range 6½ in. to 13 in.)—four toes, two of them united as far as the second joint, and two as far as the first; remiges 22; third primary longest. Genera, *Alcedo* and *Ceryle;* the Kingfishers. 151, 152.

ALCIDÆ (range 8½ in. to 32 in.)—three toes, united as far as the claws; wings fin-like; tail rudimentary. Genera, *Alca, Uria, Mergulus* and *Fratercula;* the Razorbill, Auks, Guillemots, and Puffin. 373-379.

AMPELINÆ—sub-family of Passeridæ (range 7 in. to 7½ in.); red waxy tips to secondaries; long erectile crest. Genus, *Ampelis;* the Waxwing. 77.

ANATIDÆ (range 13 in. to 60 in.)—four toes, three of them united as far as the claws; bill broad and lamellate, or toothed. Genera, *Anser, Bernicla, Cygnus, Tadorna, Anas, Spatula, Dafila, Querquedula, Mareca, Fuligula, Clangula, Harelda, Cosmonetta, Somateria, Œdemia,* and *Mergus;* the Geese, Swans, and Ducks. 217-262.

ARDEIDÆ (range 12 in. to 42 in.)—four toes, two united; bill long and straight; legs long; middle claw pectinate. Genera, *Ardea, Nycticorax,* and *Botaurus;* the Herons and Bitterns. 202-211.

CAPRIMULGIDÆ (range 10 in. to 13 in.)—four toes, three of them united no further than the first joint; phalanges, 2, 3, 4, 3; bill gaping. Genus, *Caprimulgus;* the Nightjars. 141-143.

CERTHIINÆ—sub-family of Passeridæ (range 4½ in. to 6 in.); first primary less than half as long as second; bill long, curved, and slender; rounded tail and long curved hind claw. Genera, *Certhia* and *Tichodroma;* the Creepers. 85, 86.

CHARADRIIDÆ (range 6 in. to 16 in.).

    I.—Three toes, united near base ; bill longer or shorter than head, and not dilated at point. Genera, *Cursorius, Eudromias, Charadrius, Ægialitis,* and *Hæmatopus;* the Courser, Dotterel, Plovers (except the Grey Plover), and the Oystercatcher. 292-295, 297-300, 303.

    II.—Four toes, three of them united near the base. Genera, *Squatarola, Strepsilas,* and *Vanellus;* the Grey Plover, which has a white tail with broad black and brown bars ; the Turnstone, which has orange legs ; and the Lapwing, which has a crest. 296, 302, 301.

CICONIIDÆ (range 39 in. to 44 in.)—four toes, three of them united no further than the first joint ; long legs ; long bill ; over 30 remiges. Genus, *Ciconia;* the Storks. 212, 213.

CINCLINÆ—sub-family of Passeridæ (range 6 in. to 6½ in.) ; two toes united ; dense, fibrous blackish plumage ; white throat ; concave wings. The only passerine birds with down. Genus, *Cinclus;* the Dippers. 47, 48.

COLUMBIDÆ (range 11 in. to 17 in.)—four toes, three in front, divided throughout ; bill deflected, thinnest in middle, expanding towards point ; nostrils in soft skin at base of bill ; no down ; feathers without aftershaft ; second primary longest. Genera, *Columba, Turtur,* and *Ectopistes;* the Doves and Pigeons. 263-267.

COLYMBIDÆ (range 21 in. to 33 in.)—four toes, three of them united as far as the claws and one webbed to tarsus ; wings short ; bill compressed and pointed ; tail very short and rounded. Genus, *Colymbus;* the Divers. 380-383.

CORACIIDÆ (range 11 in. to 12 in.)—four toes, three in front divided throughout ; bill compressed ; upper mandible decurved at tip ; 23 remiges ; tarsus scutellate in front, reticulate at back. Genus, *Coracias;* the Roller. 153.

CORVINÆ—sub-family of Passeridæ (range 14 in. to 24 in.) ; remiges 19 to 22 ; first primary quite half as long as second, fifth and sixth longest, first four graduated ; plumage close and glossy ; two toes united. Genera, *Pyrrhocorax, Nucifraga, Garrulus, Pica,* and *Corvus;* the Chough, Nutcracker, Jay, Magpie, Jackdaw, Crow, Rook, and Raven. 122-131.

CUCULIDÆ (range 12 in. to 17 in.)—four toes, divided throughout, two in front and two behind ; bill short or moderate. Genera, *Cuculus, Coccystes,* and *Coccyzus;* the Cuckoos. 157-160.

CYPSELIDÆ (range 7 in. to 8½ in.).

    I.—Four toes, divided throughout, all in front ; remiges 18 ; phalanges, 2, 3, 3, 3. Genus, *Cypselus;* the Swifts. 138, 139.

    II.—Four toes, divided throughout, three in front ; tail feathers with sharp, protruding spines. Genus, *Acanthyllis;* the Needle-tailed Swift. 140.

EMBERIZINÆ—sub-family of Passeridæ (range 4¾ in. to 7 in.)—first primary obsolete ; bill short and conical ; gape line angular ; knob on palate. Genera, *Emberiza, Calcarius,* and *Plectrophanes;* the Buntings. 109-118.

FALCONIDÆ (range 10 in. to 36 in.)—Birds of Prey ; bill strong, sharp, and curving, and with a cere at base ; claws powerful ; feathers on crown. Genera, *Circus, Buteo, Archibuteo, Aquila,*

Haliaëtus, Accipiter, Milvus, Elanoides, Elanus, Pernis, Falco,
and *Pandion;* the Harriers, Buzzards, Eagles, Hawks, Kites,
Falcons, and Osprey. 173-198.

FRINGILLINÆ—sub-family of Passeridæ (range 4¼ in. to 9 in.) ;
remiges rarely more than 18 ; first primary obsolete or minute ;
bill short and conical ; gape line straight or arched.   Genera,
*Carduelis, Serinus, Ligurinus, Coccothraustes, Passer, Fringilla,
Linota, Pyrrhula,* and *Loxia;* the Finches, Sparrows, Linnets,
Grosbeaks, and Crossbills. 87-108.

GLAREOLIDÆ (range 8½ in. to 9 in.)—four toes, two united ; bill
short ; wings long ; legs short ; tail forked.   Genus, *Glareola;*
the Pratincole. 291.

GRUIDÆ (range 39 in. to 48 in.)—four toes, two united ; bill long ;
legs long, middle claw smooth. Genus, *Grus;* the Cranes. 285, 286.

HIRUNDININÆ—sub-family of Passeridæ (range 4½ in. to 8½ in.) ;
nine primaries ; secondaries broad and notched ; wide bill ; short
legs ; long wings ; forked tail. Genus, *Hirundo;* the Swallows
and Martins. 81-84.

IBIDIDÆ (range 21 in. to 22 in.)—four toes, three united as far as the
claws ; bill long, slender and decurved, point rounded ; 27 remiges.
Genus, *Ibis;* the Ibis. 215.

ICTERINÆ—sub-family of Passeridæ (range 8½ in. to 9 in.) ; glossy
black with scarlet wing coverts. Genus, *Agelæus;* the Red-winged
Starling. 119.

LANIINÆ—sub-family of Passeridæ (range 7½ in. to 9 in.) ; remiges
19 ; first primary less than half as long as second ; bill short and
deeply toothed ; two toes united. Genus, *Lanius;* the Shrikes and
Woodchat. 73-76.

LARIDÆ (range 8½ in. to 33 in.)
   I.—Three toes, united as far as the claws ; wings long ; remiges
      31; tail forked or square. Genus, *Rissa;* the Kittiwake. 367.
   II.—Four toes, three united and one webbed to tarsus ; bill short.
      Genus, *Pagophila;* the Ivory Gull. 368.
   III.—Four toes, three of them united as far as the claws, the fourth
      very short.   Genera, *Hydrochelidon, Sterna, Anous, Xema,
      Rhodostethia,* and *Larus;* the Terns and Gulls. 241-366.

MEROPIDÆ (range 10 in. to 11 in.)—remiges, 23 ; second primary
longest ; four toes, three united, two as far as the second joint and two
as far as the first ; tail long. Genus, *Merops;* the Bee-eaters. 154, 155.

MOTACILLINÆ—sub-family of Passeridæ (range 5½ in. to 8 in.) ; two
toes united ; first primary obsolete or minute ; narrow, slender bill ;
long legs ;.long tail.   Genera, *Motacilla* and *Anthus;* the Wagtails
and Pipits. 60-71.

MUSCICAPINÆ—sub-family of Passeridæ (range 5 in. to 5½ in.) ;
remiges 19 ; first primary less than half as long as second ; bill
broad, flat, and bristled at base. Genus, *Muscicapa;* the Flycatchers. 78-80.

ŒDICNEMIDÆ (range 16 in. to 17 in.) ; three toes united as far as
the second joint ; remiges 29 ; Genus, *Œdicnemus;* the Stone
Curlew. 290.

ORIOLINÆ—sub-family of Passeridæ (range 9 in. to 9½ in.) ; golden
yellow bird with black wings ; remiges often 20 ; first primary half
as long as second. Genus, *Oriolus;* the Golden Oriole. 72.

OTIDIDÆ (range 16 in. to 45 in.) ; three toes united near base and edged with membranes. Genus, *Otis;* the Bustards. 287-289.

PANURINÆ—sub-family of Passeridæ (range 6 in. to 6½ in.) ; black pointed moustache ; long rufous tail. Genus, *Panurus;* the Bearded Tit. 49.

PARINÆ—sub-family of Passeridæ (range 4 in. to 6 in.) ; first primary less than half as long as second ; three toes united as far as the second joint ; long hind claw. Genera, *Acredula* and *Parus;* the Tits. 50-57.

PASSERIDÆ (range 3½ in. to 24 in.)—four toes, three united or two united, or all divided ; remiges 18 to 22 ; indexed under the different sub-families—Alaudinæ, Ampelinæ, Certhiinæ, Cinclinæ, Corvinæ, Emberizinæ, Fringillinæ, Hirundininæ, Icterinæ, Laniinæ, Motacillinæ, Muscicapinæ, Oriolinæ, Panurinæ, Parinæ, Sittinæ, Sturninæ, Troglodytinæ, and Turdinæ. 1-137.

PELECANIDÆ (range 27 in. to 36 in.)—four toes, all united ; bill long ; tarsus compressed ; third claw pectinate. Genera, *Phalacrocorax* and *Sula;* the Cormorant, Shag, and Gannet. 199-201.

PHASIANIDÆ (range 7 in. to 36 in.)—four toes, three united no further than first joint ; eleventh wing feather shortest ; short legs ; short bill. Genera, *Tetrao, Phasianus, Perdix,* and *Coturnix;* the Capercaillie, Grouse, Ptarmigan, Pheasant, Partridge, and Quail. 269-276.

PHŒNICOPTERIDÆ (range 50 in. to 70 in.)—four toes, three united as far as the claws ; web incised ; bill bent half way. Genus, *Phœnicopterus;* the Flamingo. 216.

PICIDÆ (range 5½ in. to 14 in.)—four toes, two in front, two behind ; bill long ; tongue long ; 12 tail feathers, two outer ones hidden under the two next. Genera, *Picus, Gecinus,* and *Iynx;* the Woodpeckers and Wryneck. 144-150.

PLATALEIDÆ (range 30 in. to 32 in.)—four toes, three united as far as the second joint ; spatulate bill ; 30 remiges. Genus, *Platalea;* the Spoonbill. 214.

PODICIPEDIDÆ (range 8 in. to 24 in.)—four toes, with pennate and entire lobes ; tail a tuft of small downy feathers; tarsus compressed. Genus, *Podiceps;* the Grebes. 384-388.

PROCELLARIIDÆ (range 5 in. to 19 in.)—nostrils in a tube ; bill unserrated and ending in a nail.
  I.—Three toes, united as far as claws. *Oceanites,* 398.
  II.—Four toes, three united as far as the claws. Genera, *Fulmarus, Puffinus, Bulweria,* and *Procellaria;* the Petrels and Shearwaters. 389-397.

PTEROCLIDÆ (range 16 in. to 20 in.)—three toes, united as far as the claws ; tail of 16 feathers, two of considerable length ; wings long; tail wedge-shaped. Genus, *Syrrhaptes;* Pallas's Sand Grouse. 268.

RALLIDÆ (range 7 in. to 16 in.).
  I.—Feet lobate. Genera, *Fulica* and *Gallinula;* the Coot and Moorhen. 283, 284.
  II.—Feet divided ; short stout beak ; large feet ; short legs ; short tail ; rounded wings. Genera, *Crex* and *Rallus;* the Crakes and Water Rail. 278-282.

SCOLOPACIDÆ (range 5½ in. to 26 in.).

I.—Three toes, united near base; tail feathers doubly notched. Genus, *Calidris;* the Sanderling.   324.

II.—Four toes, three united as far as the second joint; bill boldly curving upwards. Genus, *Recurvirostra;* the Avocet.   304.

III.—Four toes, three·united near base. Genera, *Himantopus, Scolopax, Macrorhampus, Limicola, Tryngites,* and *Numenius;* the Black-winged Stilt, the Woodcock, Red-breasted Snipe, Broad-billed Sandpiper, Buff-breasted Sandpiper, Curlews, and Whimbrel.   305, 308, 312, 313, 325, 338-340.

IV.—Four toes, three in front, two united. Genera, *Machetes, Bartramia, Limosa,* and *Totanus;* the Ruff, Bartram's Sandpiper, the Godwits, the Sandpiper, the Spotted, Green, Wood, and Solitary Sandpipers, the Redshanks, Greenshank, and Yellow-shank.   323, 326-337.

V.—Feet lobate; lobes narrowly denticulate. Genus, *Phalaropus;* the Phalarope.   306.

VI.—Feet divided; long slender bill. Genera, *Gallinago* and *Tringa;* the Snipes, Stints, and other Sandpipers.   309-311, 314-322.

SITTINÆ—sub-family of Passeridæ (range 5 in. to 6 in.); first primary less than half as long as the second; third, fourth, and fifth longest; long straight bill; large powerful feet; two toes united. Genus, *Sitta;* the Nuthatch., 58.

STRIGIDÆ (range 7 in. to 27 in.)—Birds of Prey; bill powerful and with a cere at base; large head; round face; eyes in front; claws well developed. Genera, *Strix, Asio, Syrnium, Nyctea, Surnia, Nyctala, Scops, Bubo,* and *Athene;* the Owls.   161-170.

STURNINÆ—sub-family of Passeridæ (range 7½ in. to 8½ in.); remiges 19; first primary minute; second primary longest in wing; plumage with metallic tints and spotted; bill straight and slender. Genera, *Sturnus* and *Pastor;* the Starlings.   120, 121.

TROGLODYTINÆ—sub-family of Passeridæ (range 3½ in. to 4 in.); first primary quite half as long as second; plumage long and soft; tail short; two toes united. Genus, *Troglodytes;* the Wren.   59.

TURDINÆ—sub-family of Passeridæ (range 3½ in. to 12 in.); remiges 19; first primary less than half as long as second; bill with or without tooth; toes united or not (see analysis of Genera). Genera, *Turdus, Geocichla, Merula, Monticola, Saxicola, Pratincola, Ruticilla, Cyanecula, Erithacus, Daulias, Sylvia, Melizophilus, Regulus, Phylloscopus, Hypolais, Aëdon, Acrocephalus,* and *Locustella.*   1-44.

TURNICIDÆ (range 6 in. to 6½ in.)—three toes divided throughout. Genus, *Turnix;* the Andalusian Bush Quail.   277.

UPUPIDÆ (range 10 in. to 12 in.)—four toes, two united; erectile crest; remiges 20; first primary small, second equal to seventh and third, fourth and fifth the longest. Genus, *Upupa;* the Hoopoe. 156.

VULTURIDÆ (range 25 in. to 40 in.)—Birds of Prey; strong, sharp, curving bill, with a cere at base; powerful claws; head bald or covered with down; wings long and rounded; tail rounded. Genera, *Gyps* and *Neophron;* the Vultures, 171, 172.

CHAPTER X.

THE GENERA,

———◦◊◦———

IN this list the families and sub-families are arranged alphabetically so as to facilitate reference ; and only such particulars are given as are needed to distinguish one genus from another as regards its representatives in the British List. For the separation of the families reference must be made to the preceding chapters, the separation of the species being given in the chapter that follows.

ACCENTORINÆ. (Plate iv.)
  Accentor—45, 46.

ALAUDINÆ. (Plate x.)
  Alauda—third primary longest ; breast spotted ; tarsus longer than middle toe. 132-136.
  Otocorys—second primary longest ; breast black ; tarsus not longer than middle toe. 137.

ALCEDINIDÆ. (Plate xi.)
  Alcedo—without a crest ; tail short. 151.
  Ceryle—with a crest ; tail long. 152.

ALCIDÆ. (Plate xxxii.)
  1. Bill unfeathered at base.
    Fratercula—bill sheathed with orange. 379.
  2. Bill feathered at base.
    Alca—bill large and compressed ; remiges 30. 373, 374.
    Mergulus—bill broader than high ; remiges 26. 378.
    Uria—bill strong, straight and pointed. 376, 377.

AMPELINÆ. (Plate vi.)
  Ampelis—long erectile crest. 77.

ANATIDÆ. (Plates xix. xx. xxi. xxii.)
  Cygnus—lores naked ; neck long ; legs short. 227-332.
  Mergus—bill narrow, with sharp teeth. 259-262.
  Somateria—bill with a central tract of feathers. 253-255.
  Spatula—bill spatulate and long. 237.
    1. Lobe of hind toe absent or rudimentary.
    2. Lobe of hind toe well developed.
      Lobe of hind toe absent or rudimentary.
        Feet webs notched.
  Dafila—tail pointed. 238.
  Querquedula—tail rounded. 239-241.
        Feet webs entire.
        Tarsus reticulate all round.
  Anser—bill nearly as long as head. 217-222.

Bernicla—bill much shorter than head. 223-226.
    Tarsus otherwise.
Mareca—bill much shorter than head. 242, 243.
Tadorna—wing shoulder white and knobbed. 233, 234.
Anas—tail wedge-shaped. 235, 236.
    Lobe of hind toe well developed.
      1. Axillaries brown.
      2. Axillaries white.
        Axillaries brown.
Œdemia—bill tumid ; body colour black or brown. 256-258.
Clangula—nostrils in middle of bill ; 16 feathers in tail. 249, 250.
Harelda—bill tapering, lamellæ exposed ; 14 feathers in tail, two middle ones very long. 251.
Cosmonetta—bill like that of a goose, lamellæ hidden ; body gaily striped and spotted ; 14 feathers in tail, which is much graduated. 252.
        Axillaries white.
Fuligula—244-248.
ARDEIDÆ. (Plates xvii. xviii.)
      1. Bill much longer than head.
Ardea—bill long and straight ; six powder down tracts ; 12 tail feathers ; tarsus scutellate in front. 202-207.
Ardetta—bill slender and pointed ; four powder down tracts ; 10 tail feathers. 208.
Botaurus—bill higher than broad ; four powder down tracts ; 10 tail feathers. 210, 211.
      2. Bill about as long as head.
Nycticorax—12 tail feathers ; six powder down tracts ; tarsus reticulate in front. 209.
CAPRIMULGIDÆ. (Plate x.)
Caprimulgus—gaping bill with large rictal bristles. 141-143.
CERTHIINÆ. (Plate vi.)
Certhia—tail feathers pointed and stiff. 85.
Tichodroma—tail feathers rounded and soft. 86.
CHARADRIIDÆ. (Plate xxvi.)
      1. With three toes.
      2. With four toes.
    Three toes.
    Bill longer than head.
Hæmatopus—remiges 29. 303.
    Bill shorter than head.
      Second primary longest ; middle toe very long.
Cursorius—tarsus long and slender, and scutellate back and front. 292.
      First primary longest.
        Inner secondaries much shorter than primaries.
Charadrius—tarsus reticulate ; tail feathers barred. 294, 295.
        Inner secondaries as long as primaries.
Ægialitis—tarsus reticulate. 297-300.
Eudromias—tarsus scutellate. 293.
    Four toes.
      Axillaries black.

Squatarola—first primary longest ; black legs. 296.
   Axillaries white.
Strepsilas—first primary longest ; orange legs ; toes cleft to base. 302.
Vanellus—head with a crest ; third and fourth primaries longest ; brown legs ; two toes webbed nearly to first joint. 301.

CICONIIDÆ. (Plate xviii.)
Ciconia—bill and legs deep red. 212, 213.

CINCLINÆ. (Plate iv.)
Cinclus—an under coating of down. 47, 48.

COLUMBIDÆ. (Plate xxiii.)
Columba—tail even ; brown and grey. 263-265.
Ectopistes—tail long and wedge-shaped ; two middle feathers black. 267.
Turtur—black and white patch on neck ; tail rounded ; two middle feathers dusky brown, tipped with white. 266.

COLYMBIDÆ. (Plate xxxii.)
Colymbus—280-283.

CORACIIDÆ. (Plate xii.)
Coracias—narrow bill and flat pointed wings. 153.

CORVINÆ. (Plate ix.)
Corvus—bill black ; tail black. 127-131.
Garrulus—crested ; blue, black and white chequer on wing. 125
Nucifraga—bill black ; tail tipped with white. 124.
Pyrrhocorax—bill red or yellow. 122, 123.
Pica—tail very long and iridescent black. 126.

CUCULIDÆ. (Plate xii.)
Coccystes—head with a crest ; tail long. 158.
Coccyzus—tail of 10 feathers, which are black and white. 159, 160.
Cuculus—tail of 12 feathers, which are black and grey. 157.

CYPSELIDÆ. (Plate x.)
Cypselus—four toes in front ; middle toe three phalanges, outer toe three phalanges. 138, 139.
Acanthyllis—three toes in front ; middle toe four phalanges, outer toe five phalanges. 140.

EMBERIZINÆ. (Plate viii.)
Calcarius—bill yellow, tipped with black. 117.
Emberiza—bill brown, grey, or buff. 109-116.
Plectrophanes—bill black. 118.

FALCONIDÆ. (Plates xiv. xv. xvi.)
   Lores feathered.
Pernis—tarsus reticulate back and front. 188.
   Lores not feathered.
   Tail forked.
Milvus—tarsus scutellate in front, reticulate behind. 184, 185.
Elanoides—white head and neck ; long black narrow wings. 186.
Elanus—grey head and neck ; black and white wings. 187.
   Tail even or rounded.
   Tarsus feathered ; fourth primary longest.

Aquila—tarsus feathered to toes ; 27 remiges. 178, 179.
Archibuteo—tarsus featherless at back ; 24 remiges. 177.
Tarsus scutellate in front, reticulate at back ; fifth primary longest.
Haliaëtus—white tail ; 27 remiges. 180.
Tarsus reticulate back and front ; first primary longer than secondaries.
Falco—legs with breeches ; outer toe not reversible ; bill deeply notched. 189-197.
Pandion—legs without breeches ; outer toe reversible ; bill faintly notched. 198.
Tarsus scutellate back and front ; first primary short.
Buteo—fourth primary longest ; first four primaries notched ; wings long. 176.
Circus—third and fourth primaries longest ; wings long ; head with a ruff. 173-175.
Accipiter—fourth and fifth primaries longest ; wings short. 181-183.

FRINGILLINÆ. (Plates vii. viii.)
Mandibles crossed.
Loxia—105-108.
Upper mandible overhanging.
Pyrrhula—102-104.
Upper mandible rather larger than lower.
Passer—tail square. 93, 94.
Serinus—tail forked. 89, 90.
Mandibles nearly equal.
Tail square.
Coccothraustes—primaries hooked at the tip. 92.
Tail forked.
Ligurinus—second, third and fourth primaries equal. 91.
Carduelis—second primary longer than third, and longest in wing. 87, 88.
Fringilla—second primary shorter than third, which, or the fourth, is the longest in the wing. 95, 96.
Linota—second and third primaries nearly equal, and the longest feathers in the wing. 97-101.

GLAREOLIDÆ. (Plate xxv.)
Glareola—291.

GRUIDÆ. (Plate xxv.)
Grus—285, 286.

HIRUNDININÆ. (Plate vi.)
Hirundo—81-84.

IBIDIDÆ. (Plate xviii.)
Ibis—215.

ICTERINÆ. (Plate ix.)
Agelæus—119.

LANIINÆ. (Plate vi.)
Lanius—73-76.

LARIDÆ. (Plates xxx. xxxi. xxxii.)
1. Three toes.
   Rissa—remiges 31 ; feet black. 367.
2. Four toes ; three all united and one webbed to tarsus.
   Pagophila—plumage pure white. 368.
3. Four toes : three united.
   Larus—tail square. 356-366.
   Rhodostethia—breast white and rose ; tail wedge-shaped. 355.
   Sterna—bill longer than head ; tail forked. 344-352.
   Anous—whole body blackish brown ; tail graduated. 353.
   Xema—bill shorter than head : tail forked ; legs long. 354.
   Hydrochelidon—bill as long as head ; tail slightly forked ; legs short ; webs incised. 341-343.
   Stercorarius—bill strong, cutting, compressed and with a cere ; remiges 26 or 28 ; tail rounded. 369-372.

MEROPIDÆ. (Plate xii.)
   Merops—wings long and pointed ; bastard primary very small ; tail long. 154, 155.

MOTACILLINÆ. (Plate v.)
   Anthus—tail short and forked. 66-71.
   Motacilla—tail long and even. 60-65.

MUSCICAPINÆ. (Plate vi.)
   Muscicapa—78-80.

ŒDICNEMIDÆ. (Plate xxv.)
   Œdicnemus—tarsus reticulate before and behind. 290

ORIOLINÆ. (Plate v.)
   Oriolus—72.

OTIDIDÆ. (Plate xxv.)
   Otis—tarsus reticulate before and behind. 287-289.

PANURINÆ. (Plate iv.)
   Panurus—49.

PARINÆ. (Plate iv.)
   Acredula—long tail, much graduated. 50, 51.
   Parus—short tail, nearly even. 52-57.

PASSERIDÆ. (Plates i. to x.)
   (See under its various sub-families.)

PELECANIDÆ. (Plate xvii.)
   Phalacrocorax—wings moderate; middle toe shorter than outer. 199, 200.
   Sula—wings long ; middle toe not shorter than outer. 201.

PHASIANIDÆ. (Plates xxiii. xxiv.)
   Tarsus feathered—
   Tetrao—tarsus without spurs. 269-272.
   Tarsus unfeathered.
   Coturnix—wings long ; tail very short. 276.
   Perdix—first primary short ; wings short ; tail short. 274, 275.
   Phasianus—wings short ; tail very long. 273.

PHŒNICOPTERIDÆ. (Plate xviii.)
Phœnicopterus—216.

PICIDÆ. (Plate xi.)
Tail feathers stiff and pointed.
Gecinus—greenish in colour. 149.
Picus—black and white or black and red. 144-148.
Tail feathers soft and rounded.
Iynx—brown and greyish white. 150.

PLATALEIDÆ. (Plate xviii.)
Platalea—214.

PODICIPEDIDÆ. (Plate xxxiii.)
Podiceps—384-388.

PROCELLARIIDÆ. (Plate xxxiii.)
Bill as long as head.
Bulweria—unspotted brownish black. 395.
Bill longer than head.
Puffinus—bill slender. 391-394.
Bill shorter than head.
Fulmarus—bill indented or curved. 389, 390.
Procellaria—bill straight to the nail. 396, 397.
Oceanites—bill small and weak ; tail square ; tarsus plated. 398.

PTEROCLIDÆ. (Plate xxiii.)
Syrrhaptes—268.

RALLIDÆ. (Plate xxiv.)
Forehead feathered ; remiges 26.
Crex—bill shorter than head. 278-281.
Rallus—bill longer than head. 282.
Forehead with a shield.
Fulica—foot lobes denticulate ; remiges 25. 284.
Gallinula—foot lobes entire ; remiges 23. 283.

SCOLOPACIDÆ. (Plates xxvii. xxviii, xxix.)
Three toes.
Calidris—324.
Four toes.
Three united as far as second joint.
Recurvirostra—remiges 30 ; bill curved upwards. 304.
Three united near base.
Himantopus—remiges 29 ; black wings ; very long legs. 305.
Limicola—bill long, flat, and wide in the middle. 313.
Macrorhampus—remiges 20; bill long and rounded ; outer web
of foot larger than inner. 312.
Numenius—bill more than twice as long as head, and curved
downwards ; 30 remiges. 338-340.
Scolopax—bill long, straight, and compressed ; 26 remiges. 308.
Tryngites—bill shorter than head. 325.
Three in front, two united.
Bartramia—remiges 26 ; bill no longer than head ; wings not
reaching tip of tail. 326.
Limosa—remiges 28 ; bill nearly twice as long as head and
curving slightly upwards 336, 337.

Machetes—male with a ruff; bill as long as head; wings reaching tip of tail. 323.
Totanus—bill rather longer than head; tail barred and short. 327-335.
Feet lobate.
Phalaropus—remiges 25. 306, 307.
Feet all divided.
Gallinago—bill very straight and long. 309-311.
Tringa—bill rather longer than head; tail without bars. 314-322.

SITTINÆ. (Plate iv.)
 Sitta—58.

STRIGIDÆ. (Plate xiii.)
 Bill straight from base, curved only at tip; 24 remiges; second primary longest.
  Strix—feet rather bristly; nostrils not in cere. 161.
 Bill curved from base.
  Tail long.
   Syrnium—facial disk complete. 164.
   Surnia—facial disk hardly traceable. 166.
  Tail short.
   Lower mandible sinuate.
   Athene—nostrils in cere; feet bristly. 170.
   Lower mandible notched.
    Head with plumicorns.
   Scops—feet bare; 22 remiges; fourth primary longest. 168.
   Asio—feet feathered; wings long; 24 remiges; second primary longest. 162, 163.
   Bubo—feet feathered; wings short; 29 remiges; third and fourth primaries longest. 169.
    Without plumicorns.
   Nyctala—ears with operculum. 167.
   Nyctea—ears without operculum. 165.

STURNINÆ. (Plate ix.)
 Pastor—crested. 121.
 Sturnus—uncrested. 120.

TROGLODYTINÆ. (Plate iv.)
 Troglodytes—59.

TURDINÆ. (Plates i. ii. iii.)
 Geocichla—axillaries chequered. 7, 8.
 Merula—axillaries black. 9, 10.
 Phylloscopus—axillaries yellow; breast whitish; legs brown. 32-35.
 Hypolais—axillaries yellow; bill stout; legs blue. 36.
 Daulias—axillaries buff; breast buff; back reddish brown; tail reddish brown. 22.
 Erithacus—chin red; lower breast white. 21.
 Melizophilus—chin chestnut; lower breast chestnut.
 Aëdon—head and back chestnut; breast buff; tail rounded and long and tipped with white. 37.
 Regulus—bright yellow crest. 30, 31.
 Saxicola—rump white; legs black; bill unnotched. 12-14.

F

Pratincola—rump whitish; legs black; bill notched; tail short and square. 15, 16.

Cyanecula—throat blue ; head brown. 19, 20.

Monticola—head bluish grey ; bill black ; breast chestnut. 11.

Ruticilla—throat black ; tail red, with black or brown on its two middle feathers. 17, 18.

Locustella—no rictal bristles ; axillaries brown ; tail pointed and shorter than wing. 43, 44.

Acrocephalus—bill large, depressed and broad at base ; axillaries whitish ; tail short and rather round. 38-42.

Sylvia—bill obscurely notched, very short and stout, but not broad at base ; breast plain or barred ; wings moderate ; first primary noticeably under half the length of second ; tail ashy or brown and white. 23-28.

Turdus—bill distinctly notched ; outer and middle toes united ; tail rather long. Range over seven inches. 1-6.

TURNICIDÆ. (Plate xxiv.)
Turnix—277.

UPUPIDÆ. (Plate xii.)
Upupa—slender curved bill ; crested head ; rounded wings. 156.

VULTURIDÆ. (Plate xiv.)
Gyps—fourth primary longest ; legs bluish. 171.
Neophron—third primary longest ; legs pinkish. 172.

CHAPTER XI.

THE SPECIES.

———◆◇◆———

IN this Chapter only such particulars are given as are needful to separate between the species. For the distinctions between the Genera, &c., reference must be made to the preceding chapters. As an aid in identification the species are arranged in order of their average size ; their accepted ornithological order will be found in the coloured plates. In the notes a few particulars are given as to flight, song, and nest. Where not otherwise stated, the plumage of the sexes is alike. The dimensions are fully given in the chapter devoted to them, and the eggs have also been dealt specially with in a similar way.

Acanthyllis.   Plate x.   *CYPSELIDÆ.*

140. *caudacuta,* 8½ in. NEEDLE-TAILED SWIFT.   Head greenish black ; forehead white ; back brown ; wings dark green with a little white on secondaries ; throat, breast, and under tail coverts white ; tail shafts ending in spines.

The Needle-tailed Swift—Dimensions, Ho—is an Asiatic, which has been added to the British List on the strength of two specimens only, one shot in 1846 and the other in 1879. Nothing is known of its eggs, but it is said to breed in Tibet and thereabouts.   As the two British victims are the only two ever heard of in Europe, and as the bird is a regular visitor to Australia, it is not unlikely that our specimens were brought home as examples of the Colonial avifauna to be promptly shot on escape, and so made into British Birds.

Accentor.   Plate iv.   *ACCENTORINÆ* (Passeridæ).

45. *modularis,* 5½ in. HEDGE-SPARROW.   Throat bluish-grey, shading into buff.

46. *collaris,* 6½ in. ALPINE ACCENTOR.   Throat white, spotted with black.

The Hedge Sparrow—Dimensions, Br ; Eggs, Da—is with us always, and is distinguishable from the House Sparrow by its bluish breast and its slenderer beak, as well as by its general bearing and behaviour.   Its gait is a shuffling hop, which has given it one of its local names— the Shufflewing—and its flight is short and direct from point to point without undulation, but it rarely crosses a field if it can work round it among the hedges.   Its note is a cheery sort of "cheep," varied by an occasional "treep."   The female is rather smaller than the male, and more thickly striped about the head and neck.   The nest is a fairly neat one, built low down in a hedge, or among evergreens, and its materials are rootlets, twigs, green moss, dry grass, and wool, lined generally with hair, feathers being present occasionally.   The pretty blue eggs are from four to six in number.

The Alpine Accentor—Dimensions, El ; Eggs, Fe—is an occasional straggler from Southern Europe.   Its flight is hasty and undulating, and occasionally soaring, somewhat like a lark's. Its note is "chich-ich-ich," with a call of "tri-tri-tri."   There are from five to six eggs in a clutch, but the nest has not yet been found in Britain.

Accipiter. Plate xv.   *FALCONIDÆ.*

183. *nisus,* 12 in. SPARROW HAWK. Greyish blue above, with a white patch on nape ; buffish below, barred with rufous brown ; tail with light and dark brown bars.

182. *atrisapillus,* 22 in. AMERICAN GOS HAWK. Ashy brown above ; below white, irregularly freckled, or marbled with brown.

181. *palumbarius,* 23 in. GOS HAWK. Ashy brown above ; below white distinctly barred with brown ; tail brown with four dark brown bars.

The Sparrow Hawk—Dimensions, Kh ; Eggs, JT—is, with the possible exception of the Kestrel, our commonest falcon. Its flight is swift and gliding, not far from the ground, in long sweeping undulations ; threading the woods in bold easy curves, and occasionally hanging in the air with quivering wings and tail. Its note is a screaming " mew." The female is larger than the male, as is the case with all the Falconidæ, though the peculiarity is not confined to birds of prey. She is greyish brown above and much whiter below than the male, though in old age she assumes the male plumage ; and she may, as a rule, be distinguished by a reddish patch of downy feathers on the flanks. The iris of the male is yellow; hers is orange. The nest is a large one of sticks, lined with rootlets and occasionally a little moss, and it is placed among rocks, or in the fork of the main trunk of a tree, or of one of the larger boughs. There are from three to six eggs.

The American Gos Hawk—Dimensions, Qd; Eggs, PH—has made three appearances in these islands, the first in 1869. Its eggs have not yet been found here.

The Gos Hawk—Dimensions, Qj ; Eggs, PP—is now but a rare visitor. Its flight is long and gliding, somewhat low, rarely circling, with the steering action of its tail very apparent. Its note is a " kurk kairk kirk," with a sharper intonation when alarmed. The female is about three inches larger than the male. The nest, on some lofty tree near the skirt of a wood, is of sticks, roots, moss, and lichens ; it is known by its hardly ever having any green leaves in it, and it grows very large by being occupied year after year and added to at each occupation. The eggs are generally four in number, but sometimes three and sometimes five have been found. The Gos Hawk obtains its specific name from the pigeon, and its popular name from the goose. The adult may be known by the narrow white line above the eye and ear coverts ; the young are buff below, streaked with blackish brown ; the full grown birds are white below, barred with ashy brown.

Acredula. Plate iv   *PARINÆ* (Passeridæ).

50. *caudata,* 5½ in. WHITE-HEADED LONG-TAILED TIT. Crown all white.

51. *rosea,* 5½ in. BRITISH LONG-TAILED TIT. Crown black, with a narrow white central patch.

The White-Headed Long-Tailed Tit—Dimensions, Bo ; Eggs, AF—has been occasionally met with in our woods in the winter. The female has a dusky lateral stripe in her crown. In every other respect this bird resembles

The British Long-Tailed Tit—Dimensions, Bn ; Eggs, Ac—which is a common resident south of the Clyde. Its flight is short and swift, with a very quick movement of the wings, flitting jerkily from tree to tree, and around the trees and blackthorn bushes, and then darting off in a series of dips, followed in single file by the wife and family. The note can be likened to " te-te," or " tse-re-re," or " zit-zit," or " zee-zee-zee." The female is blacker than the male, and the young have not so much red about them. The nest is the best built in Britain. It is generally ten feet or more from the ground, in tall hedges or trees ; it is oval in shape, and the materials are moss, lichens, wool, and cobwebs, all beautifully felted together with a lining of hair and feathers; it is entered by a hole in the side, which is generally closed with a feather when the bird is away. The eggs are from 6 to 20 in number, and have fewer spots than those of any other of the Parinæ.

Acrocephalus. Plate iii.   *TURDINÆ* (Passeridæ).

41. *aquaticus,* 4½ in. AQUATIC WARBLER. Crown stripes buff and brown.

42. *phragmitis,* 4¾ in. SEDGE WARBLER. Crown stripes all brown.

38. *streperus,* 5½ in. REED WARBLER. Eyes brown , legs purplish brown.

39. *palustris,* 5½ in. MARSH WARBLER. Eyes hazel ; legs flesh colour.

40. *turdoides,* 8 in. GREAT REED WARBLER. Eyes brown ; legs horn colour ; second primary longest in wing.

The Aquatic Warbler—Dimensions, Ah ; Eggs, BG—readily recognisable by the buff streak down the middle of the crown, is one of our very occasional spring and summer visitors. The female has much the same plumage as the male. The eggs are either four or five in number, but the nest has not yet been found in this country.

The Sedge Warbler—Dimensions, Ap ; Eggs, Ba—comes amongst us every spring to breed, and remains with us till September. Its flight is hardly worthy of the name, for it rarely flies, as it contents itself with skulking amongst the rushes and undergrowth. Indeed, it is curious how a bird with so poor a flight can cross the English Channel. Its note is a vehement "cheep" or a "churr"—as if it had a brogue in it. The female is much duller in colour than the male. The nest is never suspended, and it is never found among reeds, and rarely among sedges, but it is built close to the ground, or even on the ground, among bushes and osiers. It is composed of moss and coarse grass, lined with horsehair, reed tufts, and dry grass. The eggs are either five or six in number.

The Reed Warbler—Dimensions, Bp ; Eggs, Bd—is not only longer but slimmer than the Sedge Warbler. It also comes about April and leaves in September, and has a skulking sort of flight, now and then just clearing the reed tops and vanishing into them. Its note is a sort of whistle, a kind of "choh-choh" in variations, which is heard at its best long after sunset. The female is of a paler brown than the male. The nest is the deep one, built over the water on two or three reed stems, which carry it up with them as they grow. It is compactly built of reeds and dry grass, moss, wool, feathers, and horsehair ; and sometimes it is attached to willows or alders, but it nearly always hangs over water, and contains four or five eggs.

The Marsh Warbler—Dimensions, Bq ; Eggs, Ca—is a somewhat rare visitor reported every summer, chiefly from the West of England. Its flight is a trifle bolder than that of the Reed Warbler, but it is marked with the same eagerness to get out of sight as soon as possible. Occasionally it can be seen singing on the top of a low willow. It sings by night as well as by day, and its note, syllabised by an admirer as "chiddy, chiddy, chiddy, chit, chit, cha, cha, cha, chit, chit," is said to be "varied and melodious, like a nightingale's, but not so loud." The female is of a very retiring disposition. The nest is never over water, but generally, though not always, near it. As a rule it is found among osier beds, and is built of leaves, round grass, and moss, felted with cobweb and seed down, and lined with horsehair. It is quite as deep as that of the Reed Warbler, and contains five, six, or seven eggs.

The Great Reed Warbler—Dimensions, Gn ; Eggs, Ep—is more often talked about than seen. He is a very rare summer visitor, and his flight is of the timid, skulking kind, avoiding observation as much as possible, though his occasional captures of insects on the wing show what he could do if he tried. His note is loud and unmusical ; a series of monotonous variations on "karry-charry-karry," with a croak as an alarm. The female is about half an inch shorter than the male. The nest is suspended from two or three reeds, but is never over water though often over mud. It is a deep cup made of reeds, leaves, and flowering scapes, and contains from four to six eggs ; but it is very rarely met with.

Aëdon.   Plate iii.   *TURDINÆ* (Passeridæ).

37.   *galactodes,*   6¾ in.   Rufous Warbler.   Chestnut above ; whitish below ; white eye stripe ; two central tail feathers tipped with black, others tipped with white.

The Rufous Warbler—Dimensions, Ep ; Eggs, Er—is a rare accidental straggler which has been found here some times since 1854. It is well-known round the Mediterranean, and gets as far south as Abyssinia. Its flight in this country is not on record, owing, probably, to its being cut short by the sportsman in his eagerness to make the bird British. The female is paler than the male.

Ægialitis.   Plate xxvi.   *CHARADRIIDÆ.*

298.   *curonicus,*   6 in.   Little Ringed Plover.   Broad black ring on white chest ; white on first primary of wing ; scapulars same colour as back ; outer tail feathers a quarter of an inch shorter than middle ones ; legs yellow.

299.   *cantianus,*   6½ in.   Kentish Plover.   White nape joining white throat ; black ring on chest not meeting in front ; legs black.

297.   *hiaticulus,*   7 in.   Ringed Plover.   Broad black ring on white chest ; white bar across wing ; white below ; legs orange.

300.   *vociferus,*   10 in.   Killdeer Plover.   Two narrow black rings on chest ; lower back and rump chestnut buff ; legs grey.

The Little Ringed Plover—Dimensions, Ds—has been recorded about half a dozen times as an unexpected straggler from the north. As in many other cases it is only a British bird by courtesy.

The Kentish Plover—Dimensions, Eo; Eggs, HE—has an undoubted claim to be considered British, inasmuch as it was first described from a specimen taken at Sandwich, and is found every summer all along the Kent and Sussex coasts. Its flight is rather slow, notwithstanding the quick beating of its wings, and it starts and alights with a run of a few yards, with its wings expanded. Its note is a sort of "pittwee" or "ptwee." The female is recognisable by her being brown where the male is black, the absence of black being especially noticeable on the fore-crown. The nest is a mere hollow in the shingle; the eggs are four in number, though occasionally only three have been found.

The Ringed Plover—Dimensions, Fn; Eggs, IR—is with us all the year round. Its flight is low or high, made up of quick flappings and long glides, straight for a time, then wheeling, and rolling leisurely from side to side so as to show first the back and then the underparts. The note is a whistle, with "penny-yet" as an alarm. The female has a much less conspicuous collar. The nest is a mere hollow in the sand or shingle. The eggs are four in number and very pointed in shape.

The Killdeer Plover—Dimensions, Iq; Eggs, IQ—is so called from its call of "killdeer." It is an American species, of which two examples have been shot in these islands, and none on the Continent of Europe. The female has much the same plumage as the male.

Ageleæus. Plate ix.   *ICTERINÆ* (Passeridæ).

119. *phœniceus,*   9 in.   RED-WINGED STARLING. Glossy black; lesser wing coverts red; legs and bill glossy brownish black; tail rounded, but with two rather short middle feathers.

The Red-winged Starling—Dimensions, Ia; Eggs, FH—is another rare visitor from across the Atlantic, probably shot on escape from confinement. The note, as pronounced with the American twang, is "kork-ker-ree." The female is unknown in this country. The nest is of the hanging purse-shape, characteristic of all the Icterinæ.

Alauda. Plate x.   *ALAUDINÆ* (Passeridæ).

135. *brachydactyla,* 5½ in. SHORT-TOED LARK. Crown fawn; bill flesh colour; brown above, unspotted below.

133. *arborea,*   6 in.   WOOD LARK. Broad white eye stripe; throat and breast more streaked than spotted; tail short, outer feathers brown.

134. *cristata,*   7 in.   CRESTED LARK. Crest pointed; outer tail feathers half buff.

132. *arvensis.*   7¼ in. SKY LARK. Faint yellowish eye stripe; throat and breast more spotted than streaked; outer tail feathers mostly white.

136. *sibirica,*   7½ in. WHITE-WINGED LARK. Secondaries white.

The Short-tailed Lark—Dimensions, Cl; Eggs, DT—is a rare visitor to the South of England. Its flight is a jerky, undulating one; its song is of the feeblest, and like its flight is generally cut short by some enthusiastic gunner. There is only one record of one of these birds being taken alive in this country, and that was at Amberley, in Sussex, in 1888. It has never been known to breed here.

The Wood Lark—Dimensions, Dq; Eggs, ED—is one of our resident birds, and migrates about the country. Its flight is not so high as that of the Sky Lark, and it soars in more of a circle. Sometimes it sings on the ground, sometimes on a tree, and often its melodious "lu-lu" will be heard far into the night. The female is much the same in plumage as the male, and like him, is of a deeper richer brown in the winter. The nest is rather a compact one, of coarse grass outside and finer grass within, mixed with moss and lined with hair; and it is generally placed on the ground under a tuft of grass or low bush. The eggs are either four or five in number.

The Crested Lark—Dimensions, Fi; Eggs, FG—is a rare visitor to our south coast. Its flight is like that of the Wood Lark, and its note is a melodious "coo-hai." The female is not so large as the male and somewhat darker. The nest has not been found in Britain.

The Sky Lark—Dimensions, Ft; Eggs, Es—is resident amongst us though reinforced in the autumn by visitors from the Continent. Its flight is fluttering and gliding, rising in long slopes, almost vertical at times, and soaring as the song is trilled forth. Sometimes the lark will sing from a tree top, sometimes from a telegraph wire. The song has been syllabised as "cherry do, cherry do, pretty joey, pretty joey, pretty joey, white hat, white hat, pretty joey," and one ornithologist, of Scottish parentage, has likened it to a bagpipe heard at a distance—of course a considerable distance. Another Scotsman gives it as, "Up in the lift go we, te-hee, te-hee, te-hee, te-hee! There's no' a cobbler on the airth can mak' a

shoe to me, to me! Why so? Why so? Why so? Because my heel is as long as my toe."
The female resembles the male in plumage. The nest is always on the ground, and is
composed of grass or herbaceous plants with a little moss, lined with dry grass, rootlets, and
hair. The eggs are from three to five in number. It is perhaps worth noting that the
larks, unlike the pipits, never bathe in water, but dust themselves clean.

The White-winged Lark—Dimensions, Gj; Eggs, Fᴅ—made one appearance in this
country and was promptly bagged as British. Curiously enough, this solitary specimen,
caught near Lewes, in 1869, was a female. Its nest has to be sought for in Siberia and
Turkestan.

Alca. Plate xxxii. *ALCIDÆ.*

373. *torda,* 17 in. RAZORBILL. Black above, white below; thin white
line from bill to eye; 12 tail feathers.

374. *impennis,* 32 in. GREAT AUK. Black above, white below; broad
white patch between bill and eye; 18 tail feathers.

The Razorbill—Dimensions, Nn; Eggs, Rᴅ—can be found in our estuaries all the year
round, but it comes ashore in its thousands in the beginning of April. Its flight is rapid and
direct, with a considerable roll so as to display its breast and back alternately; and when the
birds are in any number they always fly in single file. Afloat it can be distinguished from
the Guillemot by its upturned tail. In winter it loses its green gloss, and its chin and throat
become white. Its note is a grunting croak, which some have syllabised as "hurray."
The female lays but one egg, and this in a crevice or on an overhung ledge, without any
attempt at building a nest. In incubation she takes watch and watch with the male, neither
of them couching across the egg, but along it. The Razorbill egg is greenish when held to
the light, while that of the Guillemot is yellowish white.

The Great Auk—Dimensions, Sk; Eggs, Ss—is said to be extinct, and is only included
here by request, in the hope that some day it may, in Miltonic phrase, return from visiting
"the bottom of the monstrous world." Like the Razorbill, it built no nest and laid a
solitary egg.

Alcedo. Plate xi. *ALCEDINIDÆ.*

151. *ispida,* 7 in. KINGFISHER. Head black and blue; back blue;
white spot on neck; chin white; breast chestnut;
legs red.

The Kingfisher—Dimensions, Et; Eggs, Dǫ—is one of the gayest in plumage of our
resident birds. Its flight is straight and unwavering, like a flash of blue flame, but
occasionally it pauses and hovers in the shade, though it never does so in the sunshine. Its
note is a shrill "pip, pip, pip." The female has the beak orange on the lower base, and is
not so bright in colour generally. The nest is in a slimy hole in a bank near water, and is
composed of ejected fish bones. The eggs are from six to nine in number, and are of a deep
pink colour until the yolk is blown out of them. They are nearly round in shape.

Ampelis. Plate vi. *AMPELINÆ* (Passeridæ).

77. *garrulus,* 7½ in. WAXWING. Brown and chestnut above; throat
black; secondaries tipped with scarlet; tail tipped
with scarlet or yellow.

The Waxwing—Dimensions, Gh; Eggs, Fʟ—only finds its way to this country in
exceptionally cold continental winters. Its eggs were first discovered by Wolley, in 1856, in
Russian Lapland. The females have fewer wax tips than the male, particularly as they get
older, when the male often has wax tips to his tail as well as his wings.

Anas. Plate xxi. *ANATIDÆ.*

236. *strepera,* 20 in. GADWALL. Wing bar white.

235. *boscas,* 24 in. MALLARD. Wing bar purple; tail of 14 feathers.

The Gadwall—Dimensions, Ph; Eggs, Oc—is resident in the eastern counties of England,
but the numbers are occasionally swollen by winter migrants. The flight is very strong, the
wings whistling as they flap. The note is a shrill "quack"—whence the specific name—
but occasionally a double "quack" is given. The female has very little chestnut on the
shoulder of the wing, and is brown in colour, but like the male is distinguishable from the
other ducks by the white wing bar or "speculum." In summer the male assumes the
female plumage, but the bill is always black with blue at the base, while the female's bill is
dusky with dull orange at the sides. The nest is placed on the ground under the shelter of
a bush, and not far from water, but in a dry place. It is formed of dry grass, leaves, and
rushes, and lined with smaller down than that of the Mallard. The eggs are from 8 to 13
in number, and of a greenish hue when fresh.

The Mallard—Dimensions, Qp; Eggs, Pʙ—is the common Wild Duck, from which our domesticated ducks are derived. As with them the drake can be distinguished by the curl of the upper tail coverts. The flight is straight and swift, and the wings work rapidly in long full strokes, without any intermission. The duck always rises first, the drake follows. The note of the male is "quork," that of the female is "quark," and the female invariably makes the most noise. The female has a dark grey bill with a black nail; the male's bill is greenish yellow. In summer the male assumes the female plumage. The nest is on the ground, and generally—but not always—near water, and sometimes the Mallard will take possession of an old crow's nest. The nest is always lined with down from the female's breast, neutral grey in colour, with small white tips. When specially built it is composed of dead grass, reeds, and leaves. The eggs are from 8 to 16 in number, and have smooth shells. The female is generally smaller than the male, and sometimes she has been found to assume the male plumage. In fact our No. 235 is a confusing sort of bird from all points of attack. To avoid calling a drake a duck, its name of Wild Duck was discountenanced in favour of Mallard, which simply means Drake.

Anous. Plate xxx. *LARIDÆ.*

353. *stolidus,* 14 in. NODDY. Crown grey; throat greyish; the rest dark sooty brown; bill black; fourth tail feather from outside longest; feet brown with yellowish webs.

The Noddy—Dimensions, Mb; Eggs, Nᴘ—is a tropical species, which in 1830 sent two representatives to be shot off the coast of Wexford. It had never been seen in Europe before nor has it been seen since. Its eggs are worth noting as being the only tern's eggs laid in a nest.

Anser. Plate xix. *ANATIDÆ.*

221. *erythropus,* 20 in. LESSER WHITE-FRONTED GOOSE. Forehead white; bill pink, with horn coloured nail; legs orange.

220. *albifrons,* 28 in. WHITE-FRONTED GOOSE. Forehead white; bill yellow, with white nail; black bars on lower breast; legs yellow.

219. *brachyrhynchus,* 29 in. PINK-FOOTED GOOSE. Bill pink with black nail; legs pink.

217. *cinereus,* 30 in. GREY LAG GOOSE. Bill pink with white nail; black bars on lower breast; legs flesh colour.

222. *hyperboreus,* 30 in. SNOW GOOSE. White; wings black and white; bill and legs red.

218. *segetum,* 34 in. BEAN GOOSE. Bill orange, with black nail; legs yellow.

The Lesser White-fronted Goose—Dimensions, Pk; Eggs, Rᴍ—is a very rare winter visitor from Scandinavia. The female is more rufescent in colour and smaller than the male.

The White-fronted Goose—Dimensions, Sc; Eggs, Rᴋ—visits us every winter, but does not breed here. It has large spots of black on the breast and below. The female is smaller than the male and has much less black on the breast.

The Pink-footed Goose—Dimensions, Se; Eggs, Sc—is another winter visitor, but much rarer.

The Grey Lag Goose—Dimensions, Sh; Eggs, Sɪ—was once resident amongst us in considerable numbers, but it is now best known as a regular visitor. Its flight is high, heavy, and sedate; in the breeding season it flies in pairs, the goose being in front; on migration it flies in families in a V formation, and the families often join company so as to make up a series of W's. The note is "gag, gag," or "kak-kak," or "gaggle." The female is a seventh shorter than the male. The nest is generally among the heather, or on a crag, or some lonely moor, and consists of a few sticks with a pile of reeds, grass, and sedge nearly a yard across, and lined with down as soon as the eggs are laid. The eggs number from six to fourteen. According to the older etymologists this bird derives its name from the grey wings which are so conspicuous in its flight.

The Snow Goose—Dimensions, Sl; Eggs, Sᴅ—is a straggler from North America, first shot in Ireland in 1871.

The Bean Goose—Dimensions, Sq; Eggs, Sғ—is one of our usual winter visitors. It has no black on the breast. It rises heavily, striking the water with its wings to begin with, and flies in lines either straight, angular, or wavy. Its note is a trumpet-like "clank." The female is rather smaller than the male.

Anthus. Plate V.   *MOTACILLINÆ* (Passeridæ).

66.	*pratensis,*	$5\frac{3}{4}$ in.	MEADOW PIPIT.	Plumage whitish; throat and chest spotted with blackish brown.
67.	*trivialis,*	6 in.	TREE PIPIT.	Plumage yellowish; hind claw shorter than toe and much curved.
71.	*obscurus,*	$6\frac{1}{4}$ in.	ROCK PIPIT.	Hind claw same length as toe and curved; tail feathers entirely dark brown.
70.	*spipoletta,*	$6\frac{1}{2}$ in.	WATER PIPIT.	Throat and chest unspotted.
68.	*campestris,*	7 in.	TAWNY PIPIT.	Hind claw same length as toe and curved; tail feathers edged with light brown.
69.	*richardi,*	$7\frac{1}{2}$ in.	RICHARD'S PIPIT.	Hind claw not less than an inch in length.

The Meadow Pipit—Dimensions, Da; Eggs, Dm—is one of our residents whose numbers are increased by migration in spring and thinned by departures for the Continent in the autumn. It is quite as well known as the Titlark—indeed all the Pipits are known as Titlarks—and like all the rest of the genus, and all the Larks and Wagtails, it runs when on the ground and does not hop. One of its distinctive marks is its nearly straight hind claw, which is longer than the hind toe. Like all the Pipits it varies very much in size, but its proportions are fairly constant. Its characteristic odour is stronger than that of any other ground bird. Its flight is at times swift and undulating, but generally wavering, as it sings on the wing, fluttering up for a short distance, and then slowly descending with expanded wings and tail. Its note is a feeble warbling "cheep-teep," with a sharper alarm or call of "whit." The female is not so spotted as the male, and in the winter resembles him in being greener above and buffer below. The nest is always on the ground and generally on a bank under a tuft of grass; it is made of moss, dry grass, and seed stalks, lined with fine grass and hair. The eggs are from four to six in number.

The Tree Pipit—Dimensions, Dk; Eggs, Eb—is a summer migrant, arriving early in April and leaving us in October. Like all its namesakes, it has the bill of a wagtail, and the long hind claw of a lark. Its flight is of the same character as that of the Meadow Pipit. It mounts nearly straight up, hovers over a tree, trilling out its canary-like song; and then, with its legs hanging and its wings almost meeting over its back, it drops in a spiral to the bush from which it rose, and from which, in a few moments, it rises to sing again. Its note is "twee, twee, twee, twee,"—longer than the Meadow Pipit's—and it has also a call of "tick-tick," and another of "tsee-a, tsee-a, tsee-a." The female is not so large as the male, and is not so spotted on the breast. The nest is placed on the ground, generally on a bank, and sometimes in a hole; and it is made of dry grass, rootlets, moss, wool, and horsehair. The eggs, of which there are from four to six in the nest, are more variable than those of any other British bird, except, perhaps, the Cuckoo and the Guillemot.

The Rock Pipit—Dimensions, Ee; Eggs, Ef—frequents our coasts all the year round, and breeds annually north of the Humber. It has no white in its tail, its axillaries are smoky brown, and its hind claw is very much curved. It is the highest flyer among the Pipits, rising 30 ft. or more in a wavering desultory way, singing as it flutters aloft, and slowly circles to the ground again. Its note is a shrill "cheep." The female has no rosy tinge on the breast. The nest is generally near the sea, under a stone or in a hole; it is made of grass, seaweed, and moss, and lined, as a rule, with horsehair; and it contains from four to five eggs.

The Water Pipit—Dimensions, Ek; Eggs, Ee—is a very occasional straggler into the south of England. Its flight is "Pipit-like," and the note is reported to be "ting-ting-ting" on the rise, and "si, si, si, si" on the fall.

The Tawny Pipit—Dimensions, Ef; Eggs, En—is another rare straggler never known to breed here.

Richard's Pipit—Dimensions, Gc; Eggs, Eh—often straggles over here in the autumn from its home in Turkestan, but it never stays the winter with us.

Aquila. Plate xv.   *FALCONIDÆ.*

178.	*clanga,*	26 in.	SPOTTED EAGLE.	Wings brown, spotted with greyish white; tail brown.
179.	*chrysaëtus.*	36 in.	GOLDEN EAGLE.	Wings brown, shaded with black; tail mottled.

The Spotted Eagle—Dimensions, Rq; Eggs, Qh—is a very rare straggler to these islands, and only about half a dozen specimens are on record, and there is some doubt as to whether these are of larger or smaller species. If they are of the smaller kind it would seem that they should be *nævia* and not *clanga*.

The Golden Eagle—Dimensions, Te; Eggs, RT—is undoubtedly a British bird, although it is not shot quite as often as is reported in the newspapers. Most of the Golden Eagles shot in England by gamekeepers are Sea Eagles, from which the Golden bird is at once distinguishable by its having the tarsus feathered right down to the toes. The Golden Eagle rarely hovers; he flies with a few powerful strokes, and then glides along with no apparent motion of the wings, his neck and feet drawn in so as to make his length seem much shorter than it really is, in proportion to the wing-spread. The note is a "yelp" and a "squeal." The female is rather larger than the male, and the young have their tails white at the base. The nest is a flat mass of sticks, often five feet across, placed on some precipitous cliff, or in a tree, or even on the ground, and it is roughly lined with moss and heather, or grass and fern. The eggs are generally two in number, but cases are on record in which three and four have been found, and sometimes there is only one.

Archibuteo.   Plate xiv.   *FALCONIDÆ.*

   177. *lagopus,*   26 in.   ROUGH-LEGGED BUZZARD. Crown and neck white, with brown patches; plumage generally brown above, white below; tail white, barred with brown; thighs barred with brown; 24 remiges, fourth primary longest, first four primaries notched.

The Rough-legged Buzzard—Dimensions, Rr; Eggs, Os—once a resident, seems to be now only a visitor. On the wing it is distinguishable from the ordinary Buzzard by the white on the tail. It is rarely seen to glide, but leisurely strokes along as if intent on a very long journey. Its note is a squealing "mew." The female is larger than the male, and like him varies considerably in size. The nest is generally placed on a cliff or on a tree, and consists of a large flat mass of sticks lined with grass; the eggs being from two to five in number.

Ardea.   Plate xvii.   *ARDEIDÆ.*

   207. *ralloides,*   18 in.   SQUACCO HERON. Head buff; crown black and white.

   206. *bubulcus,*   20 in.   BUFF-BACKED HERON. Head buff; crown buff.

   205. *garzetta,*   22 in.   LITTLE EGRET. All white; bill black.

   203. *purpurea,*   33 in.   PURPLE HERON. Crown black; crest black.

   202. *cinerea,*   36 in.   HERON. Crown white; crest black.

   204. *alba,*   42 in.   GREAT WHITE HERON. All white; bill yellow.

The Squacco Heron—Dimensions, Oh; Eggs, Jo—is one of our occasional stragglers, apparently arriving in the spring and summer and, once at least, staying here till November.

The Buff-backed Heron—Dimensions, Pe; Eggs, Lm—appeared in Devonshire in 1805, and was promptly shot and sent to the British Museum where it now is. Two other appearances are recorded and that is all.

The Little Egret—Dimensions, Qb; Eggs, Le—occasionally straggles here from the Lower Danube, and a specimen was shot on the Exe, in 1870.

The Purple Heron—Dimensions, Sn; Eggs, On—is more frequently met with in this country than the three last species, but it is still very rare.

The Heron—Dimensions, Tb; Eggs, Pt—is the only species of Ardea breeding in this country. Its flight is a slow, steady flap, with the wings much arched, the legs held out, the neck doubled back, and the beak out straight like a bowsprit. Its cry is a croaky sort of "kronk." The female is duller in plumage, and has a smaller crest and shorter plumes. The nest is a flat one, built of twigs, turf, moss, roots, and wool, and is generally placed in tall trees. The eggs are from three to five in number.

The Great White Heron—Dimensions, Th, Eggs, Qd—has straggled over here about eight times, probably on a voyage from the Crimea. The bird, which has been found as far east as Japan and as far south as the Transvaal, has a black bill when in summer plumage.

Ardetta.   Plate xvii.   *ARDEIDÆ.*

   208. *minuta,*   13 in.   LITTLE BITTERN. Crown and back black; four powder-down tracts; primaries and tail brownish black; legs greenish yellow.

The Little Bittern—Dimensions, Km; Eggs, Ig—has put in one or two appearances in nearly every county in England at all seasons of the year, and is even said to have bred here. Its flight is low, but very quick and strong, and its note is a peculiar "wof-wof." The female has no green gloss in the crown, which is brownish, and the primaries are dark brown instead of black. The nest is generally hung to reeds, a little above the water, or built in pollards, and it is composed of flags and grass, and holds from five to nine eggs. This bird has been known to breed in a Magpie's nest.

Asio. Plate xiii. *STRIGIDÆ.*

162. *otus,* 14 in. LONG-EARED OWL. Plumicorns nearly upright, and exceeding an inch.

163. *accipitrinus,* 15 in. SHORT-EARED OWL. Plumicorns nearly upright, but not exceeding half an inch.

The Long-eared Owl—Dimensions, Mf; Eggs, KP—is generally found in fir woods. It is orange buff in colour, with a good many blackish bars and streaks. Its flight is buoyant and silent, like that of all the Owls, but very undecided, and the bird is hardly ever seen out in broad daylight. The note is a mew and a bark, not a hoot, and the bark is often given when on the wing. The female is rather redder than the male, and she is a little larger. She never builds her own nest, but adds a few sticks to a crow's or a wood-pigeon's, or something of the sort, and lines the cavity with rabbits' fur. The eggs are from four to seven in number, and are without any gloss.

The Short-eared Owl—Dimensions, Mq ; Eggs, JP—is a bird of very different habits. It haunts the open moor, and comes abroad in the daytime. Its flight is soft and silent, but not unlike the Gull's. Its numbers are increased by migrants in the winter, who come with the Woodcock, and, from being about during the daytime, it is the most frequently noticed Owl we have, though not, perhaps, the commonest. Its note is a scream. The female is larger, but much the same as the male ; but the young are darker in plumage, and very pale in the eye. The nest is a hollow on the ground, among the reeds or heather, and consists of a few sprigs or broken leaves ; the eggs are smooth, and vary from four to seven in number. It may be worth noting that the ear opening on the right of this bird is directed upwards, while that on the left is directed downwards.

Athene. Plate xiii. *STRIGIDÆ.*

170. *noctua,* 8 in. LITTLE OWL. Greyish brown above ; whitish with brown streaks below ; tail barred with white ; toes covered with bristles instead of feathers.

The Little Owl—Dimensions, Hd ; Eggs, JB—is known to have been frequently imported and turned loose here, but has never been proved to come here of its own free will. Its first primary is equal to its sixth, its second to its fifth, and its third is the longest, and, like most of the Owls, it perches with two toes in front and two behind. It is generally about in the daytime ; its cry is "cuckoo, vah-ee" ; and its nest is a mere scratching of rubbish low down near the ground.

Bartramia. Plate xxviii. *SCOLOPACIDÆ.*

326. *longicauda,* 12 in. BARTRAM'S SANDPIPER. Head and breast rufous with angular spots ; chin white ; lower breast white and spotted ; under-surface of wings barred black and white ; remiges 26 ; tail long and wedge-shaped.

Bartram's Sandpiper—Dimensions, Kf ; Eggs, LN—is an American very occasionally met with on this side of the Atlantic. Its axillaries are white, barred with brown, and its tail feathers are barred with black. It has a habit of flying in large circles, and its call is a soft whistle. The female is always bigger than the male.

Bernicla. Plate xix. *ANATIDÆ.*

226. *ruficollis,* 22 in. RED-BREASTED GOOSE. Head black ; white patch in front of eye.

223. *brenta,* 23 in. BRENT GOOSE. Head black ; white patch on each side of neck.

224. *leucopsis,* 25 in. BARNACLE GOOSE. Head white ; crown and nape black ; black stripe from eye to bill.

225. *canadensis,* 41 in. CANADA GOOSE. Head black ; white patch under chin.

The Red-breasted Goose—Dimensions, Qf ; Eggs, QT—has appeared on the east coast about half a dozen times during the last hundred years. It is a handsome bird with chestnut throat and breast. Its home is in Siberia, where it is known as the Shakvoy, from its call. The female is much the same as the male, but rather smaller.

The Brent Goose—Dimensions, Qi ; Eggs, RB—is one of our regular winter visitors, but is seldom found inland. It never dives. Its call has been variously rendered as "rot," "cronk," and "torock." It breeds within the Arctic Circle.

The Barnacle Goose—Dimensions, Rh ; Eggs, RL—is another winter visitor, much rarer on the east coast than on the west. Like the Brent, it breeds somewhere in the far north.

The female, as with all the other Geese, is not so large as the male. The note has been rendered as "halm, halm," or "a-what." The popular name is due to the popular notion that it is bred not from eggs but from barnacles.

The Canada Goose—Dimensions, Tg ; Eggs, Sj—is almost as big as a Swan. It has often been imported but has never been proved to find its way across the Atlantic on the wing, and it owes its place in the list to the fact of its having been shot when escaped from confinement.

Botaurus. Plate xvii. *ARDEIDÆ.*

211. *lentiginosus,* 27 in. AMERICAN BITTERN. Crown black ; primaries all brown.

210. *stellaris,* 30 in. BITTERN. Crown brown ; primaries chestnut barred with brown.

The American Bittern—Dimensions, Sa; Eggs, Nf—has occasionally straggled here during the winter, but has not yet got as far as the Continent. It can be distinguished from the Common Bittern by its primaries having no bars. Its call is "like the noise made by driving a stake in boggy soil," whence its local name of the Post-driver.

The Bittern—Dimensions, Sg ; Eggs, Ne—does not often breed here now. Its flight is low, slow, steady, and silent. Its note is a deep "boom," a sort of bellowing " proomb," with a sharper call of " ca-wak." The female is like the male in size and plumage. The nest is generally placed on the mud in the thick of a reed bed, and it is composed of dead reeds and flags, with no sign of interlacement or regular arrangement. It contains three, four, or five eggs.

Bubo. Plate xiii. *STRIGIDÆ.*

169. *ignavus,* 26 in. EAGLE OWL. Facial disk obsolete over eyes ; plumicorns large and falling , no operculum ; plumage dark brown above, yellowish below, mottled and patched ; bill black ; 29 remiges, third primary generally longest, but rarely much longer than fourth ; claws black.

The Eagle Owl—Dimensions, Rp ; Eggs, Qg—is a very doubtful resident in this country, except in confinement. Its cry is a deep "oo-hoo," which is rarely heard except in the spring. The female is about two inches longer than the male, and never makes a nest.

Bulweria. Plate xxxiii. *PROCELLARIIDÆ.*

395. *columbina,* 10 in. BULWER'S PETREL. Plumage black ; tail wedge-shaped.

A Bulwer's Petrel—Dimensions, Is ; Eggs, Kj—was found floating dead on the Ure in that year of Accession, 1837. Its home is on the Desertas, near Madeira ; the species had never been seen in this country before nor has it been seen here since. The case is worth noting as showing that is not even necessary for a bird to be seen here alive to secure its admission to the British list.

Buteo. Plate xiv. *FALCONIDÆ.*

176. *vulgaris,* 23 in. BUZZARD. Remiges 25 ; fourth primary longest, third almost as long, first as long as the eighth, and second longer than the sixth, first four notched ; tail whitish brown with ten or more dark brown bars ; legs yellow ; claws black.

The Buzzard—Dimensions, Ql; Eggs, Or—is still resident in this country, but is not often met with. The plumage is very variable, being sometimes nearly white, but the size and tail and short legs are enough to know him by. His flight is low, heavy, and leisurely, with a spiral rise. His note is like a long-drawn scale of vowels, "a-e-i-o-u." The female is like the male, but larger. The nest is on some tall tree in the thick of a wood ; it is about two feet across, built of large sticks outside, twigs within, and lined with fresh beech leaves. The eggs are either two, three, or four.

Calcarius. Plate viii. *EMBERIZINÆ* (Passeridæ).

117. *lapponicus,* 6¼ in. LAPLAND BUNTING. Black head ; white eye stripe ; chestnut collar ; black and brown spotted back ; spotted wings ; tail brown and white ; throat black ; under parts white, joined by thin white line to eye stripe.

The Lapland Bunting—Dimensions, Ed ; Eggs, Dp—is occasionally met with in the autumn among a flock of larks. It was first found here, in Leadenhall Market, in 1826. The female has a brown head instead of a black one.

Calidris. Plate xxviii. *SCOLOPACIDÆ.*

324. *arenaria*,   8 in.   SANDERLING. Under parts white, except the breast, which, like the head and neck, is of pale chestnut spotted with dark brown.

The Sanderling—Dimensions, Gr; Eggs, Im—visits us twice a year, in spring and autumn, on its way to and from its breeding haunts in the far north. In the spring its upper parts are rufous and black; in the autumn they are grey. The young are buffish white above and below.

Caprimulgus. Plate x.   *CAPRIMULGIDÆ.*

141. *europæus*,   10 in.   NIGHTJAR. Ashy grey, pencilled and spotted; small whitish spots on wings and tail.

143. *ægyptius*,   11 in.   EGYPTIAN NIGHTJAR. No whitish spots on upper surface of wings or tail.

142. *ruficollis*,   13 in.   RED-NECKED NIGHTJAR. Rufous collar; large whitish spots on wings and tail.

The Nightjar—Dimensions, It; Eggs, Ht—arrives here in the middle of May and leaves us in September; but being a bird of the night he is more often heard than seen. He is the latest of our summer migrants, and the only night bird among them. His three first primaries have a white spot near the end, and his two outer tail feathers have broad white tips. His palate is faintly transparent; and he has the curious pectinate middle claw, which, according to some people, he uses to hold on by as he sits sideways on a branch, and according to others uses as a small-tooth-comb for the special discomfort of the species of Nirmus with which he is infested. He begins to sing exactly at sundown, the note being a "churrrrr," and an occasional "wh-ip, wh-ip," which may, or may not, be due to the rapid movement of his wings. His flight is soft and gliding, with his tail well out, so as to show off its white spots. He feeds entirely upon insects; he does not suck goats; he is not a Hawk; neither is he an Owl; but he generally falls a prey to some owl of a gamekeeper. The female has the spots on the wing and tail pale buff. She makes no nest, but lays her eggs on the ground under a fern or furze bush. The eggs are two in number, and have both ends equally rounded.

An Egyptian Nightjar—Dimensions, Jn; Eggs, Ht—was shot by the usual gamekeeper, in 1883, in Nottinghamshire, and so made into a British bird. That is the only appearance of the species in these islands.

A Red-necked Nightjar—Dimensions, Kt; Eggs, Ht—was shot at Killingworth, of railway fame, in 1856; the species had never been recognised here before, nor has it been heard of here since.

Carduelis. Plate vii.   *FRINGILLINÆ* (Passeridæ).

88. *spinus*,   4½ in.   SISKIN. Blackish forehead; plumage yellowish green above; chin black; throat and cheeks yellow; sides of neck yellowish.

87 *elegans*,   5 in.   GOLDFINCH. Scarlet forehead; plumage ruddy brown above; upper throat and cheeks scarlet, the scarlet mask with a broad black edging wings black, barred with yellow and tipped with white; tail black, tipped with white.

The Siskin—Dimensions, An; Eggs, Ap—occasionally breeds here; it visits us in late and early winter, on its way to and from its northerly haunts within the limit of the pine forests, and it is imported, in cages, in large numbers, from Germany. Its tail is blackish, though all but the two middle feathers have yellow bases; its lower breast shades into white. Its flight is undulating and irregular, and its note is "tit-tit-tit-tit," with a sharp call not unlike its name. The female has a whitish throat, and no black on the head and chin, which are marked with brown, and she is not so large as the male. The nest is generally in a fir tree, in a fork, about 20 feet from the ground, and it is made from grass-stalks, heather twigs, and pine needles, lined with rootlets, moss, and rabbits' fur—a very similar nest to that of the greenfinch; it contains from four to six eggs.

The Goldfinch—Dimensions, Bf; Eggs, Ar—is a resident, partially migrating about the country, and reinforced by migrants from the Continent, but yearly becoming rarer, owing to the efforts of the bird-catcher. He is the "Thistlefinch," and is not often found where thistles are not close handy. His red mask distinguishes him from every other British bird. His flight is light and buoyant, but somewhat drooping and jerky, with a good deal of wheeling up and down as he travels. His song is loud, sweet, and canary-like and his call is a sharp "glit." The female has a slenderer bill, no yellow on the breast, less red on the forehead and upper throat, and is much duller in plumage altogether. The nest is generally in a garden or orchard, or among evergreens ; it is even neater than the Chaffinch's, and smaller, and it has no lichens, but consists of rootlets, grass, moss, and wool, woven together and lined with willow down ; there are either four or five eggs.

Certhia. Plate vi.   *CERTHIINÆ* (Passeridæ).

85. *familiaris,*   5½ in.   TREE CREEPER.   Spotted brown above, buffish white below ; bill slender and decurved ; tail brown and long, with stiff points.

The Tree Creeper—Dimensions, Cb ; Eggs, As—is well known in nearly all our woodland districts. His flight is quick and direct, and almost always downwards. He hops up the tree trunks spirally, but keeps on the further side when observed, pressing his pointed tail against the trunk to support him, much as if he were a bracket ; when he reaches the top of a tree, or the extremity of a branch, he dives down to the root of another tree, and works up that to dive again to another, and so on. The note is a shrill " tree-tree-tree," with a crisp "cheep," as an alarm. The female does not differ from the male in plumage. The nest is in a hole in the tree, or in a gap between the bark and trunk ; tiny twigs are woven to narrow the entrance, and the nest always has a bit of bark in it, generally birch, besides the usual roots and feathers and moss. The eggs are from three to nine in number.

Ceryle. Plate xi.   *ALCEDINIDÆ.*

152. *alcyon,*   13 in.   BELTED KINGFISHER.   Crested ; slaty blue with a white collar and rufous band on breast ; wings spotted and barred ; tail long.

The Belted Kingfisher—Dimensions, Ld ; Eggs, Il.—is a North American bird, of which two specimens, unfortunately for themselves, and for writers of bird books, strayed into Ireland, in 1845, to be forthwith shot for the Dublin Museums. This was the first time the species was ever heard of at large on this side of the Atlantic, and apparently it was also the last. It is hardly likely to visit us without recognition, for its call is described as a noisy edition of the twirl of a watchman's rattle !

Charadrius. Plate xxvi.   *CHARADRIIDÆ.*

295. *fulvus,*   9 in.   EASTERN GOLDEN PLOVER.   Throat and breast black ; axillaries grey.

294. *pluvialis,*   10 in.   GOLDEN PLOVER.   Throat and breast black ; axillaries white.

The Eastern Golden Plover—Dimensions, Ic ; Eggs, Mi—otherwise the Lesser Golden Plover, has been found here three or four times, generally in Leadenhall Market. It is a remarkable bird, for, according to Morris, it has been seen in the Land o' the Leal !

The Golden Plover—Dimensions, Ir ; Eggs, Nr—visits us on his migration from the north in August and September, and calls again on his way home during March, leaving a few representatives here throughout the year. The flight is very high, powerful and sustained, flapping fast and steadily, sweeping to the ground and up again, and always circling before alighting. The note is " kelleeee " or " kloveeee," with a call of " klee," and an alarm of " ko." The female is not so black below as the male, her breast being mottled with white. The nest is a little heather and moss scratched together in a hollow of the ground, or in a clump of cotton grass, and is generally found on the moors and in mountain districts. The male helps in incubation. The eggs, like most pyriform eggs, are four in number.

Ciconia. Plate xviii.   *CICONIIDÆ.*

213. *nigra,*   39 in.   BLACK STORK.   All iridescent black except from lower breast to tail, which is white ; remiges 32.

212. *alba,*   42 in.   WHITE STORK.   All glossy white except primaries, secondaries, scapulars, and great wing coverts, which are black ; remiges 34.

The Black Stork—Dimensions, Tf ; Eggs, Qq—has appeared in England about a dozen times. He is not really black, but black and white, and like the White Stork, who is not really white, but white and black, he has a red bill and red legs. Like his relative he generally stands on one leg, and hangs his legs down as he flies.

The White Stork—Dimensions, Ti ; Eggs, Rn—is another occasional visitor, but has never been known to breed here. He has a patch of bare skin round his eye, which is black, while the corresponding patch in the Black Stork is red. It is a very curious thing that a large bird so common in Holland should so rarely find its way across the Channel.

Cinclus. Plate iv.   *CINCLINÆ* (Passeridæ).

47. *aquaticus,*   7 in.   DIPPER. Blackish brown head; dark grey back; chest white; breast brown.

48. *melanogaster,*   7 in.   BLACK-BELLIED DIPPER. Blackish brown head; dark grey back; chest white; breast black.

The Dipper—Dimensions, Fb; Eggs, Fo—otherwise the Water Ouzel, is one of the most interesting of genuine British birds. Wherever there is a roar of waters, his short cheery song is almost sure to be heard. Although he is not web-footed, he is truly aquatic in his habits, and floats, and swims, and dives, and actually flies under water, as if water were his true element. He flies like a Kingfisher, but with rather more labour, but he never plunges direct at a fish, but alights on the shore, and wades in until he is out of his depth. Dippers generally go in pairs, the sexes being alike in plumage. The nest is a beautiful felt-work of green moss, lined with dry grass and withered leaves, and is always domed when it is not in a hole. There are from four to six eggs.

The Black-bellied Dipper—Dimensions, Fc; Eggs, Fp—only differs in colour from his relative, and is generally found in East Anglia.

Circus. Plate xiv.   *FALCONIDÆ.*

175. *cineraceus,*   17 in.   MONTAGU'S HARRIER. Greyish above, whitish below; outer web of fifth primary without a notch; inner web of outer tail feathers barred white and brown.

174. *cyaneus,*   18 in.   HEN HARRIER. Greyish above, whitish below; outer web of fifth primary with a notch; head greyish, streaked with brown; wings brown and whitish; throat grey.

173. *æruginosus,*   22 in.   MARSH HARRIER. Brownish above, whitish below; outer web of fifth primary with a notch; head buff; wings brown and grey; throat buff.

Montagu's Harrier—Dimensions, Oa; Eggs, Km—is a rarer resident than formerly. His white breast feathers have a narrow central streak of chestnut. He flies lightly and gracefully, darting with his wings half closed, sailing in widening circles with them outspread, and turning with one wing higher than the other, as if to help his tail in steering. Like all the Harriers, he chiefly feeds on reptiles. The female is brown above, not grey, and the tail feathers are brown, with broad grey and buff bars and pale tips. She is rather larger than the male. The nest is always on the ground, made of heather twigs, and lined with grass; and the eggs are from four to six in number.

The Hen Harrier—Dimensions, Oo; Eggs, Lq—is larger, but shorter in the wing-spread, than Montagu's bird. Like it, it is resident, but rare. Its flight is lower, and the whitish rump is unmistakable, as the bird flaps leisurely along, somewhat like a heron, hovering with its tail half spread, swaying from side to side, and now and then giving its tail a twist in the manner of the Kite, to steer in a wide circle. The female is rather larger than the male, and is brown above, with white streaks on the nape; the ruff being very distinct, and the tail being very much like that of Montagu's Harrier. The nest is always on the ground, and when in a reed bed, or other wet place, it is of considerable size; it is made of sticks and heather, wool, and dry grass, and contains four, five, or six eggs.

The Marsh Harrier—Dimensions, Qg; Eggs, Nl—has almost disappeared from this country. It varies very much in plumage. The flight is very low and spiritless, the bird just skimming the tree-tops in a leisurely laboured way, as if not caring to exert himself more than necessary. His note is a sort of "pitz-pitz." His eyes are yellow; those of his mate are hazel. The female is larger than the male, and has a white edge on the shoulders of the wings. She is brown below, and has a brown tail, while the male's tail is ashy grey. The nest is sometimes in the lowest branch of a tree overhanging a marsh, but more usually on a clump of sedge, or in a reed patch on the ground; it is of considerable size, it is made of reeds and grass and dry flags, and contains three or four eggs. As in the other two Harriers, the powder down tracts extend up to the shoulders in this species. The Harriers, owing to their ruff, are the most owlish-looking of the Falconidæ.

Clangula. Plate xxii.   *ANATIDÆ.*

250. *albeola,*   15 in.   BUFFEL-HEADED DUCK. White patch on nape forming an erectile crest.

249. *glaucion,*   18 in.   GOLDENEYE. White spot at base of bill; wing speculum white; remiges 26.

The Buffel-headed Duck—Dimensions, Mh; Eggs, Mr—is a North American which v ry rarely indeed straggles over here across the Atlantic. The male's bill is greyish blue, the female's blackish grey.

The Goldeneye—Dimensions, Oi; Eggs, Pd—is one of our regular winter visitors. It makes a great splash as it rises, and a great noise as it flies with its whistling wings. Its note is a loud "kr-kroak." The male's bill is black, the female's brown. This duck lays its eggs in the hole of a tree as if it were a Woodpecker. There is no nest beyond the chips of wood that may be in the hole. The clutch ranges from 10 to 19.

Coccothraustes.   Plate vii.   *FRINGILLINÆ* (Passeridæ).

    92. *vulgaris,*   7 in.   HAWFINCH.   Chestnut brown above ; nape grey ; wings purplish black ; five inner primaries jagged or hooked at the tips ; black patch on chin ; bill bluish or pinkish and very large.

The Hawfinch—Dimensions, Fe; Eggs, Fb—is a resident reinforced in winter by migrants from the north. It is at once recognisable by its large beak. Its flight is generally an undulated one, but often it is straight and rapid. Its song is a whistle of four notes in an ascending scale, and its call is a "click." The female has much less black on the throat than the male, and has the secondaries edged with bluish grey. The nest is a large edition of the bullfinch's, usually in an old tree from 5 to 25 feet from the ground, built of small twigs and grey lichens lined with rootlets and hair, but with a very shallow cavity for the eggs, which are from four to six in number.

Coccystes.   Plate xii.   *CUCULIDÆ.*

    158. *glandarius,*   16 in.   GREAT SPOTTED CUCKOO.   Crest, head, and nape bluish grey streaked with black ; plumage brown above, white beneath ; wings spotted with white.

A Great Spotted Cuckoo—Dimensions, Nb; Eggs, Ia—appeared off the coast of Connemara, in 1842, and another was bagged in Northumberland in 1870. These are the only two instances on record of the species ever visiting these islands.

Coccyzus.   Plate xii.   *CUCULIDÆ.*

    159. *americanus,*   13 in.   YELLOW-BILLED CUCKOO.   Dark drab above, greyish white below ; tail black and white ; bill yellow.

    160. *erythrophthalmus,*   13 in.   BLACK-BILLED CUCKOO.   Brown above, white below ; bill black.

The Yellow-billed Cuckoo—Dimensions, Kq; Eggs, Hp—is really the Cow-cow, it being the American Cow-bird, so called from its cry of "cow, cow, cow, cow, cow." Unlike our Cuckoo it builds its own nest and hatches its own eggs. It has only been recognised in Britain twice, and twice in Ireland.

The Black-billed Cuckoo—Dimensions, Kp; Eggs, Gm—is another American of normal breeding arrangements. Only once, however, has he crossed the Atlantic, and that was to be shot at Belfast, in 1871. Like the Yellow-bills he probably came by steamboat.

Columba.   Plate xxiii.   *COLUMBIDÆ.*

    265. *livia,*   11 in.   ROCK DOVE.   Bill black ; plumage bluish grey ; rump white ; two broad black bars on wings ; axillaries white ; legs dark red.

    264. *œnas,*   13 in.   STOCK DOVE.   Bill red at base, white at tip ; plumage bluish grey ; green patch on neck ; one bar only on wing and that brown and incomplete ; axillaries grey ; legs coral red.

    263. *palumbus,*   16 in.   RING DOVE.   Bill red at base, yellow at tip ; plumage brownish grey ; white patch on neck ; white on outer wing coverts ; legs bright red.

The Rock Dove—Dimensions, Jp ; Eggs, Jd—is to be found all the year round on our coasts wherever there are high cliffs and deep caves. It rarely is seen on a tree, as it always alights on a rock or on the ground. Like all the pigeons it bobs its head as it walks. As it rises it beats the ground with its wings and produces a peculiar crackle by doing so ; its flight is rapid ; and so powerfully are the wings worked that they whistle as they flap. Its note is "coo-coo-roo-coo." The female is smaller than the male and duller about the neck.

The nest is always in caves, and often dry only at low water ; it is a very slight flat arrangement of seaweed, grass, and sticks, with now and then a sprig of heather. There are two eggs.

The Stock Dove—Dimensions, Kr ; Eggs, Jg—is most abundant in the Midlands. Its note is a short "coo-oo." Its flight is light and swift, with busy beats and a glide downwards. The female is not so pink on the chest as the male. The eggs are laid in a rabbit-burrow, or in a hole in a tree, and generally no nest is built, but sometimes a few twigs and roots are scratched together.

The Ring Dove—Dimensions, Ng ; Eggs, Kn—is the well known Wood Pigeon. Its note is "coo-oo-coo, coo-oo-coo," and it is easily recognisable on the wing by its white collar and wing bars. Its flight is light, deliberate, and persistent, and its gait is of the strutting, head-bobbing variety. Its nest is generally in a tree, and so lightly built of sticks that the two eggs can be seen in it from below. The female has a fainter collar than the male.

Colymbus. Plate xxxii.   *COLYMBIDÆ.*

383. *septentrionalis*, 24 in.   RED-THROATED DIVER. Throat grey and red ; head streaked black and white and patched with grey ; bill black.

382. *arcticus*, 26 in.   BLACK-THROATED DIVER. Throat black ; head streaked with black and white and patched with grey ; bill black.

380. *glacialis*, 33 in.   GREAT NORTHERN DIVER. Throat with two black rings, and two black and white rings streaked vertically ; bill black.

381. *adamsi*, 36 in.   YELLOW-BILLED DIVER. Throat with black and black and white rings ; bill pale yellow.

The Red-throated Diver—Dimensions, Qo ; Eggs, Ro—is the commonest of the family in this country and breeds in the North of Scotland and the islands off the coast. Its dusky brown back is streaked with oval spots. Its legs are greenish black, and its feet are yellowish. In autumn the red on the throat is not always present. In winter the browns become greys, and the underparts are pure white. This bird is the Rain Goose, whose call of "ak-ak-kakera-kakera," is rarely heard except when rain is approaching. The female is similar in plumage to the male. There is no nest as a rule, although now and then the hollow in which the eggs are laid may be lined with a few leaves. There are two eggs, and they are generally laid so near the water as to be wet underneath.

The Black-throated Diver—Dimensions, Rm ; Eggs, Sg—is rarer, but is also found breeding in the north country. It may be known from the Red-throat by its having red eyes instead of brown. In winter it is brown above, with white spots, and pure white below. There are about a dozen white bars on the scapulars, which are constant all the year round. The sexes are alike in plumage. The flight is very swift and so is the diving. The note is a noisy "deoch ! deoch ! deoch ! tha'n loch a traoghadh," which is the Gaelic rendering of "drink ! drink ! drink ! the loch is nearly dry !" The nest is of reeds and water plants, lined with grass, and is generally so near the water as to be half afloat. There are two eggs.

The Great Northern Diver—Dimensions, Sm ; Eggs, Sm—loses the throat band in the winter and becomes brown above, with a great increase of the white spots. Its eyes are red. It breeds in the Western Isles. The flight is rapid and straight, and the cry a "who ? who ?" generally heard at night, with an occasional "karok." There are two or three eggs ; the nest is of reeds and water plants, and can be recognised by the bird making a path to it from the water. The sexes are alike in plumage.

The Yellow-billed Diver—Dimensions, Ss ; Eggs, Sk—sometimes called the White-billed Diver, is an American straggler of which only a few specimens have been identified in this country, the first having been shot at Lowestoft, in 1852.

Coracias. Plate xii.   *CORACIIDÆ.*

153. *garrula*, 13 in.   ROLLER. Head and nape green or blue ; mantle chestnut ; wings black, and light and dark blue ; chin white ; underparts blue or green ; 23 remiges ; first primary short, second, third, and fourth longest ; tarsus scutellate in front and reticulate at back.

The Roller—Dimensions, Ks ; Eggs, Jc—has been noticed here about a hundred times since it was first recorded by Religio Medici Browne, in 1644. Its flight is like a Tumbler

Pigeon's, rapid and acrobatic. It would seem to be the total abstainer of the bird-world, for we are gravely assured that "it has never been known to drink." Not unnaturally, its cry is a peculiarly dry and thirsty "rakker-rakker-crea." This handsome but eccentric straggler seems to prefer a telegraph wire as a perch.

Corvus. Plate ix. *CORVINÆ* (Passeridæ).

127.	*monedula*,	14 in.	JACKDAW. Cindery black, with grey collar.
128.	*corone*,	18 in.	CARRION CROW. Greenish black ; nostrils always feathered.
129.	*cornix*,	19 in.	HOODED CROW. Grey and black ; hood black, wings black, tail black, other parts grey.
130.	*frugilegus*,	20 in.	ROOK. Purplish black, with blue reflections ; bald over nostrils, lores, and throat.
131.	*corax*,	24 in.	RAVEN. Glossy steel black, with green and purple reflections ; bill black and strong ; lanceolate throat feathers.

The Jackdaw—Dimensions, Mc ; Eggs, Ji—is one of our most popular residents. When on the wing its progress is of the yawing, unsteady variety. Its call is a "kae," which some have imagined to resemble "Jack," while others will have it that it is "daw,"—but, then, a Jackdaw will say anything, and do anything, to oblige. The female is smaller than the male, and has the grey collar somewhat obscure. The nest, in which there are from four to six eggs, is an untidy heap of miscellaneous matter, in some tower, or wall, or chimney, or tree, or in any hole—even in a rabbit-burrow ; and where there is one there are generally many.

The Carrion Crow—Dimensions, Om ; Eggs, Kr—is generally found in woods near the sea and inland waters. It has whitish bases to its body feathers ; it has a stouter bill than the Rook, and a more laboured flight, besides a quicker walk, and a curious habit of keeping its bill to the ground ; and it is generally found alone or in pairs. Its cry is a "croak-uk-uk" ; or "There's a hog dead ! Where ? where ? Up the burn ! up the burn ! Is't fat ? Is't fat ? It's a creesh ! It's a creesh !" Its nest is of sticks, with the twigs inside plastered over with mud, the lining being of wool and feathers ; and it is generally placed in the fork of the main trunk of a tree, or on a rocky ledge. There are from three to six eggs. The female is rather browner than the male.

The Hooded Crow—Dimensions, Pb ; Eggs, Kg—is retained in the list, though generally admitted to be a variety of *C. corone*, not breeding true to colour. Its eggs are said to be smaller, and they appear as such in our table ; but the birds themselves, in measured specimens, are certainly larger on the average.

The Rook—Dimensions, Pi ; Eggs, Ke—has a feathered beak during its first year, but the young can be distinguished from those of the two preceding Crows by the inside of the mouth being of dark flesh-colour, turning to purplish, instead of being of a very pale tint. The bases of its body feathers are grey, with no white. The flight is straight and assured, easy and regular, with the primaries extended so that their tips look like short fingers. The Rook is often very noisy on the wing, with his well-known "caw"—the characteristic call of the Corvidæ. Rooks are not often alone ; they are generally in straggling flocks ; and they build in colonies. The nest, in the top of a tall tree, is a large one of sticks and twigs, plastered with mud, and lined with grass and moss and wool ; the cavity is rather deep, and contains from three to five eggs.

The Raven—Dimensions, Rc ; Eggs, Mm—is yearly becoming rarer. It has the boldest flight of all the Corvidæ ; with its neck and feet drawn in, it floats high over the mountain-tops, leisurely, steady, and self-possessed, and then sweeps off, as if to be punctual to an appointment. Its note is a hoarse "cawruk," or a "craugh," with a bark when attacked, and an occasional "gorbel." The nest, now generally found on some rocky cliff, but formerly more frequent in lofty trees, is an unplastered mass of sticks, lined with twigs and grass and wool. The eggs are from four to six in number. The female is not so iridescent in plumage as the male, and she is generally smaller.

Cosmonetta. Plate xxii. *ANATIDÆ.*

252.	*histrionica*,	17 in.	HARLEQUIN. Gaily striped and spotted ; wing speculum purple.

The Harlequin Duck—Dimensions, Np ; Eggs, Oo—has a beak like a goose, with a small lobe at each side, and its tail is not nearly so long as that of the Long-tailed Duck for which it is occasionally mistaken. It is an Iceland species usually visiting us in the winter. It has a swift and powerful flight, and is the most daring of swimmers among rapids and waterfalls. Its note is a loud croak, a sort of "eck, eck." The female is of smaller size, and is brown in plumage, with a white patch on the forehead, and a brown stripe across the eye-patch.

Coturnix. Plate xxiv. *PHASIANIDÆ.*

276. *communis,* 7 in. QUAIL. Back light brown, marked with black and streaked with buff.

The Quail—Dimensions, Fl ; Eggs, GE—is a resident, reinforced by spring migrants which in some years are very numerous. It is one of those birds who are never seen to perch ; and its flight is short, quick, whirring, about a yard from the ground. Its note is the flute-like " weet-my-feet," or " clook-look-leek," for which it is occasionally kept as a song bird. The female is larger than the male, and has a buff throat, while that of the male is black. The nest is a mere hollow in the ground. It contains from 5 to 12 eggs.

Crex. Plate xxiv. *RALLIDÆ.*

281. *bailloni,* 7 in. BAILLON'S CRAKE. Bill olive ; under tail coverts black and white ; legs flesh colour.

280. *parva,* 8 in. LITTLE CRAKE. Bill green ; no white on first primary ; flanks grey ; legs green.

279. *maruetta,* 9 in. SPOTTED CRAKE. Bill yellow ; axillaries barred with white ; under tail coverts buff ; legs green.

278. *pratensis,* 10 in. CORN CRAKE. Bill flesh colour ; axillaries chestnut ; legs flesh colour.

Baillon's Crake—Dimensions, Fa ; Eggs GK—is a rarity said by some to be resident, by others to be only a spring visitor. It lurks about pools and marshes, is an excellent swimmer, diver, walker, and runner, and has a short heavy flight, hanging its legs down as if they were broken. The base of its bill is red ; its eyes are red ; the outer web of its first primary is white ; and its flanks are black and white in bars. Its note is a whistle, with a " kik, kik," as an alarm. The female has a white chin. The nest is loosely made of water plants, and is placed in a swamp ; and there are from five to eight eggs.

The Little Crake—Dimensions, Gp ; Eggs, HM—has been found here a few times in spring and autumn. It has a low unsteady flight, and runs well over land and over water plants, and swims well and dives boldly, and, like all the rails, hides itself in the water with only its beak above the surface. Its note is a loud whistle, with a " kek, kek " alarm. The female has a pearly grey patch round the eye.

The Spotted Crake—Dimensions, Hr ; Eggs, Ic—is generally said to be a spring visitor, though some claim it as a resident. It hangs its legs as it flies, and makes the most of its broad wings, but its flight is low and wavering, and rarely prolonged, as it will always run if it can, taking very long strides. The nest is generally on a tussock surrounded by water, a mass of leaves and dead reeds, in which the eggs are often quite wet. There are from 8 to 12 eggs. The female is a smaller and browner bird than the male.

The Corn Crake, otherwise the Land Rail—Dimensions, Jh ; Eggs, JA—is one of our summer migrants. It is a short-tailed bird, with a flight of the brief and fluttering kind, which becomes unexpectedly vigorous when in full swing. When pursued, this bird prefers to run and to climb, and it never runs straight, but makes as many turnings as a hare. Its note is the "crake-crake," from which it takes its name. The nest is on the ground, in a cornfield or meadow ; it is generally in a hollow and is made of grass and lined with grass. The eggs are from 7 to 12 in number. The female is smaller and not so grey as the male.

Cuculus. Plate xii. *CUCULIDÆ.*

157. *canorus,* 14 in. CUCKOO. Slate grey and brown above ; wings slightly spotted with white ; tail tipped with white ; lower parts buffish white, barred with black, similar to Sparrow Hawk ; remiges, 19 ; first primary short, fourth and fifth longest ; tail feathers, 10 ; contour feathers with no aftershaft.

The Cuckoo—Dimensions, Md ; Eggs, FA—is a summer migrant, appearing here in April, and generally leaving us early in August, though the young ones linger on till well into September. The male Cuckoos come first, and the males are always in a majority. The Cuckoo ranges as far eastward as Japan, and as far south as Abyssinia. The note in April and May is the familiar " cuck-oo," but in June this changes to " cuck-cuck-oo," and in July to " cuck-oo-oo " ; but the bird has another note, a sort of chuckle ; and the female has a cry of her own, a chattering " kwow-ow-wow." The cuckoo calls on the wing, and also when at rest. The flight is hurried and straight, with an occasional twist and swoop, the long tail being held out horizontally, the white in the plumage being well shown. Sometimes the grey of the plumage is brown, but the brown bird is not necessarily a female, although she can always be recognised by a rufous tinge on the breast. Instances are on record of the Cuckoo's hatching its own eggs, but the evidence is not generally accepted ; usually there is no nest, the egg being laid on the ground, and then carried in the mouth, and placed in the nest of some other bird. As a rule, the nest chosen is that of a Meadow Pipit or a Pied Wagtail ; but Hedge Sparrows, Warblers, Wrens, Redstarts, Magpies, Jays, Shrikes, Finches, Buntings, Pigeons, and even Little Grebes, have been made to do duty as foster parents of the Cuckoo. The eggs are laid at intervals of a week or more. and there are several of them : they vary much in colour, but not so much as those of the Guillemot. They are often somewhat of the colour of the eggs among which they are placed ; the Cuckoo does not, however, colour her egg to suit the nest, but wanders about with it until she finds a suitable clutch ; and she would seem to be easily satisfied. for the egg is in nine cases out of ten unmistakable, and can be instantly distinguished from the rest by its colour, as well as by its shape and size.

Cursorius. Plate xxvi. *CHARADRIIDÆ.*

292. *gallicus*, 10 in. CREAM-COLOURED COURSER. Sandy buff, spotted and edged with black ; black streak from eye to nape ; primaries black ; outer web of secondaries buff ; axillaries black ; bill black ; tail not forked ; legs grey ; tarsus scutellate.

The Cream-coloured Courser—Dimensions, Ip ; Eggs, IH—is a Mediterranean species now and then straying here during the last three months of the year.

Cyanecula. Plate ii. *TURDINÆ* (Passeridæ),

19. *wolfi*, 5½ in. WHITE SPOTTED BLUE-THROAT. Blue throat, white centre.

20. *suecica*, 5½ in. RED SPOTTED BLUE-THROAT. Blue throat, red centre.

The Blue-Throats—Dimensions, Cc and Cd ; Eggs, BM—only differ from each other in the colour of the spot. They are not often seen in this country ; in fact, there is a doubt as to whether the white one comes here at all. The flight is a short, dipping one, and the bird sings as he flies, and as he alights with outspread wings. The song is said to be recognisable by its always ending with "ting-ting."

Cygnus. Plate xx. *ANATIDÆ.*

232. *bewicki*, 50 in. BEWICK'S SWAN. Bill, as far as nostrils, yellow ; the rest black.

230. *americanus*, 55 in. AMERICAN SWAN. Orange patches at base of bill,

228. *immutabilis*, 60 in. POLISH SWAN. Bill red, with small black tubercle,

229. *musicus*, 60 in. HOOPER SWAN. Bill, to below nostrils, yellow ; the rest black ; remiges 34.

231. *buccinator*, 60 in. TRUMPETER SWAN. Bill black.

227. *olor*, 60 in. MUTE SWAN. Bill all reddish yellow, with large black tubercle ; remiges 31.

Bewick's Swan—Dimensions, Tl ; Eggs, Sp—is an occasional visitor to this country from its breeding haunts in Siberia. Its note is "tong," or "a-kloong."

The American Swan—Dimensions, Tm—owes its place on the list from its having been found in a poulterer's shop at Edinburgh.

The Polish Swan—Dimensions, To—is generally considered to be merely a variety of the Mute Swan. It owes its specific name to the fact of the cygnets being white; although called Polish it is unknown in Poland, and, in fact, has only been found once outside the British Islands, and that was in the case of a solitary specimen from Haarlem, in 1840.

The Hooper Swan—Dimensions, Tq ; Eggs, SQ—was at one time one of our residents, but is now only a winter visitor. It was formerly called the Whistling Swan, from its call of "hoop," like the base note of a trombone.

The Trumpeter Swan—Dimensions, Tp—is an American, claimed as British on the strength of four birds shot at Aldeburgh, in 1866.

The Mute Swan—Dimensions, Tr ; Eggs, SR—is *the* Swan, the largest and handsomest of British birds, said by some to have been brought here from Cyprus over seven hundred years ago. No bird dare attack the swan when on the wing. He flies high and fearlessly, with his neck out at full stretch, and his wings audibly swishing in a flap somewhat like a heron's. Swans journey in files or *en echelon*, the birds taking it in turns to lead, and falling to the rear as they tire. The Swan is only mute by name. He hisses like a goose, gives a low trumpetlike "maul," and according to some people, even "sings" at other times than just before his death. The Swan's nest is usually on a small island, and it is a large mass of reeds and other water plants. There are from five to eight eggs. The female has a smaller tubercle than the male, and swims much lower in the water. The young are grey, with bluish beaks and legs.

Cypselus. Plate x. *CYPSELIDÆ.*

138. *apus,* 7 in. SWIFT. Plumage black ; chin and upper throat greyish white.

139. *melba,* 8 in. ALPINE SWIFT. Plumage dark brown ; white below, with a broad brown band on chest.

The Swift—Dimensions, Fp ; Eggs, Fk—comes in April, and is occasionally found as late as November. In flight the narrow wings are almost at a right angle, rapidly beating for a moment or so, and then held motionless, as the bird glides along, curving and swaying in response to the working of the tail. The note is a screaming "swee-ree-ee." The sexes are alike in plumage, the young having rather more white about them than the adults. The nest is in a hole in some cliff or building, generally high up ; and it is returned to year after year. It is made of straw and dry grass, and other light materials, stuck together with saliva as if with glue, and lined with feathers ; it is flat in shape, and contains from two to four eggs.

The Alpine Swift—Dimensions, He ; Eggs, Ho—is a rare summer visitor, never known to breed here. The note is a louder scream than that of the Swift, and the flight is more powerful, with a glide " like the shoot of a Kestrel."

Dafila. Plate xxi. *ANATIDÆ.*

238. *acuta,* 26 in. PINTAIL. Wing bar iridescent green ; tail of 15 feathers and pointed ; neck long.

The Pintail—Dimensions, Rn ; Eggs, Ns—is an uncommon resident, whose numbers are greatly reinforced in the winter by migrants from the north, and in spring by migrants returning from the south. The male's beak is black, with pale blue under the nostrils, while the female's beak is greyish black above, and reddish brown below. The male has the long tail which has given him his name of Sea Pheasant ; the female is a brown bird with a brownish wing bar, and is not so large as the male. In summer the male is not unlike the female, and his beak is blue. The flight is of the ordinary duck character. The note is a low " quaark." The nest is on the ground ; it is made of dead grass and sedge, and lined with brown down having faint white tips. There are from five to nine eggs.

Daulias. Plate ii. *TURDINÆ* (Passeridœ).

22. *luscinia,* 6¼ in. NIGHTINGALE. Reddish brown above : buffish below ; tail reddish brown ; first primary longer than primary coverts.

The Nightingale—Dimensions, Ea ; Eggs, Ec—comes in the second week of April, and leaves us in September, although the song generally ceases in the first week in June. He sings only until the eggs are hatched, and then he croaks ; but if the brood be destroyed, he sings again, to wind up with a croak again. The best rendering of the famous song is the French one quoted by Macgillivray: " Le bon Dieu m'a donné une femme, que j'ai tant, tant, tant, tant battue ; que s'il m'en donne une autre, je ne la batterais plus, plus, plus, plus, qu'un petit, qu'un petit, qu'un petit ! " The Nightingale is not the only bird that sings at night ; and he often sings in the daytime. His flight is buoyant and quick and smooth, and generally short, for he skulks in the underwood, among the hazels, and rarely takes to the open. The female is like the male, but the young are spotted like young robins. The nest is near the ground, sometimes on it, in a hedge-bank, or under a bush ; and is generally of dead oak leaves and grass, lined with rootlets and hair ; there are from four to six eggs.

Ectopistes. Plate xxiii. *COLUMBIDÆ.*

267. *migratorius,* 16 in. PASSENGER PIGEON. Head slate blue ; throat, breast, and sides reddish hazel ; back dark slate ; wings black, brown, and white.

The Passenger Pigeon—Dimensions, Nd ; Eggs, Jj—is an American bird, whose best claim to be British seems to be based on some specimens brought over here in a basket and shot when they escaped. According to Seebohm, "there is no reason why this bird should not cross the Atlantic if it felt so disposed ; but there is not the slightest evidence that it has ever done so."

Elanoides. Plate xv. *FALCONIDÆ.*

186. *furcatus,* 25 in. SWALLOW-TAILED KITE. Bill black ; cere blue ; head and neck white ; back black and rump white ; under parts white ; wings greenish black and very long ; tail purplish black, very long, and much forked.

The Swallow-tailed Kite—Dimensions, Rj; Eggs, Ml—is an American from the Mississippi known in no other country of Europe than Britain, and only known here by two specimens, the first of which arrived in 1772 and the other in 1823.

Elanus. Plate xv.   *FALCONIDÆ.*

187. *cæruleus,* 13 in. BLACK-WINGED KITE. White forehead; white eye stripe; grey above; white below; small wing coverts black.

The Black-winged Kite—Dimensions, Lf—sent a solitary representative from the tropics to be made into a British bird by an untimely death in County Meath, in 1862.

Emberiza. Plate viii. *EMBERIZINÆ* (Passeridæ).

115. *pusilla,* 4¾ in. LITTLE BUNTING. Head chestnut, striped with black; throat reddish white; breast streaked with black.

114. *rustica,* 5½ in. RUSTIC BUNTING. Head brown, with black crown and sides; throat white; rufous band on chest.

116. *schœniclus,* 5¾ in. REED BUNTING. Head black, eye stripe white; throat black; lower breast white.

112. *cirlus,* 6 in. CIRL BUNTING. Head olive brown, eye stripe yellow, lores and ear coverts black; throat black and yellow; breast chestnut and yellow.

113. *hortulana,* 6¼ in. ORTOLAN BUNTING. Head greenish grey; throat yellow; breast reddish buff; a yellow ring round eye.

111. *citrinella,* 6½ in. YELLOW BUNTING. Head yellow; throat yellow; breast yellow—all with chestnut streaks.

109. *melanocephala,* 6¾ in. BLACK-HEADED BUNTING. Head and ear coverts black; throat yellow; breast yellow.

110. *miliaria,* 7 in. CORN BUNTING. Head brown, spotted and streaked; throat whitish, with angular brown spots at side.

A Little Bunting—Dimensions, Aq; Eggs, Bn—was found by a boy in Sussex, in 1864; the first, and apparently the last, to be identified in this country.

The Rustic Bunting—Dimensions, Cf; Eggs, Ds—has been found here three times, the first record being in 1867.

The Reed Bunting—Dimensions, Cr; Eggs, Cb—is with us all the year round. It is known by its monotonous double note repeated several times and ended with a long drawl. Its flight is a dipping one, ending in a flutter of the wings and a sudden spread of the tail so as to show the white. The female has no black on the head and throat which are reddish brown. In winter the black and white of the male are edged with brown. The nest is on the ground, or near it, always in a swampy place; and it is made of moss, grass, and reeds, lined with reed flowers and horsehair. The eggs are from three to six in number.

The Cirl Bunting—Dimensions, Dh; Eggs, Eg—was discovered by Montagu, at Kingsbridge, in 1800, and is a not uncommon resident south of the Thames. Its note is "tirrilirrilul," and its call "chea-chee." Its flight is swift and graceful, with a long dip and a rise. Its nest, in which there are four or five eggs, is generally on the ground, or in a furze bush, and consists of dried grass, moss, and roots, often, but not always, lined with hair. The female has black in the crown, and the eye stripe pale yellow, but in winter the plumage of male and female is much duller than in spring.

The Ortolan Bunting—Dimensions, Ec; Eggs, Dr—occasionally comes here in the spring, but does not breed here. Most of those recorded are probably escapes from the poulterer's.

The Yellow Bunting—Dimensions, Ej; Eggs, Eq—is the Yellow Ammer (so called to distinguish it from the other Ammers grouped under the Latinisation of Emberiza), to which some cockney humorist prefixed an "h" which seems so difficult to remove that it has been thought better to give the bird its older name. Its flight is quick and undulating, with a characteristic wheel in the air, and a jerk of the tail on alighting. Its note is the often quoted "little bit of bread and no cheese!" with an emphasis on the "no" and the "cheese;" or in its Scottish form, "deil, deil, deil, tak' ye!" The call is a "chick, chick, churrr." It is asserted that this bird invariably sings at three o'clock in the afternoon, and certainly a good many of them seem to do so. The streaks in the male's crown are brown; in the female's they are black, and there is much less yellow about her. In summer the male's crown is often pure yellow. The nest is generally on a hedge bank, and always near, or on, the ground. It is made of dry grass and moss, with finer grass, and roots, and horsehair; and contains four or five eggs.

The Black-headed Bunting—Dimensions, Eq; Eggs Ei—is an Asiatic, occasionally straying here.

The Corn Bunting—Dimensions, Fd ; Eggs, Fɴ—is one of our uncommon, but widely distributed and partially migrating residents. It has a whirring, slightly undulating flight, with the legs dangling until it gets fairly under way ; and on the ground it both hops and runs. Its note is a "tees-ees-ees," with a peculiar skirl described as resembling a jingling chain, the alarm being "tzit-kaak." The sexes are alike in plumage, and in the winter both are darker above and buffer below. The nest is generally on or near the ground, often in the middle of a field, among coarse grass or young corn. It is a loose affair of straw and grass, with perhaps a little moss, lined with roots and hair, and contains four, five, or six eggs.

Erithacus. Plate ii. *TURDINÆ* (Passeridæ).

21. *rubecula,* 5¾ in. ROBIN. Olive brown above ; throat and upper breast chestnut red ; lower breast white.

The Robin—Dimensions, Cp : Eggs, Dɢ—is the most popular of British birds. According to a French author, "this beautiful songster is very good with bread crumbs " ; but it is not cooked in this country. The song is a mellow "yoop ! tirry lil, tirry lil, tirry lirry lirry lil," and is heard till very late in the evening, the Robin being one of the last birds to go to bed, as he is one of the earliest to get up. His flight is rapid and straight from bush to bush. The sexes are alike in plumage. The nest is rather large, with the cup out of the centre ; it is found in many strange positions, but oftenest in a hole or on the ground, under ivy ; it is made of dead leaves, grass, and moss, lined with rootlets, hair, feathers, and now and then a little wool. The eggs are from five to seven in number.

Eudromias. Plate xxvi. *CHARADRIIDÆ.*

293. *morinellus,* 9 in. DOTTEREL. Black crown ; white eye stripe ; rufous breast ; black below ; grey axillaries.

The Dotterel—Dimensions, Ie ; Eggs, Kᴛ—has its numbers reinforced in spring and autumn by migrants to and from the north. It has a hurried sort of flight, and its call is the "dot, dote," which gives it its name. The female is larger than the male, and much more brilliantly marked, especially below. The eggs are laid on the ground on some unfrequented moor ; there are generally three of them, but occasionally four have been found, as one would expect from their shape.

Falco. Plate xvi. *FALCONIDÆ.*

194. *æsalon,* 10 in. MERLIN. Above slaty blue and black ; below rufous, with blackish brown streaks ; throat white ; tail with a broad black band.

195. *vespertinus,* 11 in. RED-FOOTED FALCON. Dark grey above ; pale grey below ; tail black ; thighs chestnut ; legs red ; feet red ; claws yellowish white.

197. *cenchris,* 12 in. LESSER KESTREL. Head and tail grey ; back unspotted chestnut ; claws white.

193. *subbuteo,* 13 in. HOBBY. Above bluish black ; black moustache ; buff below, with black stripes ; thighs reddish ; two middle tail feathers black.

196. *tinnunculus,* 14 in. KESTREL. Head and tail slaty grey ; back chestnut, spotted with black ; legs yellow ; claws black.

192. *peregrinus,* 17 in. PEREGRINE FALCON. Bluish grey above ; black moustache ; buffish, barred with brown, below ; crown black.

189. *gyrfalco,* 21 in. GYR FALCON. Grey above ; whitish below ; crown slate-coloured ; moustache slate-coloured ; breast streaked with black ; tail barred with slate.

190. *candicans,* 22 in. GREENLAND FALCON. Bill yellowish white ; plumage white, with dark brown markings above ; white below ; tail white.

19 *islandus,* 23 in. ICELAND FALCON. Brownish grey above ; whitish below ; head white, but finely streaked ; throat white ; flanks barred ; breast spotted ; bill blue.

The Merlin—Dimensions, Ja ; Eggs, Jɴ—is the smallest of our Falcons. It can be recognised on the wing by its tail being longer than the Hobby's in proportion to its body, and by its body being bulkier. Its flight is low and gliding, and rather slow, but persistent, as it flies down its prey. The "mew" is a tremulous scream like the Kestrel's. The female is like the young male, and is brown where the adult male is grey, and her tail is barred with brown and tipped with white ; she is larger than the adult male, whose plumage she occasionally assumes. The nest is generally a hollow in the moor, lined with a few twigs of ling, although the deserted nest of some other bird, in a tree, is used. There are four or five eggs.

The Red-footed Falcon—Dimensions, Jr ; Eggs, Js—is occasionally found here in the summer, but its visits have been few and far between.

The Lesser Kestrel—Dimensions, Ki ; Eggs, Jf—has put in two appearances in this country during the last quarter of a century, and it was never heard of here before.

The Hobby—Dimensions, Lg ; Eggs, Kq—when on the wing looks like a miniature Peregrine, with its slender form and long, narrow, pointed wings, flying swiftly, swooping, and hovering, and then swooping again to catch the insects on which it feeds. The "mew" is a "pree, pree." The female is like the male, but larger. The young are buffish on the head and thighs. The nest is generally the deserted one of a Crow or a Magpie, and is always in high trees. There are three or four eggs.

The Kestrel—Dimensions, Lo ; Eggs, Kk—is our commonest Falcon, and can be recognised by its hovering (whence its name of Windhover), head to windward and hanging down, tail downwards and slightly spread, feet hidden, and wings quivering, the hover changing into a swift, easy flight, with a few rapid flaps, a glide, and then another hover to carefully examine the ground. One of the most interesting of experiences is that of standing on a lofty, precipitous hill, and looking down on to a Kestrel as he hovers over the deep valley below. The call is a screaming "keelie-keelie, kee, kee, kee," and a chatter. The male is grey above, the female is brown ; his tail is tipped with white, while hers has a broad brown tip. She is two inches longer than he is, and sometimes assumes his plumage. The eggs, from four to six in number, are generally laid in the deserted nest of a Crow or Pigeon ; but occasionally a nest is specially made in a hole in a cliff, of a few twigs and heather, with a lining of grass.

The Peregrine—Dimensions, Nt ; Eggs, Oe—is the Blue Hawk, with the strong, rapid, circling flight, who screams "hek, kek, kek," and gracefully sweeps out of view. The female is also blue, but is from three to four inches longer. The eggs, from two to four in number, are either deposited in a deserted nest of a Crow or Heron, or else laid in a hollow on a ledge.

The Gyr Falcon—Dimensions, Po ; Eggs, Ot—is the "gyr"-ating bird etymologically, but not in any other sense. There is only one record of his having been seen in this country. His flight is so swift as to make a noise in the air, and he is very seldom seen to glide. His cry is a loud shrill "mew."

The Greenland Falcon—Dimensions, Qe ; Eggs, Ot—is a rare winter visitor here.

The Iceland Falcon—Dimensions, Qk ; Eggs, Ot—is another occasional winter visitor whom some ornithologists consider to be, like the Iceland Falcon, merely a Gyr in a different state of plumage.

Fratercula. Plate xxxii. *ALCIDÆ.*

379. *arctica,* 12 in. PUFFIN. Head and back black ; collar black ; under parts white ; bill sheathed with orange ; legs orange.

The Puffin—Dimensions, Kd ; Eggs, Pn—has no colour on its bill in winter. It visits our coasts in summer and breeds here. It has a whirring flight when on the wing, and dives and flies under water for long distances. When wounded its mates swarm around it and push it with their bills to encourage it to fly or dive out of danger. Its call is "orr-a-orr." The female is like the male but has a smaller bill. The egg, for there is only one, is laid in a rabbit burrow or in a crevice in the rock, which is occasionally lined with a little grass or a few rootlets.

Fringilla. Plate vii. *FRINGILLINÆ* (Passeridæ).

95. *cœlebs,* 5¾ in. CHAFFINCH. Forehead black ; head greyish ; back chestnut ; rump green ; wings black, white, and yellow ; tail brown and white ; bill bluish.

96. *montifringilla,* 6 in. BRAMBLING. Forehead black ; head black spotted with brown ; back black ; rump white ; wing with a white spot ; white below, reddish on throat, and with black spots on the flank ; bill horn colour.

The Chaffinch—Dimensions, Ct ; Eggs, Cg—is one of our commonest birds. Its flight is a rapid undulating one, with many pauses, and an abrupt sort of alighting, the male raising his head feathers when in safety. The note is a ringing "tol-de-rol, lol, chickweedo," or a "tol, lol, lol, kiss me dear," with an occasional "wee, wee, wee," or a snore as of some drunken man. The female has the head and back ashy brown, the rump yellowish green, and the breast yellowish grey. The nest is a beautiful, compact, structure of rootlets, moss, and grass, lined with hair and feathers, and generally with some chips of decayed wood outside. There are four or five eggs.

The Brambling—Dimensions, Dp; Eggs, Cᴛ—visits us in the winter. It has a rapid undulating flight. Its note is a flute-like "chip-a-way." The female has a dark brown head and shoulders, and has no black and chestnut. The nest is higher in the trees than a Chaffinch's, and nearly always has birch bark in it, the other constituents being green moss, lichens, cobwebs, and thistle down, forming a rather large accumulation. There are from five to seven eggs.

Fulica. Plate xxiv. *RALLIDÆ.*

284. *atra,·* 15 in. Cooᴛ. Broad white shield on forehead ; plumage blackish grey, with narrow white wing bar ; remiges 25, third primary longest ; tail feathers, 14.

The Coot—Dimensions, Mk; Eggs, Nᴍ—can swim, dive, walk, and run. It can fly strongly, but prefers to skim along, touching the water every now and then with its feet. The call is "kew." The sexes are alike in plumage. The nest is a bulky structure of rushes and flags, often two feet high, built up from the bed of the water to form an island, and occasionally afloat or moored to a reed. It is lined with dry dead reeds ; and the eggs, which number from 6 to 12, are of the colour of the reeds among which they are laid.

Fuligula. Plate xxi. *ANATIDÆ.*

246. *nyroca,* 16 in. Wʜɪᴛᴇ-ᴇʏᴇᴅ Ducᴋ. Head ferruginous ; back brown ; lower breast white ; eye white ; 18 feathers in tail.

247. *cristata,* 17 in. Tᴜꜰᴛᴇᴅ Ducᴋ. Crest and head black ; back black.

245. *ferina,* 18 in. Pocʜᴀʀᴅ. Head chestnut ; back grey ; wing speculum grey.

248. *marila,* 20 in. Scᴀᴜᴘ. Head, neck, and shoulders black ; back white or speckled.

244. *rufina,* 21 in. Rᴇᴅ-cʀᴇsᴛᴇᴅ Pocʜᴀʀᴅ. Crest and head chestnut ; back brown ; eye brown ; 16 feathers in tail.

The White-eyed Duck—Dimensions, Na ; Eggs, Nɢ—has not only a white eye but a white wing bar or speculum. Its bill is dark blue with a black nail. It is almost as well known as the Ferruginous Duck. It has been occasionally found here, generally in Leadenhall Market.

The Tufted Duck—Dimensions, Nq, Eggs, Pꜰ—is very common in Nottinghamshire. Its bill is greyish blue with a black nail. The female is brown where the male is black, and the white wing patch is smaller. They are capital divers. The flight is a strong, steady one, close to the water for some distance and then with a considerable rise. The call is a "kr-kr-kurra." There are from 8 to 12 eggs. The nest is in a tuft, generally on the brink of a pond, and it is built of dry reeds and grass, lined with small down, which is greyish black, with an obscure white centre.

The Pochard—Dimensions, Od ; Eggs, Pɪ—is another of the Diving Ducks now increasing in this country. Its bill is black, blue and black, the blue being a stripe in the middle. The sexes are alike in plumage, except that the female has a dull brown head and neck, and a white chin. Both sexes have a grey wing bar. The flight is straight, rapid, low, and noisy, and the call is a "kr, kr, kr," with a whistle. The nest is always near water, and is made of dry grass and sedge, lined with brownish grey down, having obscure white centres.

The Scaup—Dimensions, Pc ; Eggs, Qᴀ—is so called from its call. It has a light blue bill with a black nail, and its tail is not longer than its closed wings. Its wing bar is white. The female, like the young male, has a white band round the base of the bill. The flight is noisy and rapid. The cry is given with a peculiar tossing of the head and opening of the bill. The nest is usually on a sloping bank, and is made of dry grass and sedge, lined with broken sedge and dark brown down without white tips, but with pale centres.

The Red-crested Pochard—Dimensions, Pn ; Eggs, Pc—has a red bill and red legs. Its wing bar is white. The female is light grey on the cheeks and throat. It is well known in Northern India, but is only a rare straggler to this country.

Fulmarus.   Plate xxxiii.   *PROCELLARIIDÆ.*

390. *hæsitatus,*   16 in.   CAPPED PETREL.   Head brown ; rump white ; white below.

389. *glacialis,*   19 in.   FULMAR.   Head white ; rump grey ; buff below.

A Capped Petrel—Dimensions, Nl—was once found by a boy in a furze bush near Swaff-ham ; it bit his hand, and he thereupon killed it, and made it into a British bird.   It is a tropical species, and its eggs are unknown.

The Fulmar—Dimensions, Ot ; Eggs, Rj—is well known to sailors as the Mollymoke, and, on the American seaboard, as the Noddy.   Its flight is like a Gull's, sweeping along with only an occasional flap, following the curves of the waves hundreds of miles out over the sea, on which it sleeps ; but, unlike a Gull, it holds its wings out straight, instead of curving them. Its first primary is the longest ; it has a short, reticulate tarsus ; and its nasal tubes join on to the maxillary margin.   Its note is a cackle.   It is said to breed in Britain, on the strength of its haunts at St. Kilda, which is rather a long way out in the Atlantic.   It makes no nest, and lays but one egg, which can be recognised by its coarse grain and strong smell.

Gallinago.   Plate xxvii.   *SCOLOPACIDÆ.*

311. *gallinula,*   7½ in.   JACK SNIPE.   Mantle glossy purple ; inside webs of scapulars glossy green ; remiges, 24 ; axillaries white ; tail feathers, 12.

310. *cælestis,*   10 in.   SNIPE.   Axillaries whitish ; tail feathers 14.

309. *major,*   11½ in.   GREAT SNIPE.   Remiges 25 ; tail feathers 16 or 18 ; four outer ones on each side whitish ; median wing covers tipped with white.

The Jack Snipe—Dimensions, Gd ; Eggs, Jk—comes to us in September, and leaves us, for his breeding haunts in the north, in April.   The flight is straight and rapid, beginning, in silence, with a few zigzags.   This bird used to be considered the male of *G. cælestis,* which was the "Jill" Snipe.

The Snipe—Dimensions, In ; Eggs, Kc—unlike the Jack Snipe, calls as he rises, the note being "chiswick," given as he zigzags up, preparatory to getting straight away.   In the breeding season the male makes a curious drumming sound as he swoops down in his flight, with his tail outspread.   The sexes are alike in plumage.   The nest is in a hollow in the ground, generally under a tuft of grass, and always in a swampy place ; it consists of a few scraps of sedge or dry grass, and there are four eggs.

The Great Snipe—Dimensions, Js ; Eggs, Ll—rises silently, like the Jack Snipe, but is a mere straggler to this country.   It has a good deal of white in its tail feathers, and keeps its tail well spread as it flies.   Its call is "bad, bad !"

Gallinula.   Plate xxiv.   *RALLIDÆ.*

283. *chloropus,*   13 in.   MOORHEN.   Red or brown shield on forehead ; plumage blackish grey ; wing with white streak ; flanks streaked with white ; under tail coverts barred with white ; remiges 23, second primary longest ; legs greenish.

The Moorhen—Dimensions, Ko ; Eggs, Lj—is almost as well known under the more appropriate name of Waterhen.   It bobs its head as it swims, and bobs its tail as it walks ; it dives readily ; and its flight is low and slow, with the legs hanging, legs, which it may be as well to note, are not webbed, although it is a water bird.   The call is "krek-rerk-rerk." The sexes are alike in plumage, both having the red frontal plate, and the white line on the wing feathers.   The nest is a mass of reeds, often on the ground, sometimes afloat on a pond, and now and then up a tree 20 feet or more above the water.   It is lined with dry grass and sedge, and contains from 4 to 10 eggs.

Garrulus.   Plate ix.   *CORVINÆ* (Passeridæ).

125. *glandarius,*   14 in.   JAY.   Crown white, buff, and black ; face with a black moustache ; throat white ; upper parts brown ; wing coverts chequered with blue, white, and black ; tail barred with blue ; under parts pale brown shading into white.

The Jay—Dimensions, Lo ; Eggs, Hk—has pale blue eyes and a peculiarly wide swallow, and is generally found where there are oak trees about.   The flight is a flopping one, with a closure of the wings preceding the downward shoot.   The call is a screeching "rake, rake," but the Jay can imitate anything except the human voice.   The sexes are alike in plumage. The nest is in the lower branches of some good sized tree, generally in the thick of a wood ; it is a bulky cup-shaped structure of twigs and roots, lined with rootlets and grass, and it contains from five to seven eggs.

Gecinus. Plate xi. *PICIDÆ.*

149. *viridis,* 13½ in. GREEN WOODPECKER. Crown grey and scarlet; moustache black and red; back green; primaries brown spotted or barred with white.

The Green Woodpecker—Dimensions, Li; Eggs, Ha—has a laughing "hyu, hyu, hyu" for a call, and a dipping flight, but is generally detected as it taps the tree trunk up which it works obliquely, while its peculiarly nicked tail feathers keep it from slipping backwards. The female has no red in her moustache. The nest is generally in a beech, or ash, or poplar tree, in a hole about a foot long, made by the bird straight into the heart wood, and then curving downwards to an enlargement, which contains a few chips of wood and the clutch of from five to eight white glossy eggs.

Geocichla. Plate i. *TURDINÆ* (Passeridæ).

8. *sibirica,* 9 in. SIBERIAN THRUSH. Axillaries white and grey; tail feathers 12; plumage olive brown and slaty grey, with brown spots; broad yellowish white eye-stripe; wings brown.

7. *varia,* 12½ in. WHITE'S THRUSH. Axillaries white and black; tail feathers 14; plumage yellowish brown above, buffish below, with dark brown crescentoid blotches; wings brown, edged with buff.

The Siberian Thrush—Dimensions, Hq—has only been heard of once or twice on this side of the Channel, although it is occasionally seen in France and Belgium.

White's Thrush Dimensions, Kk; Eggs, Hb—or White's Ground Thrush, as it is better called, is named after Gilbert White, of Selborne, who died five and thirty years before the first specimen was heard of in Great Britain. It is unknown in this country except as a rare winter visitor. Its nest has only been found once, and that was at Ningpo, in North China. Its flight is like a Woodcock's, and its note is a plaintive "see!"

Glareola. Plate xxv. *GLAREOLIDÆ.*

291. *pratincola,* 9½ in. PRATINCOLE. Olive brown above; tail coverts white; wings blackish; axillaries chestnut; throat buff, with a narrow black edging; remiges 26; tail much forked; bill black, red at base.

The Pratincole—Dimensions, Ik; Eggs, Hi—is an African species occasionally visiting us in spring or autumn. It has long wings and flies like a Tern, and it calls "bedree, bedree!"

Grus. Plate xxv. *GRUIDÆ.*

286. *virgo,* 36 in. DEMOISELLE CRANE. Tuft of white feathers behind the eye; innermost secondaries straight; bill green.

285. *communis,* 48 in. CRANE. Crown naked and red; no tuft of white feathers; innermost secondaries plumed; bill brown; remiges 33, first primary as long as fourth, second and third longest.

A Demoiselle Crane—Dimensions, Td; Eggs, Sh—was once shot in the Orkney Islands, and thereby became a British bird.

The Crane—Dimensions, Tk; Eggs, Sn—is said to have bred in the Fens in the days of Elizabeth. It certainly does not do so now; but it straggles here very occasionally. It flies with its head and neck out straight, and its legs out straight. Its call is "coorrr!"

Gyps. Plate xiv. *VULTURIDÆ.*

171. *fulvus,* 42 in. GRIFFON VULTURE. Head and neck downy; plumage ashy; ruff white; wings and tail dark brown; bill pale brown; legs bluish.

A Griffon Vulture—Dimensions, Tj; Eggs, So—in the springtime of 1843, sat on a rock near Cork Harbour, and is now to be seen, duly stuffed, in Trinity College, Dublin. He was the first and the last of the Griffons on record in the British Islands; and in many bird books he proudly heads the British list.

Hæmatopus. Plate xxvi.   *CHARADRIIDÆ.*

303. *ostralegus,*   16 in. OYSTERCATCHER. Black and white : bill orange ; remiges 29, the 26th at the elbow, and equal in length to the third primary ; legs flesh-colour ; tarsus reticulate all round.

The Oystercatcher—Dimensions, Nf ; Eggs, Om—derives its generic name from its red foot, and its specific name from its gathering shells with which to line the hollow in the beach it uses as a nest. In the spring there are chestnut markings on the back, which are absent in the winter plumage. The flight is a strong, skimming one, with rapid wing work. The call is a shrill " keep, keep." There are from two to four eggs, in colour resembling the pebbles with which, and the shells, it lines its nest.

Haliaëtus. Plate xv.   *FALCONIDÆ.*

180. *albicilla,*   34 in. SEA EAGLE. Bill yellow ; head ashy brown ; brown above ; dark brown below ; 27 remiges ; fifth primary longest, first primary equal to eighth, and second longer than seventh ; tail wedge-shaped and white.

The Sea Eagle—Dimensions, Sr ; Eggs, R1—is the bird beloved of sculptors and plasterers, who will never feather an eagle to the toes if they can help it. In its flight its wings seem to curve upwards at the points, as it gives a few regular flaps, and then sails along with feet and head short in, and wings full out. Its cry is a peculiar " yelp." The sexes are alike in plumage. The nest is occasionally in a tree, but generally on a lofty ledge in some precipitous cliff ; and it is built of sticks and twigs, and turf and seaweed, being sometimes six feet across. There are one, two, or three eggs, and these are much rougher in texture than those of the Golden Eagle.

Harelda. Plate xxii.   *ANATIDÆ.*

251. *glacialis,*   26 in. LONG-TAILED DUCK. Head white ; cheeks brown ; back black ; remiges 26 ; tail blackish.

The Long-tailed Duck—Dimensions, Rl ; Eggs, Ob—is one of our regular winter visitors, and is generally recognisable by its peculiar cry, which has been rendered as " coal an' candle licht ! " The male's beak is black and orange ; the female's is bluish grey. The male is unmistakable in winter, owing to his two long black tail feathers. The female is browner than the male, with a brown patch on the side of the neck. Both sexes have a swift and rolling flight.

Himantopus. Plate xxvii.   *SCOLOPACIDÆ.*

303. *candidus,*   13 in. BLACK-WINGED STILT. Head and neck white ; black and white above ; white below ; bill black, pointed, and straight, and twice as long as head ; remiges 29 ; legs pink, web extending down the toes but incised almost to the base.

The Black-winged Stilt—Dimensions, Lc ; Eggs, Ls—has come here at long intervals for a very long time, but has apparently never bred here. Its very long legs render it unmistakable.

Hirundo. Plate vi.   *HIRUNDININÆ* (Passeridæ).

83. *riparia,*   5 in. SAND MARTIN. Brown above ; rump brown ; white below ; brown band across chest ; legs brown.

82. *urbica,*   5½ in. MARTIN. Blue black above ; rump white ; white below ; no band across chest ; toes feathered.

84. *purpurea,*   6¾ in. PURPLE MARTIN. Purplish blue body ; brownish black wings and tail ; small white patch under wings ; legs purple.

81. *rustica,*   7½ in. SWALLOW. Blue black above ; rump blue ; white below ; throat chestnut ; legs black.

The Sand Martin—Dimensions, Bg ; Eggs, Bh—arrives here during the last week of March and leaves us in October. It has a light, skimming, fluttering flight. The song is a twitter, and the alarm a " share." The female's throat band is narrower than the male's, but otherwise the sexes are alike, both having a characteristic tuft of feathers just above the hind toe. The nest is in a hole in a sandbank, the hole sloping upwards and generally swarming with fleas, the nest a mere bed of grass and feathers. There are four, five, or six eggs, which are white, smooth, and glossy.

The Martin—Dimensions, Dm ; Eggs, Br—comes at the end of April and lingers on till December. He flies in shorter curves than the Swallow, and not so swiftly. His note is "screeb," often uttered when on the wing. The sexes are alike in plumage. The nest is built under the eaves of a roof, and on walls and cliffs, and consists of a ball of mud, having a hole just large enough for a doorway, and lined with dry grass and feathers. There are four, five, or six eggs.

A Purple Martin—Dimensions, Es ; Eggs, Fi—was once shot near Dublin. It is an American, and beyond the fact of its having once been shot in the British Islands has no claim to be considered a British bird.

The Swallow—Dimensions, Gf ; Eggs, Cp—arrives in the first half of April and leaves us in November. The female differs from the male in having the tail not so forked, and the throat bands narrower. The flight is bold and graceful, wavering at times, but usually in easy curves and long undulations. The Swallow has a gentle warbling song, and a call of "whit, ceep, cheep." The nest is of mud like the Martin's, but it is open at the top, and is larger and more loosely made. It is lined with dry grass and feathers, and contains from four to six eggs.

Hydrochelidon. Plate xxx.　　*LARIDÆ.*

342. *leucoptera,* 9½ in. WHITE-WINGED BLACK TERN. Black, with broad white edge to wings ; tail white ; bill red ; legs red.

341. *nigra,* 10 in. BLACK TERN. Black, with slaty wings and tail ; bill black ; legs brown.

343. *hybrida,* 11½ in. WHISKERED TERN. Crown and nape black ; cheeks white ; grey above ; wings whitish below ; tail white ; lower breast brownish ; bill red ; legs red.

The White-winged Black Tern—Dimensions, Il ; Eggs, Hs—is occasionally found on the east coast, generally in May or June. It is a widely distributed species, having been recorded in Sweden, North China, Celebes, New Zealand, and the Transvaal.

The Black Tern—Dimensions, Jb ; Eggs, Io—is better known as a spring and autumn migrant than as a resident. Like all the Terns it is recognisable by its forked tail ; and it carries its wings crossed one over the other as it walks. The sexes are alike in plumage, though the female is generally lighter in colour below than the male. The note is a shrill "hear! hear!" The nest is a mass of decaying vegetable matter on a mud flat, a floating raft, or a marshy island, and contains three eggs.

The Whiskered Tern—Dimensions, Ka ; Eggs, KF—has been recorded in this country about half a dozen times. It is the rarest of the Marsh Terns as far as Europe is concerned, for though it breeds along the Danube, it breeds more freely in the Orange Free State, forming a curious, but not the only, instance of a bird nesting both north and south of the Equator.

Hypolais. Plate iii.　　*TURDINÆ* (Passeridæ).

36. *icterina,* 5 in. ICTERINE WARBLER. Olive green above ; greenish yellow below ; greenish yellow eye stripe ; legs blue.

The Icterine Warbler—Dimensions, Be ; Eggs, Cd—has only been recorded three times in this country.

Ibis. Plate xviii.　　*IBIDIDÆ.*

215. *falcinellus,* 22 in. GLOSSY IBIS. Bronze brown with green and purple reflections ; bill decurved ; face bare ; 27 remiges ; legs dark green.

The Ibis—Dimensions, Qa ; Eggs, No—was once made out to be the Liverpool Liver, and it certainly seems to be the Black Curlew of East Anglia ; but its visits are at very distant intervals. It gives its name to the magazine under whose auspices the list we are working to was originally compiled.

Iynx. Plate xi.   *PICIDÆ.*

150   *torquilla,*   6½ in.   WRYNECK. Above greyish brown, much spotted ; throat buff with many narrow blackish bars ; remiges 21 ; first primary short, second and third longest ; tail soft and rounded, greyish, with five or six rippling dark brown bars ; 12 tail feathers, the two outer ones hidden under the two next.

The Wryneck—Dimensions, Eh ; Eggs, Do—gains its name of Iynx from its shriek, and its popular name from its habit of twisting its neck round. Its call is " oh, dear, dear, dear, dear, dear ! " It is a summer migrant, often known as the Cuckoo's mate from coming at the same time as the Cuckoo. Its flight is a short and quick one, but it is generally seen at rest. It lays its eggs in a hole in a tree, but, unlike the Woodpecker, it never bores the hole in which they are laid. The eggs are from 6 to 10 in number, and are laid among a few chips of rotten wood.

Lanius. Plate vi.   *LANIINÆ* (Passeridæ).

76.   *pomeranus,*   7 in.   WOODCHAT. Crown and nape chestnut ; head black ; back black ; rump white ; white below ; wings black, tipped with white ; two middle tail feathers black, the rest black and white.

75.   *collurio,*   7½ in.   RED-BACKED SHRIKE. Head grey ; back chestnut ; chin white ; lower breast buff ; wings black, edged with chestnut ; two middle tail feathers black.

74.   *minor,*   8½ in.   LESSER GREY SHRIKE. Grey above ; whitish below ; forehead black ; wings black, with one white spot ; first primary very short, third primary longest.

73.   *excubitor,*   9½ in.   GREAT GREY SHRIKE. Pearl grey above ; whitish below ; forehead whitish ; wide black stripe through eye ; wings black, with one or two white bars ; two middle tail feathers black, with white tips.

The Woodchat—Dimensions, Fg ; Eggs, Et—is a rare visitor, recorded as having bred in the Isle of Wight. The flight is swift and curving, with an occasional hover. The call is a " kra, kra," but there is also a somewhat musical song, mostly mimetic of the birds in the neighbourhood. The female has red margins to the wing coverts, but is otherwise much duller in plumage than the male. The nest is a conspicuous one in the fork of a tree ; it is made of twigs, and grass, and wool, and generally has a few flowers of Gnaphalium, and there are four, five, or six eggs.

The Red-backed Shrike—Dimensions, Gb ; Eggs, Eo—arrives in May, and is our commonest representative of the Butchers, for such is the meaning of Lanius, the name being derived from the way in which these birds kill their victims and hang them up on thorns, so as to form a larder near the nest. The flight is a dipping one, with many a poise and hover ; and in times of danger the bird can be recognised by a characteristic twirl of its tail. A Shrike never pursues its prey, but it will attack and kill any bird under its own size. The note is " tst-tst-tsook-tsook," but the male can mimic the song of his neighbours. The female is brownish red above, with very pale edges to the secondaries. The nest is about seven inches across and easily found ; it is made of twigs and plant stems, and lined with hair and wool, and contains from four to six eggs.

The Lesser Grey Shrike—Dimensions, Hh ; Eggs, Fm—is an accidental straggler to our shores.

The Great Grey Shrike—Dimensions, Ig ; Eggs, Gh—is a regular winter visitor. It dangles its legs as it flies, works its wings rapidly, dips and swoops, and frequently hovers. It is called *excubitor,* or the sentinel, from sitting on some conspicuous branch. Its alarm note is a " shake ; " its call a " trui." The female is duller in plumage, and has grey crescents on the breast. It breeds in Northern Sweden.

Larus. Plate xxxi.   *LARIDÆ.*

357.   *minutus,*   11 in.   LITTLE GULL. Head changing from black to white ; back grey ; primaries tipped with white without black bars, and being black below ; remiges 28.

356. *philadelphia,* 15 in. BONAPARTE'S GULL. Head changing from greyish black to white ; back grey ; inner webs of the two outer primaries edged with white.

358. *ridibundus,* 16 in. BLACK-HEADED GULL. Head changing from dark brown to white ; back grey ; remiges 30 ; outer primaries with white centres ; inner webs edged with black.

359. *melanocephalus,* 17 in. MEDITERRANEAN BLACK-HEADED GULL. Head black ; back grey ; wings white ; first primary with black line on outer web ; bill red, with a dark band in front of the angle.

361. *canus,* 18 in. GULL. Head white or spotted with brown ; back grey ; primaries brown with white spot ; bill tipped with yellow ; legs greenish yellow ; remiges 31.

363. *fuscus,* 21 in. LESSER BLACK-BACKED GULL. Head white ; primaries dark brown ; back blackish ; legs bright yellow.

366. *leucopterus,* 22 in. ICELAND GULL. All white ; legs and wings very long.

362. *argentatus,* 23 in. HERRING GULL. Head white or spotted with grey ; back grey ; bill yellow ; remiges 34 ; legs flesh-colour.

360. *ichthyaëtus,* 27 in. GREAT BLACK-HEADED GULL. Head black ; white patch round eye ; bill yellow with a black bar ; legs greenish yellow.

364. *marinus,* 28 in. GREAT BLACK-BACKED GULL. Head white ; back blackish ; remiges 34 ; legs flesh-colour.

365. *glaucus,* 32 in. GLAUCOUS GULL. All white ; legs and wings rather short.

The Little Gull—Dimensions, Jq ; Eggs, KI—is the smallest of the Gulls, and only visits our coasts occasionally. The first specimen on our record was shot on the Thames, at Chelsea.

Bonaparte's Gull—Dimensions, Mm ; Eggs, Ms—is an occasional straggler from across the Atlantic. It is, perhaps, worth noting that this bird builds its nest in tall trees.

The Black-headed Gull—Dimensions, Nk ; Eggs, MT—is best known by its brown head, which is only black by courtesy. It flies buoyantly, with much circling and hovering, spreads its tail, raises its wings, and pats at the water as it drops to its prey. Its call is a varied "hyuk-kak-kah," which has the fancied resemblance to a laugh, from which comes the specific *ridibundus,* and the popular "Laughing" Gull. In winter the head is white, with a grey patch round the eye and on the ear coverts. The sexes are alike in plumage. The nest is a mere hollow in a swamp, or on an island ; it is lined with a little grass or weed, and contains two or three eggs.

The Mediterranean Black-headed Gull—Dimensions, Nr ; Eggs, MK—has been here twice.

The Gull—Dimensions, Op ; Eggs, OR—is well known for its beautifully buoyant flight, now busily flapping, and now sailing and swaying on its long arched wings, which are mottled with brown below. The first six primaries are grey, brown, and white ; the secondaries are grey and white ; the coverts are all grey ; the first and second primaries are equal, and the longest in the wing. In summer the head is white ; but in winter the head is streaked with brown, and the yellow of the legs darkens considerably. The call is a "kyah," and a laughing "kree." The nest is a large one, usually on a low grassy island, but occasionally on a cliff ; it is made of grass, heather, and seaweed, and shore plants, and contains three eggs.

The Lesser Black-backed Gull—Dimensions, Pq ; Eggs, QN—is as common a bird as the last, and can be distinguished from it by the black back and small feet. In winter the white head is streaked with brown. The call is an "ah-ah-ah," and the alarm is "jock." The nest is always on the ground, but at any height above the water ; it is a large mass of grass and dead leaves, with a little seaweed and other plants ; it contains two or three eggs.

The Iceland Gull—Dimensions, Qh ; Eggs, Rc—has occasionally been recorded as a winter visitor.

The Herring Gull—Dimensions, Qm ; Eggs, RG—is known, all the year round, all round the coast—flying like a heron, following the herring, and stealing the eggs of every sea bird it meets with. Its outer primaries are mainly black with a grey wedge down the inner webs, increasing till the feathers are mainly grey. *In winter* the head and neck have grey streaks.

Its call is a croak and a "peewheel." Its nest is generally on a ledge of rock, but sometimes on level ground, and is a bulky construction of seaweed, lined with straw and shore plants. There are two or three eggs.

A Great Black-headed Gull—Dimensions, Sb ; Eggs, Rr—straggled from the Persian Gulf into the estuary of the Exe, in 1859, and, after a few foolish "croawks," fell a victim to an excited gunner, and thus became a British bird.

The Great Black-backed Gull—Dimensions, Sd ; Eggs, Rp—is a not uncommon resident, a "murderous thief," feeding on fish and the eggs and young of other birds, recognisable by his great size and Eagle-like flight. His cry is a yelping " kyauk." The nest is on some crag or islet—a big untidy mass of grass and seaweed, lined with a few feathers, or wool, and containing two or three eggs.

The Glaucous Gull—Dimensions, Sl ; Eggs, Sa—is the Burgomaster of the whalers, and is distinguished by the enormous spread of its wings. It is the largest of our Gulls, but is only an irregular visitor. It has grey streaks on its head in winter.

Ligurinus. Plate vii. *FRINGILLINÆ* (Passeridæ).

91. *chloris,* 6 in. GREENFINCH. Crown and back olive green ; wings greyish brown, edged with yellow ; axillaries bright yellow ; outer tail feathers black, yellow at base, and tipped with greyish brown.

The Greenfinch—Dimensions, Dm ; Eggs, Ef—is one of our common residents, yearly becoming commoner. It has a rapid drooping flight, with occasional glides. It has a twittering song of its own, but generally imitates that of other birds. Its call is "meay," or "yik, yik, yik." The female is not so green as the male, and has the tail feathers tipped with yellow on the outer webs only. The nest is generally in a tree which has a good deal of lichen on it, but frequently it is among evergreens. It has moss outside, with grass and wool, and it is lined with hair and feathers, and contains four, five, or six eggs.

Limicola. Plate xxvii. *SCOLOPACIDÆ.*

313. *platyrhyncha,* 6 in. BROAD - BILLED SANDPIPER. Blackish brown above ; white eye stripe ; brown spot in front of eye ; bill broad in the middle and longer than head ; little or no white on secondaries and upper tail coverts.

The Broad-billed Sandpiper—Dimensions, Dr ; Eggs, Hr—occasionally straggles here from its Swedish home.

Limosa. Plate xxix. *SCOLOPACIDÆ.*

336. *lapponica,* 15½ in. BAR-TAILED GODWIT. Back spotted brown ; rump whitish ; axillaries white, faintly barred with black.

337. *belgica,* 19 in. BLACK-TAILED GODWIT. Back spotted chestnut ; rump spotted chestnut ; axillaries white, or brown and white ; tail feathers black with white bases.

The Bar-tailed Godwit—Dimensions, Mr ; Eggs, Ok —visits us in autumn and spring on its way from and to its breeding grounds. It has a call like the bleat of a goat ; and another which has been syllabised as "Poor Willie." In summer it is red below ; in winter it is white below. The females are much larger than the males.

The Black-tailed Godwit—Dimensions, Or ; Eggs, Od—is also a spring and autumn visitor. The females are also much larger than the males. In winter its back is ashy brown. Its cry is a " yelp." It has two flights, a leisurely one with the wings fully spread, and a hurried one with the wings shortened in.

Linota. Plate vii. *FRINGILLINÆ* (Passeridæ).

99. *rufescens,* 4½ in. LESSER REDPOLL. Crown red ; rump brown ; throat pink ; chin black ; bill horn colour and small.

98. *linaria,* 5 in. MEALY REDPOLL. Crown red ; rump white ; throat pink ; chin black ; bill horn colour and small.

100.	*hornemanni,* 5¼ in.	GREENLAND REDPOLL. Crown red ; rump rosy ; throat pink ; chin black ; bill brown and large.
101.	*flavirostris,* 5½ in.	TWITE. Crown brown ; rump red ; throat brown; chin buff ; bill yellowish and short.
97.	*cannabina,* 5¾ in.	LINNET. Crown reddish, streaked with grey and blackish brown ; rump pale brown ; throat yellowish grey with red and brown streaks ; chin brownish white ; tail dark brown and white ; bill brownish or blue.

The Lesser Redpoll—Dimensions, Ak ; Eggs, Al—is our smallest Finch. He is darker than the Mealy Redpoll, and has whitish red bands on his wings. He has a jerky, swimming sort of flight, generally starting off with a chattering rattle and continuing with a prolonged trill. His call has been syllabised as "honree." The female is smaller than the male, and, unlike him, has no red on the breast and rump. The young birds have no red at all. The nest is generally low down among willows, or in a hedge or bush ; it is neatly made of slender twigs, grass, and moss, and lined with hair or willow catkins or cotton grass, and contains four, five, or six eggs.

The Mealy Redpoll—Dimensions, Bd ; Eggs, Ak—has a longer tail than the last, and it is deeply forked, but as he is only an irregular visitor the chances of his being met with are somewhat remote.

The Greenland Redpoll—Dimensions, Bk ; Eggs, Am—put in a first appearance among us at Whitburn, in 1855, and has not been seen here since.

The Twite—Dimensions, Ce ; Eggs, Bf—is a native found mostly among the northern moors and hills, whence its other name of Mountain Linnet. "Twite" comes from its call, which has otherwise been syllabised as "twah-it." Its flight is the jerkily buoyant one, characteristic of the Linnet family, with a little "chatter" to start with, a "twitter" on the wing, and a circling sweep before alighting. The female has no red on the rump, and is tawnier above and buffer below than the male ; she has a dusky brown tip to her beak. The nest is either on the ground or near it, among heather or furze as a rule, beautifully made of heather and grass, and lined with roots, feathers, wool, hair, and thistledown. It contains from four to six eggs.

The Linnet—Dimensions, Db ; Eggs, Bj—is one of our most popular songsters, with a sweet and mellow "twit, twit," and "tye wee, tye wee," of his own, to which he adds whatever he thinks best of the notes and calls of other birds. He has a rapid, wavy flight, with alternating flappings and pausings, glidings and wheelings, displaying all the white in his wings, and in his full spread tail, as he alights. In summer he has a good deal of red in his plumage, on his crown and breast, and chest, but this disappears in the autumn. The older he gets the redder he gets. The female has no red in her plumage at any time, and has little white on her wings, and many more brown stripes below than the male has, although in the winter he is much more streaked than in the summer. The Linnet in confinement loses much of the little bright colour he possesses, and is not unlike a hen sparrow. The nest is generally in a furze bush, occasionally it is in a thorn hedge, or even in a tree, and more rarely it is on the ground. It is a well built little affair of twigs, grey moss and wool, and grass, lined with rootlets, hair, feathers, and thistledown, and it contains from four to six eggs.

Locustella. Plate iii. *TURDINÆ* (Passeridæ).

| 44. | *luscinioides,* 5½ in. | SAVI'S WARBLER. Back russet brown ; throat white ; under tail coverts pale chestnut. |
| 43. | *nævia,* 5¾ in. | GRASSHOPPER WARBLER. Back greenish brown ; throat brownish white ; under tail coverts buffish brown. |

Savi's Warbler—Dimensions, Bt ; Eggs, Cq—has not been seen in this country since 1856, but was formerly a regular visitor to the Fen district. Its nest was a deep cup of interwoven sedge blades.

The Grasshopper Warbler—Dimensions, Co ; Eggs, Bo—is one of our spring visitors, arriving at the end of April, and leaving us in September. It is more often heard than seen. It skulks about the underwood, running like a Sandpiper, and only occasionally takes to the wing. Its note is like the sound made by a grasshopper, whence its name, a sort of trilling "tric-tric-tric," shrill and monotonous. The female is like the male, with the brown barred rounded tail, which is characteristic. The nest is compactly built and deep, and generally has some Galium in it. It is, as a rule, in a clump of grass, or at the bottom of a furze bush, and, with the bedstraw, has a good deal of flat grass and moss. It is lined with grass, and contains five, six, or seven eggs.

II

Loxia. Plate viii.   *FRINGILLINÆ* (Passeridæ).

108. *lifasciata,*   6 in.   TWO-BARRED CROSSBILL. Pale scarlet spotted with brown ; wings black with two white bars.

105. *curvirostra,* $6\frac{1}{4}$ in.   CROSSBILL. Dull crimson, brighter on chest and rump ; wings and tail brown ; under tail coverts white with brown centres.

107. *leucoptera,* $6\frac{1}{2}$ in.   WHITE-WINGED CROSSBILL. Dull crimson, with blackish scapulars and wings mostly white ; bill slender.

106. *pityopsittacus,* 7 in.   PARROT CROSSBILL. Similar to *curvirostra* but with bill longer, more arched, and very strong.

The Two-barred Crossbill—Dimensions, Do ; Eggs, CR—has a stouter beak than the White-winged Crossbill, which it somewhat resembles. Only a few stragglers have been noticed in this country, and it has never bred here.

The Crossbill—Dimensions, Eg ; Eggs, EM—is a winter visitor, occasionally remaining here to breed among the pine forests. It is generally seen on the wing when fluttering round the pine cones, on which it feeds. Its note is a "tsip, tsip," or "tsoc, tsoc." The female is dull yellow, where the male is red. The nest is always in a fir tree, and generally at the top. It is built of fir twigs, dry grass, lichens, and wool, and contains four or five eggs.

The White-winged Crossbill—Dimensions, En ; Eggs, Cs—is an American classed as British on the strength of a few escapes.

The Parrot Crossbill—Dimensions, Fj ; Eggs, EL—is occasionally met with. It is larger than the others, and has a stouter bill.

Machetes. Plate xxviii.   *SCOLOPACIDÆ.*

323. *pugnax,*   11 in.   RUFF. White axillaries.

The Ruff—Dimensions, Jl ; Eggs, LK—is an uncommon and perhaps doubtful resident, reinforced twice a year by flocks on migration to and from the north. It varies very much in the colour of its plumage, ringing almost every change on chestnut, black, and white. In spring the feathers of the face are moulted, to be replaced by hard pimples, and a ruff is developed which lasts through June. The pimples come in useful as a protection during the cock-fights which begin daily at sunrise during May and June, whence the bird's names of *Machetes,* a fighter ; and *pugnax,* fighting—for he fights much, but only with his beak, and does little damage. His cry is "kick-kick." The female, known as the Reeve, which is merely another form of Ruff, is a smaller bird, and has no ruff or occipital tufts, and is black and brown above. The nest is always in a swamp ; it consists of a few leaves of grass or sedge, and contains four eggs.

Macrorhampus. Plate xxvii.   *SCOLOPACIDÆ.*

312. *griseus,* $10\frac{1}{2}$ in.   RED-BREASTED SNIPE. Remiges 20 ; first primary white ; axillaries white ; tail coverts barred with black and white.

The Red-breasted Snipe—Dimensions, Je ; Eggs, LB—is an American, occasionally straggling across the Atlantic.

Mareca. Plate xxi.   *ANATIDÆ.*

242. *penelope,*   18 in.   WIGEON. Crown white ; cheeks and neck chestnut ; 14 feathers in tail.

243. *americana,*   19 in.   AMERICAN WIGEON. Crown buff ; a green stripe passing backward from eye.

The Wigeon—Dimensions, Oj ; Eggs, Nc—breeds in the north of Scotland, but arrives here in thousands in September, and leaves us in March. The flight is a rapid and vigorous one. The call is the "wee-ju," or "wigeon," from which it gets its name. The female has a bluish bill, tipped with black, like the male, and also the green wing bar, which is rather greyer ; but she is greyer above and buffer below. The nest is in a clump, always near water, and is made of grass and sedge, lined with down, which is sooty brown with white tips. It contains from 7 to 12 eggs.

An American Wigeon—Dimensions, Os ; Eggs, OL—was once found in Leadenhall Market ; but it is doubtful if it was ever seen elsewhere in these islands.

Melizophilus. Plate iii.   *TURDINÆ* (Passeridæ).

29. *undatus,*   5 in.   DARTFORD WARBLER. Dark brown above; chestnut brown below; tail dark grey, half as long as the bird, with its outside feathers tipped and edged with white; legs brown; eyes orange yellow.

The Dartford Warbler—Dimensions, As; Eggs, Be—is an uncommon but undoubted British bird. The first specimen on record was discovered near Dartford, in 1773. On the wing it looks like a black Wren. It has a curious way of working up a bush in search of insects, and then flying off to the base of another bush, and working up that, spreading its long tail as it settles after each change. The note is "pitchoo," with a chiding "cha, cha." The female has a cinnamon breast. The young have yellow eyes; those of the adult are almost red. The nest is generally in a furze bush, and is so loosely made of bedstraw, furze, and grass as to be seen through. It is small and deep, and lined with moss and wool. There are four, five, or six eggs.

Mergulus. Plate xxxii.   *ALCIDÆ.*

378. *alle,*   8½ in.   LITTLE AUK. White spot over eye; edges of scapulars white; remiges 26; primaries 11; tail feathers 12; legs brown.

The Little Auk—Dimensions, Hl; Eggs, Mf—is a winter visitor, generally found afloat, swimming much by the stern, and occasionally calling "try, try, try."

Mergus. Plate xxii.   *ANATIDÆ.*

261. *albellus,*   17 in.   SMEW. Rump grey; bill grey; 16 tail feathers.

262. *cucullatus,*   19 in.   HOODED MERGANSER. Rump white; head white; 18 tail feathers.

260. *serrator,*   24 in.   RED-BREASTED MERGANSER. Rump white; head black; 18 tail feathers.

259. *merganser,*   26 in.   GOOSANDER. Rump grey; bill vermilion; 18 tail feathers.

The Smew—Dimensions, No; Eggs, Ni—is a winter straggler from Finland. It is really a white bird, with black, and a few grey, markings, and a crest. It has a rapid, noiseless flight, and its call is "kr, kr." The female has a black patch on the lores. She is slate grey above; and her beak, like the male's, is bluish.

The Hooded Merganser—Dimensions, Oq; Eggs, Nk—is an American bird found here occasionally, but unknown elsewhere on this side of the Atlantic.

The Red-breasted Merganser—Dimensions, Qq; Eggs, Qm—is with us all the year round. His flight is powerful and quick, and his wings whistle as he goes. His call is a "karr, karr." The female has a white speculum divided by a black bar, while the male has two bars. The nest is generally near water, and always on the ground, in some dry place. It is made of heather and dry grass and leaves, and lined with brownish grey down, having dull pale tips and centres. It contains from 6 to 12 eggs.

The Goosander—Dimensions, Rk; Eggs, Ra—breeds in Scotland, and is known all round the coast in the winter. When in flight its wings are conspicuously long. Its call is "karr, karr," and it has a cry like a whistle. The male's head is black, the female's chestnut; both have crests. The nest is in a hole of some tree, or on the ground, generally in a tree, and it is lined with pale grey down, and contains from 8 to 12 eggs.

Merops. Plate xii.   *MEROPIDÆ.*

154. *apiaster,*   10¼ in.   BEE-EATER. Chestnut, gold, and green above; gold and black below; forehead white, lores black; wings green, black and chestnut; tail green; two central feathers an inch longer than the others.

155. *philippinus,*   12 in.   BLUE-TAILED BEE-EATER. Blue tail; chestnut throat and no black band on breast.

The Bee-eater—Dimensions, Jg; Eggs, Gc—has been occasionally shot in this country, but it is very rare.

The Blue-tailed Bee-eater—Dimensions, Kq—is even rarer, for it has only been seen here once.

Merula. Plate i. *TURDINÆ* (Passeridæ).

9. *merula,* 10 in. BLACKBIRD. Plumage brownish or glossy black ; bill orange or brown.

10. *torquata,* 11 in. RING OUZEL. Plumage brownish black, with white crescent on chest ; bill orange or brown, but black at tip.

The Blackbird—Dimensions, Im ; Eggs, GL—might have a better name, for it is not the only bird that is black ; and the female is brown, and the young are spotted. He has a hasty, fitful flight, low, but straight across open ground, making a spurt at the finish, and cocking up his tail as soon as he settles. His note is a deep contralto warble and pipe, with a call of "pic, pic, pic." He has a yellow bill ; the female has a brown one until she ages. The young male has a blackish bill ; the young female a brown one ; and the male is darker generally than the female. The nest is among evergreens or in a hedgerow, and is within a few feet of the ground. It is made of twigs and roots plastered with mud, and lined with dry grass and moss. There are from four to seven eggs.

The Ring Ouzel—Dimensions, Jk ; Eggs, GT—is a bird of the wilderness, resident in a few favoured localities all the year round, but mostly coming in April and leaving his moorland haunts in December. Like the Blackbird he raises his tail as he settles, and his flight is strong and straight. The song is flute-like and melodious, but not so musical as a Blackbird's ; and the call is a sharp "tac, tac, tac." The female is chocolate brown instead of black, and the gorget (whence the name *torquata,* collar wearer) is not clear white. The nest is on the ground, and generally by the side of a stream. It is made of coarse grass and heather and twigs, plastered with mud and lined with dry grass, and it contains four or five eggs.

Milvus. Plate xv. *FALCONIDÆ.*

185. *migrans,* 23 in. BLACK KITE. Bill black ; wings brown beneath ; tail dark brown and moderately forked.

184. *ictinus,* 26 in. KITE. Bill horn colour ; wings whitish beneath with a broad black patch ; tail rufous, barred with brown, and much forked.

The Black Kite—Dimensions, Qo ; Eggs, OH—was unknown in this country until 1866, and it has not been seen here since.

The Kite—Dimensions, Ro ; Eggs, PK—is now a rarity in this country, though at one time it used to be our commonest bird of prey. It is very reddish in plumage, and has yellow eyes and cere, and feet and legs. Its gliding flight gave it its old name of Glead. It seems to swim in the air, steering itself with its forked tail, in long sweeps and shorter curves, much as does the schoolboy's toy to which it gave its name. Its cry is a "whew," with an occasional "keh, keh." The female is larger than the male, and is greyer above and redder below, and shorter in the tail. The nest is in a tall tree ; it is built of twigs and many other things, including rags and paper ; it is very large for the size of the bird, and contains two, three, or four eggs.

Monticola. Plate i. *TURDINÆ* (Passeridæ).

11. *saxatilis,* 8 in. ROCK THRUSH. Axillaries chestnut ; tail chestnut, with two darker central feathers ; bill black ; legs black.

A Rock Thrush—Dimensions, Gs ; Eggs, GA—was shot in Hertfordshire, in 1843. There is no other authenticated record.

Motacilla. Plate v. *MOTACILLINÆ* (Passeridæ).

63. *flava,* 6 in. BLUE-HEADED YELLOW WAGTAIL. Bluish head, white eye stripe ; white chin ; white throat ; yellow breast.

64. *viridis,* 6¼ in. GREY-HEADED YELLOW WAGTAIL. Grey head, no eye stripe ; white chin ; yellow throat ; yellow breast.

65. *raii,* 6½ in. YELLOW WAGTAIL. Yellow head, with brownish crown.

60. *alba,* 7¼ in. WHITE WAGTAIL. White head ; black cap ; black throat ; greyish back.

61. *lugubris,* 7½ in. PIED WAGTAIL. White head ; black cap ; black throat ; black back.

62. *melanope,* 8 in. GREY WAGTAIL. Grey head ; narrow white eye stripe ; black patch on throat ; green rump.

The Blue-headed Yellow Wagtail—Dimensions, Dj ; Eggs, CN—has occasionally bred in

Durham, but generally straggles over here on migration. It has a buoyant, airy flight, a shrill call of "chit-up," and a twittering song. The female is a paler bird than the male, with the eye stripe less marked.

The Grey-headed Yellow Wagtail—Dimensions, Dt ; Eggs, Cɪ—once sent two specimens to Penzance, but they proceeded no further into the country owing to their being made British in the usual tragic manner. *M. viridis* has not been seen here since.

The Yellow Wagtail—Dimensions, Ei ; Eggs, Cɪ—arrives here annually shortly after Lady-day, and leaves just before Michaelmas. It has a fluttering flight with long, bold undulations, and an occasional soar, and as it drops to settle it spreads its tail so as to show off its white. As it starts it gives its call of "gee-up," in addition to which it has a short and rather cheery song. The female is browner on the back than the male, and is much paler below. The nest is usually on the grass, or on a bank, or else at the foot of a wall. It is made of dry grass, moss, and rootlets, and lined with hair, or feathers, or fur. It contains five or six eggs.

The White Wagtail—Dimensions, Fq ; Eggs, Dʜ—is a rare summer visitor, first noticed in 1841, and probably often mistaken for the common Water Wagtail, which it resembles in its flight, its song, and its nesting arrangements. The female has less white on her head, and less black on her throat than the male, and the throat patch is mottled with white.

The Pied Wagtail—Dimensions, Ga ; Eggs, Dᴅ—is the Water Wagtail so often alluded to as the "smallest bird that walks," which it very nearly is. It stays with us all the year round. It is generally found near water, running about with much bobbing of the tail to balance itself, and then taking to flight with a few rapid flaps, to soon ease its wings and float off in curves "like Hogarth's line." The note, loud and short, is often given when on the wing ; the call is "which is it ?" The female has a shorter tail than the male, and less black about her. The nest is in a hole in a wall, or bank, or tree, or among a heap of stones ; it is rather a large mass of moss, grasses, and leaves, lined with wool, hair, and feathers, and it contains four, five, or six eggs.

The Grey Wagtail—Dimensions, Gm ; Eggs, Cꜰ—is one of our less commoner residents. It has the Wagtail walk, with the tail jerking and the head nodding ; and its flight has the long bold curves of its congeners, with a similar spreading of the tail as it comes to the ground. It is more of a percher than its fellows, and has a longer tail. Its note is shriller but just as short, its call being "who? he? 'tis he ! 'tis he !" The female has little or no black on the throat, and more green in her plumage, and her tail is shorter. The nest is generally under a ledge in a quarry, or on a bank near running water ; it is made of rootlets, grass, and moss, and lined with white cowhair ; and it contains five or six eggs. It may be worth noting that Motacilla is merely wag-tail Latinised.

Muscicapa. Plate vi. *MUSCICAPINÆ* (Passeridæ).

85. *parva,* 4¾ in. RED-BREASTED FLYCATCHER. Olive brown above ; red throat.

79. *atricapilla,* 5 in. PIED FLYCATCHER. Black above ; white throat.

78. *grisola,* 5¼ in. SPOTTED FLYCATCHER. Brown above ; streaked or spotted throat.

The Red-breasted Flycatcher—Dimensions, Ar ; Eggs, Aɴ—was first noticed in this country in 1863, and since then there have been several records. The female has no grey in her plumage. The nest is to be found on the shores of Lake Baikal.

The Pied Flycatcher—Dimensions, Bc ; Eggs, Cc—arrives annually in April, and leaves in September. Its flight is not unlike that of the butterfly. It catches insects on the wing, but, as a rule, picks them off the leaves, or lays in wait for them at the end of a bough and darts down at them. Its song is short and weak, and rather like the Redstart's. The female has no white on the forehead, and has brown where the male has black, and her inner secondaries have thin white edges. The nest is generally in a hole in a tree—oak, birch, or poplar for choice—but sometimes it is in a hole in a wall ; it is a loose collection of dead leaves, moss, feathers, wool, and hair, and contains from five to eight eggs.

The Spotted Flycatcher—Dimensions, Bl ; Eggs, Bᴛ—is the common one in this country, and stays here from the end of April to September. Its flight is low, jerky, and hovering, in order that it may take its food on the wing. It has a feeble twittering song, and a call of "chick, fee, chack, chack." The female has the male's winter plumage—grey above, and ashy white below. The small nest is about 10 feet from the ground, on almost anything that will hold it, and it is neatly built of moss, dry grass, cobwebs, hair, and feathers ; it contains from four to six eggs. Just as Motacilla is the Latin for Wagtail, so Muscicapa is the Latin for Flycatcher.

Neophron. Plate xiv. *VULTURIDÆ.*

172. *percnopterus,* 25 in. EGYPTIAN VULTURE. Plumage buffish white ; head and neck yellowish ; wings black and brown ; legs pinkish ; claws black.

The Egyptian Vulture—Dimensions, Ri ; Eggs, Qᴊ—has been shot on two occasions on British ground—once in Bridgewater Bay, in 1825 ; and once, 43 years afterwards, near Burnham-on-the-Crouch.

Nucifraga.   Plate ix.   *CORVINÆ* (Passeridæ).

   124. *caryocatactes*, **13** in.   NUTCRACKER.   Plumage brown, spotted with
white ; outer tail feathers tipped with white ; a
dark brown crown ; bill black ; tail black.

The Nutcracker—Dimensions, La ; Eggs, I<small>N</small>—has been noticed south of the Tweed about
twenty times. Its call has a fancied resemblance to "crack, crack," and it has a leisurely,
undulating flight.

Numenius. Plate xxix.   *SCOLOPACIDÆ.*

   340. *borealis*,   14 in.   ESKIMO CURLEW.   Crown dark brown with a paler
stripe ; no white on rump ; axillaries chestnut
barred with brown.

   339. *phæopus*,   18 in.   WHIMBREL.   Crown dark brown with a whitish
stripe ; axillaries white barred with brown ; lower
back and rump unstreaked white.

   338. *arquata*,   24 in.   CURLEW.   Crown pale brown ; rump white with
black streaks ; axillaries white barred with brown ;
tarsus more than three inches long.

The Eskimo Curlew—Dimensions, Lq ; Eggs, N<small>Q</small>—is an American species occasionally
straggling across the Atlantic.

The Whimbrel—Dimensions, Og ; Eggs, Pj—breeds in the northern islands, and gets as
far south as Cornwall, in May, whence its name of May Bird. When on migration it flies
higher than at other times, as is the case with all birds, but as a rule its flight is low and quick,
with its wings held bent and motionless as it alights. Its note is a whistling "titterel,"
repeated seven times, from which it receives its names of Titterel and Seven Whistler ; it
owes its more popular name to the "whimbrel," which its note is also said to resemble. The
female is larger than the male. The nest is a mere hollow in the ground, generally near the
sea, lined with a few heather twigs and grass blades, and containing four pyriform eggs.

The Curlew—Dimensions, Ra ; Eggs, Qo—is to be found on the coast all the year round.
Its bill is very long but its tongue is rather short. It is a very wary bird, with a stately walk
and a swift flapping flight, ending in a long glide as it settles. Its cry is the wild scream of
"cur-lew." The female is larger than the male and her bill is longer in proportion ; in winter
she also resembles the male in being nearly white below. The nest is a hollow in the ground
on a heath or moor near the sea. It is lined with a few twigs and leaves, and contains four
eggs which are not pyriform.

Nyctala. Plate xiii.   *STRIGIDÆ.*

   167. *tengmalmi*,   9 in.   TENGMALM'S OWL.   Brown above, lightly spotted
with white ; greyish white below, barred with
brown ; feet with long white feathers.

Tengmalm's Owl—Dimensions, Id ; Eggs, I<small>I</small>—has its home in the far north, and has now
and then straggled here in a very cold winter, either on its way to the south or on its return
to the north. This owl is remarkable for having one ear larger than the other, not only
externally but internally.

Nyctea. Plate xiii.   *STRIGIDÆ.*

   165. *scandiaca*,   24 in.   SNOWY OWL.   Plumage white, barred with blackish
brown ; disk incomplete ; 29 remiges, third primary
longest, first equal to the fifth, and second equal to
the fourth ; feet feathered.

The Snowy Owl—Dimensions, Rf ; Eggs, P<small>L</small>—occasionally appears in this country when
an unusually severe winter drives it from its home within the Arctic Circle. It flies more
swiftly and less buoyantly than any other owl ; and it does not hoot, but cries " krau-aw ! "

Nycticorax. Plate xvii.   *ARDEIDÆ.*

   209. *griseus*,   24 in.   NIGHT HERON.   Crown black ; plumes white ;
bill black ; six powder down tracts ; wings and
tail grey.

The Night Heron—Dimensions, Qr ; Eggs, Mc—was first noticed in this country in 1782,
and has been recorded about once every two years since then. It is quite a globe-trotter, and
has been reported from all quarters, except Australia, where it is represented by a brighter-
coloured species. It has a noiseless flight, and a noisy cry, described as "a mournful
qua-a," otherwise "cow-ow."

Oceanites. Plate xxxiii. *PROCELLARIIDÆ.*

398. *oceanicus,* 7½ in. WILSON'S PETREL. Black, with a white bar on upper base of tail, and white spots on the flanks; tail square; legs long.

Wilson's Petrel—Dimensions, Gl; Eggs, HQ—has been occasionally noted among our visitors since 1838. It is recognisable at once by its long legs. In flight it seems invariably to cross the waves at right angles, leaping from one to the other in the Petrel way, Petrel being Peterel, or Little Peter, from the Apostle who tried to walk on water. Its eggs have been found on Kerguelen Island.

Œdemia. Plate xxii. *ANATIDÆ.*

256. *nigra,* 20 in. SCOTER. All black; remiges 26; tail of 16 feathers.

258. *perspicillata,* 21 in. SURF SCOTER. All black, except patches of white on forehead and nape.

257. *fusca,* 22 in. VELVET SCOTER. All black, except a white patch on wing.

The Scoter—Dimensions, Pf; Eggs, QK—is our common black Sea Duck, so plentiful in the winter. Its black and yellow bill, with the knob at the base, at once distinguishes it. It dives well, and flies rapidly. The note of the male is "tu, tu, tu"; to which the female replies with a louder, grating "kre-kr-kre." The nest is a mere hollow on the shore, hidden among the bushes, lined with dead grass and leaves, and much down; the down in colour is like the Wild Duck's, but the quantity is far greater. There are from six to nine eggs.

The Surf Scoter—Dimensions, Pm; Eggs, Qc—is a North American, occasionally wandering over here. It is the "Coot" of the American magazines, having received the name from the white patch on the forehead, which is a very different sort of thing from that of the shield of Fulica.

The Velvet Scoter—Dimensions, Ps; Eggs, RF—is one of our doubtful residents. It is never very numerous, but appears every winter, mostly along the east coast. Its diving propensities have led to its being taken, in fishing nets, under water. It is occasionally seen inland. It flies rapidly, and is the boldest of the Scoters. The nest is a mere hollow, lined with leaves, and a large quantity of down, browner than that of the Black Scoter, darker in the centre, and larger in size. The eggs are from 8 to 10 in number.

Œdicnemus. Plate xxv. *ŒDICNEMIDÆ.*

290. *scolopax,* 15 in. STONE CURLEW. Greyish brown above; whitish below; eye very large; bill half yellow half black; remiges 29; breast boldly streaked; dark band across wing, with pale narrow band inside it, between the lesser and greater coverts, the latter of which are tipped with white; central feathers of tail more than one inch longer than the outer ones; tarsus reticulate.

The Stone Curlew—Dimensions, Mn; Eggs, OA—is often called the Thicknee, which may have its advantages as suggestive of the Œthickneemidæ, but is otherwise misleading, as it is not the bird's knee which is thick, but its ankle. It is also known as the Norfolk Plover. It is a resident, whose numbers are increased by migrants in the summer. The Stone Curlew always runs for a few yards before taking to flight, and as it flies the markings on its secondaries are conspicuous. It has a loud plaintive cry. The nest is a mere hollow among shingle, and the eggs, like all those laid on a beach, are found by looking for two stones alike.

Oriolus. Plate v. *ORIOLINÆ* (Passeridæ).

72. *galbula,* 9 in. GOLDEN ORIOLE. All yellow except wings, which are black with a yellow bar, and the central tail feathers; black spot between bill and eye; remiges 20; first primary half the length of the second.

The Golden Oriole—Dimensions, Ib; Eggs, Hc—is too conspicuous a bird to be left in peace, although it still breeds in Cornwall every year, and is frequently reported from the eastern counties. It does not walk, but is one of our largest birds that hop, and it is noticeable that its folded wings reach to within an inch of the end of its tail. Its flight is easy and undulatory. Its call is "Ah! How d'ye do?" and its alarm is a "khrr." The female is greener than the male, and her tail is brown, with a narrow yellow tip. The nest is a suspended one, hanging from two forking branches, and formed of interwoven bark strips and sedge leaves lined with grass flowers. There are four or five eggs.

Otis. Plate xxv.   *OTIDIDÆ.*

  288. *tetrax*,   16 in. LITTLE BUSTARD. No crest; chest striped with white and black bands.

  289. *macqueeni*,   29 in. MACQUEEN'S BUSTARD. Head with a crest; chest pale grey.

  287. *tarda*,   36 in. GREAT BUSTARD. No crest; chest chestnut and grey.

The Little Bustard—Dimensions, Ne; Eggs, Oo—is an occasional straggler, generally appearing in the winter months. The female has black blotches on the back.

A Macqueen's Bustard—Dimensions, Sf; Eggs, Qi—was shot in Lincolnshire, in 1847, the first and last appearance of what is really an Indian species.

The Great Bustard—Dimensions, Tc; Eggs, Rs—was once a resident, but is now one of the rarest of stragglers.

Otocorys. Plate x.   *ALAUDINÆ* (Passeridæ).

  137. *alpestris*,   7 in. SHORE LARK. Erectile black crest on each side of head; a black band across upper breast.

The Shore Lark—Dimensions, Fk; Eggs, Ff—was first recorded in 1830, and occasionally appears during the winter months on the east coast.

Pagophila. Plate xxxi.   *LARIDÆ.*

  368. *eburnea*,   17 in. IVORY GULL. All white; bill greenish yellow; legs black.

The Ivory Gull—Dimensions, Ns; Eggs, Pq—appears on the north coasts when severe winters have driven it south from Spitzbergen and thereabouts.

Pandion. Plate xvi.   *FALCONIDÆ.*

  198. *haliaëtus*,   23 in. OSPREY. Purplish brown above; white below; crown and nape white, streaked with brown; legs and feet blue, reticulate, and prickly below.

The Osprey—Dimensions, Qn; Eggs, Pr—still breeds here, but to nothing like the extent it used to do, and it is best known as an autumnal visitor. There is only one species in the world of this bird. Its contour feathers have no aftershaft and are small and short, and hence its legs have no breeches. It flies with its legs out straight, and its flight is a hovering and gliding one with little wing work. Its wings look very long as they are stretched out apparently motionless. The Osprey feeds on fish, and catches it with a sudden swoop, bearing it away in its claws. The call is "kai, kai, kai;" the alarm a scream. The female is browner on the breast than the male, and larger. The nest is a big one of twigs and turf, lined with moss, and situate on a tree-top or some lofty ledge. There are from two to four eggs.

Panurus. Plate iv.   *PANURINÆ* (Passeridæ).

  49. *biarmicus*,   6 in. BEARDED TIT. Crown grey; long black moustache; back orange tawny; tail fawn coloured and over three inches long.

The Bearded Tit—Dimensions, De; Eggs, Bl—is resident but rare. It has a varied undulating flight, with many glides and pauses. Its note is "ping, ping," its call is "chirrrr," and its alarm "hear, hear." The female has no black feathers on her neck or in her under tail coverts. The male's beak is orange; the female's is yellow. The nest is always near water, but is never hung from reeds. It consists of dry leaves of reed and grass, and is lined with reed flowers. There are from four to seven eggs.

Parus. Plate iv.   *PARINÆ* (Passeridæ).

  53. *ater*,   4¼ in. CONTINENTAL COAL TIT. Nape with white patch; back greyish blue; two white bars on wing.

  54. *britannicus*, 4¼ in. BRITISH COAL TIT. Nape with white patch; back olive brown; two white bars on wing.

  57. *cristatus*,   4½ in. CRESTED TIT. Black and white crest.

  56. *cœruleus*,   4½ in. BLUE TIT. Crown light blue edged with white.

  55. *palustris*,   4½ in. MARSH TIT. Nape greyish black without a white patch; back greyish brown; no bars on wings.

  52. *major*,   6 in. GREAT TIT. Black apron from chin to vent.

The Continental Coal Tit--Dimensions, Ae ; Eggs, Bc—is said to be born abroad, and only to come here on migration.

The British Coal Tit—Dimensions, Af ; Eggs, Bb—is resident here and seemingly increasing. It has a short fluttering flight. The note is a shrill " ping, ping," or " che, chee." The female is duller than the male in colour. The nest is in a hole either in a stump, or the ground, or a wall, and is loosely made of dry grass, feathers, moss, hair, and wool ; the eggs are from five to nine in number.

The Crested Tit—Dimensions, Ag ; Eggs, AQ—is resident among the Scottish pine forests. It has the usual fluttering flight of the tits. Its note is " ptur-re-re-ree," with a call of " si-si-si." The female has a shorter crest than the male, and is not so black on the throat. The nest is in a hole, and is a felted mass of grass, moss, wool, fur, and feathers. Sometimes a deserted Crow's nest is adapted. There are from four to seven eggs.

The Blue Tit—Dimensions, Ai ; Eggs, Ae—is the commonest of the family. It has not only a blue crown, but blue wing coverts. The flight is a fluttering uncertain one, with rapid flappings and sudden undulations. The note is " chee, chee, chicka, chee," with an occasional " chirr-r," and a call of " si, si, si." The female is not so bright in plumage as the male. The nest is generally in a hole, but it does not seem to matter where the hole is. It is rather loosely built of moss, grass, wool, hair, and feathers ; and it contains from 5 to 12 eggs.

The Marsh Tit—Dimensions, Aj ; Eggs, AJ—is resident, but rather uncommon. It has a short, fluttering flight ; its call is " ti, ti, ti," and its note is " sis, sis, sis, would ye, would ye." The female is indistinguishable from the male. The nest is in a hole, which the bird has been seen to make in some decayed stump, though rat holes are sometimes adapted to suit the purpose. The nest is a felted mass of moss, wool, fur, and willow down ; and contains from five to eight eggs.

The Great Tit—Dimensions, Bm ; Eggs, Bk—is one of our commoner birds. It is often called the Oxeye, and its note has been described as resembling " oxeye, oxeye, oxeye, oxeye, twink, twink !" which same " oxeye " has also been compared to the sharpening of a saw. The call is "teeta tee." The flight is a short, irregular flutter. The female is not so bright in plumage as the male. The nest is in holes and elsewhere, and is a felted mass of grass, moss, hair, feathers, and wool, containing from 5 to 11 eggs.

Passer. Plate vii. *FRINGILLINÆ* (Passeridæ).

94. *montanus,* 5 in. TREE SPARROW. Crown chocolate ; ear coverts whitish with a black patch behind them.

93. *domesticus,* 6 in. HOUSE SPARROW. Crown grey, bordered with chestnut ; ear coverts whitish with no black patch.

The Tree Sparrow—Dimensions, Ba ; Eggs, Ea—seems to be on the increase, though still far less numerous than the House Sparrow. Its flight is easy and swift ; its note is " see-you-eat," and its call a " chirrup." The female is like the male. The nest is domed when it is not in a hole or under shelter, and it is often found in quarries and rocks. It is built of straw, grass, and wool, lined with hair and feathers, and contains from four to six eggs.

The House Sparrow—Dimensions, Df ; Eggs, EJ—is said to be the friend of man, probably from his making as much use of him as possible. He is never seen to walk beyond one or two steps, but hops and jumps, as do all the finches ; and he is said to cock his tail in wet weather and droop it in dry. His is a rapid and direct flight as a rule, though he often undulates and flutters. He has a twittering note ; a call of " Philip, Philip, get up !" and a chirpy alarm. The female wants the grey crown and black on the throat. The nest is domed when in a tree, but is oftener built under cover on some outside part of a house. It is an untidy collection of straw, grass, wool, hair, string, rags, paper, and sundries, lined with feathers, and containing from five to seven eggs.

Pastor. Plate ix. *STURNINÆ* (Passeridæ).

121. *roseus,* 8½ in. ROSE-COLOURED STARLING. Crest, head, and neck violet black ; back and breast rose-coloured ; wings and tail black ; bill red ; legs brown.

The Rose-coloured Starling—Dimensions, Hk ; Eggs, Gf—was first recognised at Norwood in 1742, and has since been a somewhat frequent spring visitor.

Perdix. Plate xxiv. *PHASIANIDÆ.*

275. *cinerea,* 12½ in. PARTRIDGE. Tail of 16 feathers ; legs blue.

274. *rufa,* 13½ in. RED-LEGGED PARTRIDGE. Tail of 14 feathers ; legs red.

The Partridge—Dimensions, Kj ; Eggs, IT—is almost as familiar as the barn-door fowl, which is not however recognised as a British Bird. The male has a horse-shoe mark on the breast, which is absent in the female. The flight begins with a noisy whirr which soon changes into a glide with the hollow wings spread out, to be whirred again when needful ; the bird rarely flying far, and always gliding to the ground. The note is a "kir-rik, kir-rik." The nest is on the ground, and is a mere scratching together of weeds and leaves, containing from 10 to 20 eggs.

The Red-legged Partridge—Dimensions, Lh ; Eggs, KA—was acclimatised in this country in 1770, and is now quite as common in the Eastern Counties as the Grey Partridge, from which it differs in its habit of perching in trees which the other never does. The male has rudimentary spurs on his legs ; the female's legs are smooth. The flight is much like the other Partridge's but lighter and not so noisy. The call has been syllabised as "cock-a-leekie" ; but this would seem to be more appropriate in another of the Phasianidæ. The nest is generally on the ground ; but sometimes on a straw stack. It is merely a scratching, and contains from 10 to 18 eggs.

Pernis.   Plate xvi.   *FALCONIDÆ.*

188.   *apivorus*,   24 in.   HONEY BUZZARD. Head grey ; lores feathered ; upper parts brown ; lower parts brown or white, blotched and barred with brown ; tail with three black bars ; tarsus finely reticulate all round.

The Honey Buzzard—Dimensions, Re ; Eggs, NJ—is a doubtful resident and not a very common summer visitor. The flight is not unlike a buzzard's, but the bird's longer tail, more pointed wings and smaller head make it easily recognisable. Its cry is "kee, kee, kee." The female has no grey on the head. The nest is like a peregrine's, but it is lined with fresh green beech leaves, which are renewed as they dry. There are from two to four eggs.

Phalacrocorax.   Plate xvii.   *PELECANIDÆ.*

200.   *graculus*,   27 in.   SHAG. No white in the plumage ; 12 feathers in tail.

199.   *carbo*,   36 in.   CORMORANT. White patch on thigh ; 14 feathers in tail.

The Shag—Dimensions, Rt ; Eggs, Ps—is very greenish in plumage, and in spring has a crest which curls forwards. The flight is very speedy and regular. The Shag swims low in the water and dives magnificently, swimming under the surface for long distances with both wings and feet, and so deep does it go that it has been caught in a crabpot one hundred and twenty feet down. The nest is generally in a cave, and is an odoriferous mass of seaweed, grass, and heather, containing from three to five eggs.

The Cormorant—Dimensions, St ; Eggs, Qs—is almost as good a diver and a better flyer, gliding straight along after a few short powerful flaps, with his wings at full stretch, his neck straight out, and his legs close under his tail. In spring he has a few hair-like feathers on his head, which disappear after the breeding season. These head feathers form a crest, and the female's crest is the larger. In the winter there is more white in the plumage round the throat. The cry is a croak. The nest is on the ledge of a cliff, and is a large mass of sticks and seaweed lined with leaves, which can generally be smelt from afar. It contains from two to five eggs. It is said that the Cormorant can swim at different draughts, but as a rule he swims very low, with the water awash across his shoulders.

Phalaropus.   Plate xxvii.   *SCOLOPACIDÆ.*

306.   *hyperboreus*, 7 in.   RED-NECKED PHALAROPE. Bill thin and tapering, and black throughout.

307.   *fulicarius*,   8 in.   GREY PHALAROPE. Bill flat and broad, and yellow, tipped with black ; middle tail feathers more than half an inch longer than the outer ones.

The Red-Necked Phalarope—Dimensions, Fh ; Eggs, Gq—is best known as a migrant from and to its northern home, but it is resident in the Western Isles. Its name is in allusion to its lobate feet, the phalara meaning fringed, and the pous, a foot. It can both fly and swim. Its note is "wick." The female is larger than the male and brighter in colour. The nest is in a tuft in a swamp, and is made of dry grass, and contains four eggs. In winter these birds have white foreheads, and are much whiter below.

The Grey Phalarope—Dimensions, Gt ; Eggs, Hf—occasionally visits us in flocks, apparently strayed down from the Arctic Circle.

Phasianus. Plate xxiv. *PHASIANIDÆ.*

273. *colchicus,* 34 in. PHEASANT. Remiges 26 ; tail long and wedge-shaped, and of 18 feathers.

The Pheasant—Dimensions, So ; Eggs, MD—was acclimatised from the Phasis, whence also the *colchicus,* a long time ago, and seems always to have been "preserved" in this country. This is the kind without a white neck-ring. The one with the white ring, *P. torquatus,* was acclimatised from China, also a long time ago, but is not yet considered to be British. The pheasant never flies if it can help it. It runs along with its tail horizontal, and it flies with its tail spread ; a heavy, rapid, whirring flight taken in short stages as a rule, but occasionally settled down into and prolonged for miles. The female is smaller than the male and much duller in plumage, and she has a shorter tail ; but pure bred specimens of the real *P. colchicus* are very rare. The nest is a mere scratching, and hardly that, amid grass and weeds ; and the eggs are from 8 to 13 in number.

Phœnicopterus. Plate xviii. *PHŒNICOPTERIDÆ.*

216. *roseus,* 60 in. FLAMINGO. Plumage rosy-white, with scarlet wing coverts and black primaries.

The Flamingo—Dimensions, Tn ; Eggs, SL—is not quite the sort of bird one would expect to see in the British List, but as some one once happened to shoot one on British ground, its inclusion was inevitable under the prevailing rule. At the same time it is only fair to note that a few flamingoes are stated to have been seen in this country outside the Zoological Gardens, and that flocks of them yearly come north and visit Southern and Central France.

Phylloscopus. Plate iii. *TURDINÆ* (Passeridæ).

32. *superciliosus,* 4 in. YELLOW-BROWED WARBLER. Six outer primaries notched ; plumage yellowish green ; distinct eye stripe ; two yellow bars on wing ; legs brown.

33. *rufus,* 4¼ in. CHIFFCHAFF. Six outer primaries notched ; plumage olive green ; faint greyish white eye stripe ; legs nearly black.

34. *trochilus,* 5 in. WILLOW WREN. Five outer primaries notched ; first primary over half an inch in length ; plumage olive green ; faint greenish eye stripe ; legs light brown.

35. *sibilatrix,* 5¼ in. WOOD WREN. Four outer primaries notched ; first primary under half an inch in length ; plumage yellowish green ; bright yellow eye stripe ; legs brown.

The Yellow-browed Warbler—Dimensions, Ad ; Eggs, AG—is a rare straggler from Siberia.

The Chiffchaff—Dimensions, Ao ; Eggs, AD—is one of the earliest of our summer migrants, and comes in the middle of March. Its wings when closed cover hardly a quarter of its tail, and its second primary is equal to the seventh and halfway in length between the sixth and ninth. It has an undulatory flight, with the wings flapping rapidly. The song from which it derives its name "Chiffchaff," is usually delivered from near the top of some good sized tree ; it has been also syllabised as "till-tell-true, jink-junk." The nest is generally within a foot of the ground—a complete oval with the hole near the top—made of grass, leaves, and moss, and lined with feathers. It contains from five to seven eggs.

The Willow Wren—Dimensions, At ; Eggs, AH—is the commonest of the warblers, and is with us from April to September. Its wings when closed cover less than half its tail, and its third and fourth primaries are the longest. It hops like a robin, and has a short, rapid, dipping flight. Its song is a descending scale of "twiu, twiu, twiu, tiu, tiu, tiu, tiu, twee, twee, twee, twee, twee, twai, twai," with an alarm of "na, na, na, na," and a call of "whit." Its nest is on or near the ground, a flattened sphere, with the rim sloped at half a right angle, of dead grass and moss, dry leaves, roots, horsehair, and feathers, particularly feathers, containing from five to eight eggs.

The Wood Wren—Dimensions, Bj ; Eggs, AT—arrives a little after the Willow Wren. Its wings when closed cover three-quarters of the tail ; the second primary is the same length as the fourth, and the third and fourth primaries are sloped off. It is generally found in beech woods, and its flight is swift, dipping, and gliding, with a spiral descent as it settles. The call is "dear, dear, dear," and its song is a rippling "chit, chit, cherry-tr-tirrerectirreree," with a rapid jarring trill and much vibration of the wings and tail. The nest is near the ground, semi-domed like that of its congeners, but it has no feathers in its lining. It contains from five to seven eggs.

Pica. Plate ix. *CORVINÆ* (1 .>seridæ).

  126. *rustica,*   18 in.   MAGPIE. head and back greenish black ; rump greyish white ; tail greenish and large ; scapulars white ; lower breast white.

The Magpie—Dimensions, Oc ; Eggs, IJ—is distinguishable by its long iridescent green tail alone, which it invariably raises as it alights. Its flight is graceful and easy, but somewhat slow. Its cry is a noisy chatter. The female is the smaller bird and is not so iridescent in the plumage. The nest is nearly a sphere, built generally of blackthorn twigs cemented with mud, and lined with rootlets and grass, the entrance to which is a circular hole. There are from six to nine eggs.

Picus. Plate xi.   *PICIDÆ.*

  145. *minor,*   5¾ in.   LESSER SPOTTED WOODPECKER. Crown red ; back white and black ; under tail coverts with no red in them.

  147. *pubescens,*   6¾ in.   DOWNY WOODPECKER. Crown black ; nape red ; back black, with a white central stripe ; legs blue.

  146. *villosus,*   8¾ in.   HAIRY WOODPECKER. Crown black ; back black with a white central stripe ; no red on under tail coverts ; legs brown.

  144. *major,*   9½ in.   GREAT SPOTTED WOODPECKER. Crown black ; back black ; under tail coverts red.

  148. *martius,*   18 in.   GREAT BLACK WOODPECKER. Crown red ; back black.

The Lesser Spotted Woodpecker—Dimensions, Dc ; Eggs, CK—is the commonest Woodpecker in the Thames Valley. Like all the Woodpeckers it has a peculiar nick in its tail feathers. It is a restless bird, with a short flight from tree to tree as it picks and taps up one, sometimes head downwards, and then flies off to the next. The note is " keek." The female has no red about her head. The nest is in a hole so small that a larger bird cannot enter, and which is often a foot deep, and contains only a few chips and the eggs, which number from five to nine.

The Downy Woodpecker—Dimensions, Er ; Eggs, FT—is a straggler from North America that once had a representative shot in Dorsetshire.

The Hairy Woodpecker—Dimensions, Hn ; Eggs, Fs—has only appeared twice in th country.

The Great Spotted Woodpecker—Dimensions, Ii ; Eggs, FR—is a resident, whose numbers are swollen by migration. It works up a tree in spirals, picks and taps at it rapidly, and then flies off to begin at another in the same way. Its call is a " chick, chink." The female has no red on her head, but the young of both sexes are red in the crown for a time. The nest is in a hole in a tree. There are from five to eight eggs.

The Great Black Woodpecker—Dimensions, Ok ; Eggs, IE—seems to have been inserted in the List out of respect for tradition.

Platalea. Plate xviii.   *PLATALEIDÆ.*

  214. *leucorodia,*   34 in.   SPOONBILL. Pale yellow crest ; plumage white, tinted with yellow and pale orange ; 30 remiges ; second primary longest.

The Spoonbill—Dimensions, Sp ; Eggs, QB—was at one time a resident, but is now only an occasional summer visitor. Its flight is slow and regular, with the wings spread to their utmost. As a call it clicks its bill. Its nest is on a grassy tussock, or in a tree, and consists of a few sticks and dead leaves, with a lining of grass. It contains four or five eggs.

Plectrophanes. Plate viii.   *EMBERIZINÆ* (Passeridæ).

  118. *nivalis,*   7 in.   SNOW BUNTING. Black, brown, and white above ; whitish below ; four central tail feathers black, two nearly black ; the others white tipped with black.

The Snow Bunting—Dimensions, Fm ; Eggs, Fc—is often called the Snowflake. It runs like a lark and flies like a butterfly, and crows and sings on the wing. The call is " tsee." The female is brown where the male is black. In winter the black in both sexes is brownish. The nest has been found in the Scottish Highlands, and it has been found in Grinnell Land, in lat. 82° 83′ at Midsummer. It is generally placed among stones, and consists of dry grass, moss, rootlets, and twigs, lined with hair, down, or feathers, and containing from four to eight eggs.

ᅟ

Podiceps. Plate xxxiii. *PODICIPEPIDÆ.*

388.	*minor,*	9 in.	LITTLE GREBE. Bill decurved.
387.	*nigricollis,*	12 in.	EARED GREBE. Bill curved upwards.
386.	*auritus,*	13 in.	SCLAVONIAN GREBE. Bill straight.
385.	*greiseigena,*	16 in.	RED-NECKED GREBE. No white eye stripe.
384.	*cristatus,*	22 in.	GREAT CRESTED GREBE. White eye stripe.

The Little Grebe—Dimensions, Hp ; Eggs, Is—otherwise the Dabchick, is our bird with the smallest tail. It has a black chin in summer and a white chin in winter. The nest is a floating one moored to a reed, and made of rotting water plants. It contains from four to six eggs.

The Eared Grebe—Dimensions, Kb ; Eggs, Mg—has the four inner primaries all white. It is an occasional winter visitor, not yet proved to breed here.

The Sclavonian Grebe—Dimensions, Kl ; Eggs, Lg—is also known as the Horned Grebe. It is a winter visitor.

The Red-necked Grebe—Dimensions, Mt ; Eggs, Mn—is another winter visitor.

The Great Crested Grebe—Dimensions, Pr ; Eggs, Oi—is a resident. It flies with its neck out and its legs out extending beyond the rudimentary tail, and flaps rapidly with its short wings. Its call is "kewawk." The female has a smaller crest and tippet than the male, and as with him, these almost disappear in the winter. Its nest is usually afloat, and consists of a wet mass of decaying vegetation, containing three or four eggs.

Pratincola. Plate ii. *TURDINÆ* (Passeridæ).

| 15. | *rubetra,* | 5 in. | WHINCHAT. Throat light reddish brown, |
| 16. | *rubicola,* | 5¼ in. | STONECHAT. Throat black. |

The Whinchat—Dimensions, Bb ; Eggs Bq—is a summer migrant, arriving in April and departing in October. Its three outer tail feathers have white bases. It roosts on the ground, but is generally seen on the top of a bush, from which it dips off in a short flight to another bush. Its note is "oo-tac, oo-tac, tac, tac, tac," and it sings on the wing. The female is heavier than the male, paler in plumage, and with a much smaller wing bar. The nest is on or near the ground, well hidden and approached by a mazy run, and built of straws, moss, and grass, with a lining of fine grass. It contains from four to six eggs.

The Stonechat—Dimensions, Bi ; Eggs Ch—is a resident. The outer web of his tail feathers has a buff edging, and he has a white stripe round the nape of his neck. He has a darting flight from bush to bush. His song is a "wheet, chook, chook," and his call is a sharp "chack." The female is a browner and plainer bird, with her upper tail coverts reddish brown. The nest is generally at the bottom of a bush, and rather large for the size of the bird, often very neatly built of moss and dry grass, lined with hair and a little wool and feathers. There are from four to seven eggs.

Procellaria. Plate xxxiii. *PROCELLARIIDÆ.*

| 397. | *pelagica,* | 5½ in. | STORMY PETREL. Black, with a broad white ring round the base of the tail ; remiges 22, second primary longest, first equal to fourth ; tail slightly rounded. |
| 396. | *leucorrhoa,* | 7 in. | FORK-TAILED PETREL. Black, with a white bar on upper base of tail ; tail much forked. |

The Stormy Petrel—Dimensions, Cn ; Eggs Gn—is the smallest web-footed bird. In its flight it follows the curves of the waves and pats them as it feeds. Its call is "kekerek-ee." Its nest is in a hole in a cliff or wall, and consists of a few blades of grass or plant stalks. It contains but one egg.

The Fork-tailed Petrel—Dimensions, Fo ; Eggs Ib—is a straggler, breeding no nearer than St. Kilda. Its call is "peer wit." Its nest is in a burrow, and it is made of a few blades of grass and a scrap of moss, and contains but one egg.

Puffinus. Plate xxxiii. *PROCELLARIIDÆ.*

394.	*obscurus,*	11 in.	DUSKY SHEARWATER. All white below ; remiges 30 ; first primary longest.
393.	*anglorum,*	14 in.	MANX SHEARWATER. Breast white ; lower breast grey.
392.	*griseus,*	18 in.	SOOTY SHEARWATER. All brown below.
391.	*major,*	19 in.	GREAT SHEARWATER. White below, but thighs and lower breast tinged with brown ; hind toe modified into, or replaced by, a sort of spur.

The Dusky Shearwater—Dimensions, Jo ; Eggs, Oj—has strayed here twice from its tropical home.

The Manx Shearwater—Dimensions, Ma ; Eggs, Po—is the commonest of the four and is here all the year round, generally in single files, gliding close to the surface of the waves and following their curves. The call is "kitty-coo-roo," or the "kitty carew," from which it gets its Cornish name. The nest is a little grass at the end of a hole or burrow, and it contains a solitary egg.

The Sooty Shearwater—Dimensions, Ol ; Eggs, Ql—has only of late been recognised as a distinct species, it having been taken to be the young of the Great Shearwater. It is a South Atlantic species, only occasionally straggling into our latitudes.

The Great Shearwater—Dimensions, Pa ; Eggs, Re—has been occasionally noticed here in the Autumn. There is a good deal of doubt as to its nesting places, and the eggs usually ascribed to it are said to really belong to another species. It "shears the water" as it alights and dives. In flight it keeps its wings bent and glides along without much flapping, rolling from side to side and just skimming the waves.

Pyrrhocorax.   Plate ix.   *CORVINÆ* (Passeridæ).

123.	*alpinus*,	15 in.	ALPINE CHOUGH. Plumage black ; bill yellow, short, and straight ; legs yellow.
122.	*graculus*,	16 in.	CHOUGH. Plumage black ; bill orange, long, and curved ; legs orange.

An Alpine Chough—Dimensions, Ml ; Eggs, Jr—was once shot near Banbury, having probably escaped from confinement. This is the only record.

The Chough—Dimensions, Ni ; Eggs, Kh—is rare, but resident, and is only found on a rocky coast. In flight it yaws like a Jackdaw, and is very laboured and irregular in its progress. Its call is "cling," or the "chough-chough," from which it is named, or a peculiar "khew, khew." The female is smaller than the male. The nest is a hole in the rock. It is built of sticks and lined with grass roots, and a good deal of wool and hair. It contains from three to six eggs.

Pyrrhula.   Plate viii.   *FRINGILLINÆ* (Passeridæ).

103.	*erythrina*,	5½ in.	SCARLET GROSBEAK. Crown red ; rump red ; breast rose pink ; legs reddish brown ; bill yellowish.
102.	*europœa*,	6 in.	BULLFINCH. Crown black ; rump white ; breast brick red ; legs dark brown ; bill black.
104.	*enucleator*,	8½ in.	PINE GROSBEAK. Crown red ; rump red ; breast vermilion ; legs blackish brown ; bill dark brown.

The Scarlet Grosbeak—Dimensions, Ci ; Eggs, Dc—has been found twice in this country, once in 1869 and once in 1870.

The Bullfinch—Dimensions, Di ; Eggs, Db—is a resident. His wings are longer than his tail, and his nostrils are hidden by the plumelets. He has a jerky dipping flight ; and his native song is not a loud one although he is taught to pipe. His call is "do you? do you?" with the accent on the "you." The female is brown where the male is red. The nest is a flat one of slender twigs with a cup of rootlets and perhaps wool or feathers. It contains from four to six eggs.

The Pine Grosbeak—Dimensions, Ha ; Eggs, Fq—visits us so rarely that his visits are doubted.

Querquedula.   Plate xxi.   *ANATIDÆ.*

239.	*crecca*,	14 in.	TEAL. Wing bar black, purple, and green, with white at one edge ; tail of 16 feathers.
240.	*discors*,	14 in.	AMERICAN BLUE-WINGED TEAL. White crescent in front of eye.
241.	*circia*,	15 in.	GARGANEY. Wing bar green, with white at both edges ; tail of 14 feathers.

The Teal—Dimensions, Ln ; Eggs, Lf—is our smallest duck. His numbers are much augmented in the winter by migrants. His flight is lighter than that of most ducks, and when in company his column of march is angular. His cry is a sharp croak or "knake." The female has only a trace of purple in the wing bar, and her upper feathers are edged with grey. The nest is generally in a swamp, and is made of dead rushes and reeds, lined with feathers and brown down, which is small and has no white tips. There are from 8 to 12 eggs.

The American Blue-Winged Teal—Dimensions, Lm ; Eggs Ko—paid us one visit, as did also the Green-Winged Teal, of which no further mention is necessary.

The Garganey—Dimensions, Mi ; Eggs, Ma—is a spring visitor, resident only where protected. He has a grey bill, while the Teal's is black, and he has bluish wing coverts. He swims high in the water, and flies high in the air and very rapidly. His call is like the Teal's, but the "crik," which the Teal gives occasionally, is his usual cry, and hence he is locally known as the Cricket Teal. The female has no gloss on the wing bar. The nest is always on the ground and often away from water, and it is built of grass and leaves, and lined with down having long white tips. It contains from 8 to 14 eggs.

Rallus. Plate xxiv. *RALLIDÆ.*

282. *aquaticus,* 10½ in. WATER RAIL. Spotted brown above ; greyish below ; axillaries black barred with white ; flanks black with narrow white bars ; bill reddish ; remiges 26.

The Water Rail—Dimensions, Jd; Eggs, If—is a bird of the marshes, never flying if it can escape by running in and out through the reeds. Its flight is low and laboured, with the legs hanging. It can swim and it can dive. Its call is "kreek," and in the breeding season it "sharms." The female is not so bright in colour as the male. The nest is always on the ground, generally amid a clump of rushes or osiers, and it is built of reeds and flags, and contains from 5 to 11 eggs.

Recurvirostra. Plate xxvii. *SCOLOPACIDÆ.*

304. *avocetta,* 18 in. AVOCET. White and black above ; white below ; bill black, long, pointed, and curved upwards ; remiges 30 ; legs grey.

The Avocet—Dimensions, Oe ; Eggs, Na—was formerly one of our regular summer migrants, but is now merely a straggler. He bobs his head as he swims ; and flies with his head in, his beak down, his legs out, and his wings arched. His call is "klint."

Regulus. Plate iii. *TURDINÆ* (Passeridæ).

30. *cristatus,* 3½ in. GOLD-CRESTED WREN. One black streak and that over the eye.
31. *ignicapillus,* 3¾ in. FIRE-CRESTED WREN. Three black streaks, the middle one through the eye, the lowest forming a moustache.

The Gold-crested Wren—Dimensions, Aa ; Eggs, Aa—is the smallest European bird. Its flight is straight and fluttering when short, but dipping and steady when long. Its call is "zit, zit," and its note "chip chirrrr, if-he, if-he," somewhat weak and distant. The female has the crest lemon yellow. The nest is hung from a horizontal branch of some coniferous tree, and is almost a sphere of felted moss, cobweb, wool, and lichen lined with feathers. It contains from six to ten eggs.

The Fire-crested Wren—Dimensions, Ac ; Eggs, Ab—is practically the same size as the Gold-crest, although our average is higher. It is merely an occasional visitor ; the first recorded specimen was killed by a cat at Cambridge, in 1832.

Rhodostethia. Plate xxxi. *LARIDÆ.*

355. *rosea,* 14 in. WEDGE-TAILED GULL. Head and neck white with a narrow black collar ; back grey ; under parts rosy ; outer web of first primary black ; bill black ; legs red.

The Wedge-tailed Gull—Dimensions, Me—once provided a specimen for the Leeds Museum, but as it is the only specimen claimed as British, we can leave to others the unravelling of the doubt as to whether it was mounted from a relaxed skin or from the flesh. It is an Arctic species.

Rissa. Plate xxxi. *LARIDÆ.*

367. *tridactyla,* 15 in. KITTIWAKE. White and grey above ; tail white ; first to fifth primaries tipped with black, sixth barred with black ; white below ; bill yellow ; remiges 31 ; legs brownish black.

The Kittiwake—Dimensions, Mp ; Eggs, Op—so called from its call or "kittiwake," is a bird of the rocks found only on the coast. It is the most graceful of the gulls in flight. In

summer its head and neck are spotless white ; in winter they are grey. The full grown
birds have yellowish bills, the young ones have black bills, and their tails have a black band.
The nests are in colonies on ledges of rock, and consist of seaweed, grass, and feathers.
They contain from two to four eggs.

Ruticilla.   Plate ii.   *TURDINÆ* (Passeridæ).

  17. *phœnicurus,* $5\frac{1}{2}$ in.   REDSTART.   Forehead white ;   back dark grey ;
                                rump chestnut ; throat black ; breast chestnut red ;
                                legs black ; bill black.

  18. *titys,* $5\frac{3}{4}$ in.   BLACK REDSTART.   Forehead black ;   back dark
                                grey ; rump chestnut ; throat black ; breast black ;
                                legs black ; bill black.

The Redstart—Dimensions, Cg ; Eggs, Bs—is one of the handsomest of our summer
migrants, and is regularly here from April to September. It is the Red-tail—Start being
Steort, the Old English for tail. Its tail is always on the jerk, for the bird is never still, and
even its flight is jerky and irregular. It sings on the wing and when perching, but the song
is not very elaborate. The call is " wheet." The female is dull brown above, with a good
deal of white on the chest. The nest is found everywhere, and is built of grass, moss, and
roots, lined with hair, wool, and feathers, and contains from four to seven eggs.

The Black Redstart—Dimensions, Cs ; Eggs, Di—is a winter visitor. It is often called
the Blackstart, which it is not, for its tail is red. It is rather quicker and easier on the wing
than the Redstart. Its second primary is equal to its seventh, while the Redstart's second
is equal to its sixth.

Saxicola.   Plate ii.   *TURDINÆ* (Passeridæ).

  13. *stapazina,* $5\frac{1}{2}$ in.   BLACK-THROATED WHEATEAR.   Throat black ;
                                tail black and white.

  14. *deserti,*   6 in.   DESERT WHEATEAR.   Throat black ; tail black.

  12. *œnanthe,* $6\frac{1}{4}$ in.   WHEATEAR.   Throat white ; tail black and white.

A Black-throated Wheatear—Dimensions, Cj ; Eggs, Dl—was shot here on one occasion
only. This was at Bury, in Lancashire, in 1875. Another Wheatear, *S. isabellina*, was once
found here at Allonby, in Cumberland, in 1887, but our list is quite long enough without it.

The Desert Wheatear—Dimensions, Dl ; Eggs, Br—has once or twice straggled here from
the Sahara, or else escaped from captivity.

The Wheatear—Dimensions, Ef ; Eggs, Dk—is one of our earliest summer migrants, and
stays with us from March to October. Its bill is black and broad, and bristly at base ; and
its axillaries have a mottled look owing to the white feathers having grey centres. Its
under wing coverts are black and white. The flight is a low and dipping one ; it generally
begins from a wall on which the bird will always perch if it can, and it ends in a characteristic
hopping. The call is " chack, chack " ; the song, often given on the wing, is a monotonous
twitter. The female differs from the male in being brown above, and having a buff eye-
stripe. The nest is on the ground, or in a hole in a low wall, or under a stone ; it is a loose
collection of grass and moss, lined with fur, hair, wool, and feathers, and contains from four
to eight eggs.

Scolopax.   Plate xxvii.   *SCOLOPACIDÆ.*

  308. *rusticola,*   14 in.   WOODCOCK.   Breast thickly barred with brown ;
                                26 remiges, 9 primaries, with webs obscurely barred ;
                                first primary longest ; tail tipped with grey above
                                and silver below.

The Woodcock—Dimensions, Lp ; Eggs, Lp—is now claimed as a resident, whose numbers
are enormously augmented by the migrants arriving in October. The woodcock rises with a
whirr, and flies with bent wings, and his beak pointed down. The flight is a straight one
with an occasional yaw, and not particularly fast. The call has been syllabised as " vessop."
In the male the first primary is spotted, in the female it is plain. The nest is a hollow in the
ground, lined with a few dead leaves. There are four eggs, which curiously enough are not
pyriform, although *Scolopax* is the type of the Scolopacidæ.

Scops.   Plate xiii.   *STRIGIDÆ.*

  168. *giu,* $7\frac{1}{2}$ in.   SCOPS OWL.   Facial disk obsolete above ;
                                plumicorns small ; bill black ; no operculum ;
                                plumage greyish brown above ; greyish white below ;
                                22 remiges, fourth primary longest ; legs feathered ;
                                toes bare and brown.

The Scops Owl—Dimensions, Gk ; Eggs, Hh—is our smallest owl, but is only an occasional
straggler amongst us. The call is the " giu " from which comes its name. The female is
redder than the male ; and, of course, larger

Serinus. Plate vii. *FRINGILLINÆ.* (Passeridæ).

90. *canarius*, 4½ in. WILD CANARY. Feathers of back edged with grey, and marked with olive green; wing coverts tipped with olive green.

89. *hortulanus*, 4½ in. SERIN. Feathers of back edged with yellow; wing coverts tipped with yellow.

The Wild Canary—Dimensions, Al; Eggs, CL—has occasionally been reported as appearing in small flocks on the Sussex Downs.

The Serin—Dimensions, Am; Eggs, Ao—occasionally appears in the same locality. But in each case there are doubts as to whether the birds are not "escapes"; and, in fact, the evidence in favour of the Canary is stronger than that in favour of the Serin.

Sitta. Plate iv. *SITTINÆ* (Passeridæ).

58. *cæsia*, 5½ in. NUTHATCH. Bluish above, buffish below; black streak through eye; remiges 19; first primary short; third, fourth, and fifth longest; two middle tail feathers slaty grey, each of the others black, white, and grey; legs pale brown.

The Nuthatch—Dimensions, Ch; Eggs, Co—is a resident. Its peculiar toe enables it to run down the tree trunks, as well as up them, and thereby it can be distinguished from the Creepers and Woodpeckers. It sleeps head downwards; and it perches across the twigs like a Nightjar. Its call is "whit, whit." The female is not so brightly coloured. The nest is in a hole of a rotten tree, which is plastered up all but a small opening just large enough to admit the bird; it consists of a few dead leaves and chips of bark, and contains from five to eight eggs.

Somateria. Plate xxii. *ANATIDÆ.*

255. *stelleri*, 20 in. STELLER'S EIDER. Crown white.

254. *spectabilis*, 24 in. KING EIDER. Crown grey, basal tubercle of beak orange red.

253. *mollissima*, 25 in. EIDER DUCK. Crown black; central line of feathers on beak reaching only half way to nostrils; remiges 26.

Steller's Eider—Dimensions, Pd; Eggs, Pa—occasionally wanders here from the Arctic Regions in the winter. It has a blue wing bar with white edges. The female is ruddy brown with a duller wing bar.

The King Eider—Dimensions, Qt; Eggs, QF—is another winter straggler from the far north. It has a narrow black chevron under the chin.

The Eider Duck—Dimensions, Rg; Eggs, SB—is a regular winter visitor, and breeds along the coast north of the Farnes. It has an easy powerful flight. The call is a rolling "kr, kr, kr." The female is dark brown with white tips to some of the secondaries and the greater wing coverts. The nest is sometimes in a hole in the rocks, sometimes on the ground, and is a mass of sea campion and grass lined with grey down. There are from five to eight eggs.

Spatula. Plate xxi. *ANATIDÆ.*

237, *clypeata*, 20 in. SHOVELLER DUCK. Bill dark slate; wing bar green; tail of 14 feathers.

The Shoveller—Dimensions, Pg; Eggs, NH—is always found in pairs. The male has a black bill; the female's is greenish brown above. The male's eyes are yellow, the female's are brown. The female has dark brown plumage, and this is assumed by the male in the summer. The flight is rapid and rather laboured. The call is "took, took." The nest is on the ground in grass or heather, and is made of dry grass lined with dark grey down, tipped faintly with white. There are seven, eight, or nine eggs.

Squatarola. Plate xxvi. *CHARADRIIDÆ.*

296. *helvetica*, 11 in. GREY PLOVER. White above barred with black and brown; black below; axillaries black; tail coverts white; bill black; tail barred; legs black.

The Grey Plover—Dimensions, Jm; Eggs, NB—calls here in July and August on its way from its northern breeding haunts, and calls again in the spring on its way back, though a good many remain here during the winter. In winter the under parts are mostly white. The female is browner on the back than the male.

I

Stercorarius. Plate xxxii.   *LARIDÆ.*

371. *crepidatus*,   20 in.   RICHARDSON'S SKUA. Two central tail feathers three inches longer than the others.

370. *pomatorhinus*, 21 in.   POMATORHINE SKUA. Two central tail feathers four inches longer than the others, and twisted upwards.

372. *parasiticus*, 22 in.   LONG-TAILED SKUA. Two central tail feathers nine inches longer than the others.

369. *catarrhactes*, 24 in.   GREAT SKUA. Two central tail feathers less than an inch longer than the others.

Richardson's Skua—Dimensions, Pj ; Eggs, PM—is the commonest of the four in this country. He is also known as the Arctic Skua, owing, apparently, to a mistake. He breeds in Caithness and the Orkneys, and comes south on migration. Like all the "pirate gulls" he has a somewhat hawk-like flight, and chases birds on the wing until they drop their food, which he catches before it reaches the sea. He never dives and rarely settles on the water. His cry is the " skuaw," from which he gets his name. The nest is a hollow, lined with grass and moss, and contains one, two, or three eggs.

The Pomatorhine Skua—Dimensions, Pp ; Eggs, PA—or as it is now more generally called the Pomarine Skua, is a regular winter visitor.

The Long-tailed Skua—Dimensions, Qc ; Eggs, NT—is often known as Buffon's. It is an Arctic species, and its visits are somewhat rare.

The Great Skua—Dimensions, Rd ; Eggs, RH—breeds on the Shetlands. It is very powerful on the wing, and is distinguishable by the white bases to its remiges. It has a loud hoarse cry of "skuah-h-h" ; and its nest is a hole perhaps a foot in diameter, lined with moss and heather, containing one or two eggs.

Sterna. Plate xxx.   *LARIDÆ.*

350. *minuta*,   9 in.   LITTLE TERN. Crown black ; forehead white ; tail white ; bill yellow ; legs orange ; remiges 26.

348. *fluviatilis*, 13½ in.   TERN. Crown black ; head white ; tail white and grey ; bill red, black at tip ; legs red ; remiges 29.

352. *anæstheta*, 14 in.   LESSER SOOTY TERN. Crown black ; nape white ; two of the toes only webbed to the claw.

344. *anglica*, 14½ in.   GULL-BILLED TERN. Head black ; tail grey ; bill black ; legs black.

349. *macrura*, 15 in.   ARCTIC TERN. Crown black ; head grey ; primaries with narrow grey band on inner webs; remiges 29 ; tail white and grey ; bill red ; legs red and short.

346. *cantiaca*, 15½ in.   SANDWICH TERN. Head black ; tail white ; bill black with yellow tip ; legs black.

351. *fuliginosa*, 16 in.   SOOTY TERN. Crown black ; nape black ; all three toes webbed to the tips.

347. *dougalli*, 16½ in.   ROSEATE TERN. Rosy breast ; bill black ; legs red.

345. *caspia*, 20 in.   CASPIAN TERN. Head black ; tail white ; bill red ; legs black ; remiges 33.

The Little Tern—Dimensions, If ; Eggs, HL—arrives early in May, and stays till nearly the end of the year, when the black on its head becomes very dull. It has a slow flight, low over the water. Its call is "kiriree." The eggs are laid in a hollow scratched on the shingly beach ; sometimes there are three of them, sometimes four.

The Tern—Dimensions, Ll ; Eggs, LH—is almost as often called the Sea Swallow, and is one of our regular summer migrants. It has a slow skimming flight with occasional hoverings. In winter its black crown is sprinkled with white, and its bill and legs are very pale in colour. The eggs are laid in a hollow of the ground in twos and threes, and there are usually a number of these "nests" together.

The Lesser Sooty Tern—Dimensions, Lt ; Eggs, MH—has only been seen here twice as yet.

The Gull-billed Tern—Dimensions, Mg ; Eggs, MQ—is a rare visitor notwithstanding its cosmopolitan range. It has a laughing cry of "ha, ha, ha."

The Arctic Tern—Dimensions, Mo ; Eggs, Kn—breeds on our northern coasts, and is with us from May to October. Its cry is "give give, give." It lays two or three eggs in a hole among the shingle, which are recognisable by being alike and thereby differing from the pebbles.

The Sandwich Tern—Dimensions, Ms ; Eggs, Nn—was first described from a specimen found at Sandwich, in Kent. It is a regular summer visitor. Its flight and nesting arrangements are similar to those of the Arctic Tern. Its call is "correct." Its tail is unusually deep in the fork.

The Sooty Tern—Dimensions, Nj ; Eggs, Nd—has strayed over here across the Atlantic two or three times.

The Roseate Tern—Dimensions, Nm ; Eggs, Lc—used to breed on the Farnes and Scillies, but is now rare. Its primaries have their inner web white throughout, and the outer feathers of the tail are six inches longer than the middle ones. Its cry is "crake," and its eggs are two or three laid in the usual hollow.

The Caspian Tern—Dimensions, Pl ; Eggs, Qe—is only occasionally seen here Its cry is "krake-kra." Its tail is only slightly forked.

Strepsilas. Plate xxvi. *CHARADRIIDÆ.*

302. *interpres,* 9 in. TURNSTONE. Black and white ; chestnut and brown on shoulders and wings ; bill short and black ; remiges 25 ; legs orange ; toes cleft to base.

The Turnstone—Dimensions, Ht ; Eggs, Kb—is a shore bird, visiting us in spring and autumn on its way to and from the north. In winter it loses the chestnut in its plumage, and its legs become of a paler yellow. Its note is a shrill whistle, with a "keet, kitterrr" when on the wing.

Strix. Plate xiii. *STRIGIDÆ.*

161. *flammea,* 13 in. BARN OWL. Facial disk complete ; no plumicorns ; operculum large ; plumage tawny buff above, face and under parts whitish ; bill yellow ; 24 remiges, second primary longest but only a little longer than first and third ; feet generally with bristles ; claws black, middle claw serrated.

The Barn Owl—Dimensions, Le ; Eggs, Ld—is our commonest owl. It has a leisurely noiseless flight. Its cry is a screech ; and it snores. The female is, as usual, the larger bird. There is no nest. The eggs are laid in some hole in a church tower or other building, there are from two to seven of them, and it is supposed that they are usually laid in pairs.

Sturnus. Plate ix. *STURNINÆ* (Passeridæ).

120. *vulgaris,* 8 in. STARLING. Plumage bronze blue and black, thickly spotted with small triangles of buff ; remiges with pale brown margins ; second primary longest.

The Starling—Dimensions, Hb ; Eggs, Go—is gregarious and only rarely found alone. He has a straight, strong flight, with a rapid flapping and then a glide, with a sudden descent ; but he can perform the most remarkable evolutions in the air when in chase of insects. The natural note is a scream and a twitter, but a Starling is a born mimic. In summer his bill is yellow ; in winter, when he is more spotted, it is horn colour. The eyes of the male are all black, those of the female have a brown iris. The female is more spotted than the male. The nest is in a hole in a house, or in a tree, or anywhere. It is a slovenly mass of grass, or of sticks, straws, and miscellaneous matter, string, paper, and rags. There are from four to seven eggs.

Sula. Plate xvii. *PELECANIDÆ.*

201. *bassana,* 31 in. GANNET. Plumage white, except head and neck, which are buff, and primaries, which are black.

The Gannet—Dimensions, Sj ; Eggs, Rq—has a curious black pencilling round the beak, which makes the gape line look much longer than it really is. The flight is rapid, but easy, with a good deal of high soaring without much effort. The call is simply "grog," given with every phase of emphasis and expression. The full plumage is not attained till the sixth year ; young birds are blackish brown with white spots, and the older they get the whiter they get. The Gannet breeds in colonies on rocky ledges. The nests are of seaweed, straw, and turf. There is but one egg.

Surnia.   Plate xiii.   *STRIGIDÆ.*

166. *ulula,*   14 in.   HAWK OWL.   No disk ; no tufts ; no operculum ;
plumage dark brown above spotted with white ;
face white ; lower parts finely streaked with brown ;
tail graduated and tipped with white ; legs covered
with greyish feathers.

The Hawk Owl—Dimensions, Lr ; Eggs, KL—is a rare visitor.   In flight he resembles a
hawk, and he hunts his prey in daylight.

Sylvia.   Plates ii.   iii.   *TURDINÆ* (Passeridæ).

24. *curruca,*   5¼ in.   LESSER WHITETHROAT.   Back grey ; throat white ;
legs bluish.

23. *cinerea,*   5½ in.   WHITETHROAT.   Back brown ; throat white ; legs
brown.

27. *hortensis,*   5½ in.   GARDEN WARBLER.   Pale eye stripe ; legs blue.

26. *atricapilla,*   5¾ in.   BLACKCAP.   Crown black ; tail brown.

25. *orphea,*   6 in.   ORPHEAN WARBLER.   Crown and sides of face
black ; tail brown and white.

28. *nisoria,*   6¼ in.   BARRED WARBLER.   Throat and breast barred
with brown.

The Lesser Whitethroat—Dimensions, Bh ; Eggs, Ai—has been found here from April to
November, but the return generally takes place in September. It is a slenderer bird than
the Whitethroat, and has yellowish white eyes and black ear coverts. It has a dipping flight
when fairly on the wing, but is generally noticed darting and hopping about the higher
branches of trees. The call is "chick," and the song a monotonous "sip, sip, sip." The
female is smaller than the male and has the head browner and the lower plumage tinged with
grey. The nest is low in a hedgerow, and is a shallow structure of grass and rootlets,
bound together with cobwebs, and cocoons, and hair. It contains four or five eggs.

The Whitethroat—Dimensions, Bs ; Eggs, CE—is one of our commonest summer migrants.
It is a busy, inquisitive, brisk sort of bird, almost as fearless as a robin, hopping about
unwearyingly on the hedge tops, fluttering after insects, and occasionally soaring up almost
perpendicularly, singing as it goes. Its call is "lueet, lueet" ; its alarm is "shuh," or
"cha, cha, cha" ; and it has a sweet little song, to give due emphasis to which when he is at
rest he raises the feathers of his crown. The female has no rosy tinge on her breast. The
nest is in thick herbage near the ground. It is a slight shallow structure of grass, galium,
and hair, and it contains from four to six eggs.

The Garden Warbler—Dimensions, Ca ; Eggs, Dn—is another of our summer migrants,
arriving in the beginning of May. It has a short, rapid flight, but is of rather retired habits
and does not often take to the wing. Its call is "check" ; its song is rather like a Blackbird's,
but more hurried and capricious. The female has buff axillaries like the male, but is rather
paler. The nest is generally among thick brambles, and close to the ground. It is a slightly
built firm affair of galium, grass, rootlets, cobwebs, and horsehair, containing four or five
eggs.

The Blackcap—Dimensions, Cq ; Eggs, Dj—is one of our residents, but is also, and to a
great extent, a summer migrant. He has a short rapid flight from bush to bush, but dips a
good deal when fully under way. His call is "tac tic." He is our best native songster,
full, deep, and wild, beginning with two or three double notes and working up to a loud,
varied, and continuous trill. "He has caught from the Blackbird his rich mellow tone, from
the Skylark his melody shrill, and the notes of the Woodlark, the Thrush, and his own he
varies and blends at will." The female has a brown cap. The nest is near the ground in
bushes and brambles ; it is neatly but slightly built of galium, grass, rootlets, and cocoons,
with a little hair, and contains from four to six eggs.

The Orphean Warbler—Dimensions, Dg ; Eggs, DE—is occasionally seen and more often
heard of in this country. It was first recorded in 1848.

A Barred Warbler—Dimensions, Eb ; Eggs, EK—was shot near Cambridge forty years
ago, and there have been a few recorded here since. It can always be identified by its
eyes, which are of such a pale yellow as to be taken to be white.

Syrnium.   Plate xiii.   *STRIGIDÆ,*

164. *aluco,*   18 in.   TAWNY OWL.   Facial disk complete ; no plumicorns ; operculum large ; plumage reddish brown
above with much white below ; 23 remiges, fourth
and fifth primaries longest ; feet feathered to the
claws, which are whitish at base and brownish at tip.

The Tawny Owl—Dimensions, On ; Eggs, ME—otherwise the Wood Owl, is our typical Owl, the one that says " Quotha ! tu whit ; tu whoo ! ch-h, h, h ! " and flies so softly, and lives in a tree, and never comes out till after dark. The eggs are often laid in the deserted nest of a dove, a crow, a magpie, or in a squirrel's drey ; but generally it is in a hole, the three or four eggs being laid on disgorged food pellets.

Syrrhaptes. Plate xxiii. *PTEROCLIDÆ.*

268. *paradoxus,* 16 in. PALLAS'S SAND GROUSE. Buff barred with dark brown above ; sandy below ; lower breast blackish ; tail of 16 feathers, with two of them long and pointed ; toes feathered to the claws.

Pallas's Sand Grouse—Dimensions, Nh ; Eggs, LA—first appeared here in 1863, on a wave of migration from the Tartar Steppes. It is now an occasional visitor. Its flight is rapid, high, and loud ; and its cry is " truk, turuk." The female is spotted with black on the head and neck.

Tadorna. Plate xx. *ANATIDÆ.*

234. *casarca,* 24 in. RUDDY SHIELD DUCK. Bill black ; tail black ; legs black.

233. *cornuta,* 26 in. SHIELD DUCK. Bill orange ; tail white ; legs orange.

The Ruddy Sheld Duck—Dimensions, Rb ; Eggs, QR—is generally shot in this country on its escape from captivity, although there is no reason why it should not come in a wild state occasionally. It is the Brahminy Duck of Anglo-Indians. The male's bill is bright red, the female's is black, and she has no black ring round the neck.

The Sheld Duck—Dimensions, Ro ; Eggs, QP—is our old friend the Sheldrake renamed, as a revenge probably for the renaming of the Wild Duck. It is our largest duck, and a handsome one, with its beautiful green head and neck, and its broad collars of white and chestnut, its white wing coverts and its green wing bar. The male's call is a whistle, the female's a loud "kor, kor," and a "quark." The female is like the male but not so brilliant, and not so large, and she has no knob at the base of her bill. The nest is in a rabbit burrow or in a burrow made specially by the bird, which is almost circular in ground plan, or among thick furze. The materials are dry grass, and moss, and pale lavender coloured down. There are from 7 to 16 eggs.

Tetrao. Plate xxiii. *PHASIANIDÆ.*

272. *mutus,* 15 in. PTARMIGAN. Primaries white ; tail rounded, with 16 feathers.

271. *scoticus,* 16 in. RED GROUSE. Primaries brown ; tail square, with 16 feathers.

270. *tetrix,* 22 in. BLACK GROUSE. Tail forked, with 18 feathers ; 25 remiges.

269. *urogallus,* 36 in. CAPERCAILLIE. Tail slightly rounded, with 18 tail feathers ; 29 remiges.

The Ptarmigan—Dimensions, Mj ; Eggs, Li—is a familiar bird owing to its being imported so largely from Norway for food purposes, but it is resident in several parts of Scotland above the forest line. In summer the male has red wattles over the eyes, and is black and brown above, except on the lower back and rump, where he is white. In autumn the blacks and browns become greys ; and in winter the plumage is almost all white. The flight is whirring and very rapid, low and straight, and it ends with a long run. The call is a croak like a frog. The male has black lores ; the female has not. The nest is a hollow on the ground, lined with some scraps of grass and heather, and a few feathers. The eggs are from 8 to 12 in number.

The Red Grouse—Dimensions, Nc ; Eggs, Lo—is the only real and original British Bird who is never seen out of Britain. He is the "Saint" to which the 12th of August is dedicated. The male has a sort of long moustache and a very large red wattle. The female is smaller in size, paler in colour, without a moustache, and with a much smaller wattle, or "comb," as it is often called. The flight is a low one, with many a glide with outstretched wings. The call of the male is "go back, go back, go go back " ; that of the female is a croak. The nest is a hollow in the ground, lined with heather, grass, and feathers, and there are from 7 to 15 eggs.

The Black Grouse—Dimensions, Pt ; Eggs, MP—is the inclusive designation of the Black Cock and Grey Hen, and is perhaps better known as Black Game. The male has a broad white bar on the wing, and he has white axillaries and tail coverts. The female is chestnut in colour, much freckled with black, and much smaller than the male. The call is a crow and a noise " as of whetting a scythe." The flight is heavy and low, but rapid and occasionally prolonged. Unlike the Grouse, Black Game are very partial to perching in trees. The nest is a hollow, often in damp ground. It is lined with heather or fern, and contains from 6 to 10 eggs.

The Capercaillie—Dimensions, Ta ; Eggs, Og—seems once to have died out in Scotland, but to have been reintroduced in 1837. It is dark ashy grey in colour with black chin feathers, forming a sort of beard. The call is " peller, peller," " klickop," and also " heed." The flight is a particularly powerful one, with a terrible whirr to start with. The female is smaller than the male, and is pale chestnut in colour, much mottled with black, and she has white tips to her tail feathers. The nest is a hollow among the heather or whortleberry bushes, lined with a few sprigs, and containing from 5 to 15 eggs.

Tichodroma. Plate vi.   *CERTHIINÆ* (Passeridæ.)

86. *muraria*,   6½ in.   WALL CREEPER. Back slaty grey ; wings grey and crimson ; five of the primaries spotted with white ; dark grey below ; tail black, tipped with grey, and almost square in shape.

The Wall Creeper—Dimensions, Em ; Eggs, Cj—has been recorded twice in this country, once in 1792 and once in 1572. It is a well known native of Central and Southern Europe.

Totanus. Plate xxix.   *SCOLOPACIDÆ.*

327. *hypoleucus*,   7¼ in.   SANDPIPER. Remiges 24, much patched with white ; eighth and ninth secondaries nearly white ; upper tail coverts brown ; wings white barred ; axillaries white ; legs olive.

328. *macularius*,   7½ in.   SPOTTED SANDPIPER. Remiges 27 ; eighth and ninth secondaries with a broad brown band across both webs ; circular greenish black spots on breast and neck.

330. *glareola*,   8 in.   WOOD SANDPIPER. Remiges 26 ; upper tail coverts white ; axillaries white, often with brown bars ; legs pale olive.

329. *ochropus*,   8½ in.   GREEN SANDPIPER. Remiges 29 ; upper tail coverts white ; axillaries white with brown bars ; legs slaty blue.

331. *solitarius*,   9 in.   SOLITARY SANDPIPER. Central upper tail coverts brown ; no bars on primaries ; axillaries brown and white ; two middle tail feathers olive brown speckled with white.

332. *calidris*,   10½ in. REDSHANK. Lower back white ; secondaries white ; legs red.

334. *flavipes*,   10¾ in. YELLOWSHANK, Legs bright yellow.

333. *fuscus*,   12 in.   SPOTTED REDSHANK. Head, neck, mantle, and underparts grey ; secondaries white and grey ; legs reddish brown.

335. *canescens*,   13½ in. GREENSHANK. Lower back white ; remiges 27 ; secondaries grey ; legs green ; no web between middle and inner toes.

The Sandpiper—Dimensions, Fs ; Eggs, Ip—is almost as well known as the Summer Snipe; and is with us from April to September every year. It is a greenish brown bird, barred with bronze. Its wings are much bent as it flies ; it glides with them half open, then flaps them rapidly and regularly for a time, and finally holds them almost upright as it alights and runs. Its call is "weet, weet, killy leepie"; and it has a cheery little song which it sings on the wing. The sexes are alike in plumage, and lose much of the dark brown in the autumn. The nest is a hollow, near water, lined with a little grass or moss, and it contains four eggs.

The Spotted Sandpiper—Dimensions, Ge ; Eggs, Hg—is an American bird of whose appearances here there are only a few somewhat doubtful records.

The Wood Sandpiper — Dimensions, Ha ; Eggs, Jм—has bred in this country but is chiefly known as an irregular straggler during its autumn and spring migrations. It has a quick shifty flight, and a call of "treacle." The nest is a hollow near a marsh, lined with a little dry grass, and containing four eggs.

The Green Sandpiper—Dimensions, Hm ; Eggs, Jl—is with us nearly all the year, except during the summer months, when it goes northward to breed. It has a rapid, hasty flight, never fully opening its wings, and almost closing them during the final turns it takes before it alights. Its call is "dlee, dlee, dlee." This sandpiper lays its eggs in some deserted nest in a tree.

The Solitary Sandpiper—Dimensions, Hs—is an American, occasionally wandering here. Its eggs are unknown.

The Redshank—Dimensions, Jf ; Eggs, Lт—is resident in many of our marshes, and has its numbers increased in the winter by migrants from the Continent. It has a quick, jerky sort of flight, its white secondaries being conspicuous. Its call is a loud "took," or "tyook." Its nest is on the ground, well hidden among the herbage, a mere hollow trodden by the bird. There are four eggs.

The Yellowshank—Dimensions, Ji ; Eggs, Ks—is an American, found here only two or three times.

The Spotted Redshank—Dimensions, Ke ; Eggs, Mj—is occasionally met with in the eastern counties on spring and autumn migration. It breeds in Finland.

The Greenshank—Dimensions, Lj ; Eggs, Mo—is a summer migrant, breeding in the north of Scotland. It has a strong quick flight, and a call of "tyu tyu." The nest is a hollow in the ground, lined with a few heather twigs and leaves. There are four eggs.

Tringa. Plates xxvii, xxviii. *SCOLOPACIDÆ.*

317.	*minuta,*	5½ in.	LITTLE STINT. Wing less than four inches ; six outer tail feathers brownish grey ; wings level with tail ; legs black.
318.	*temmincki,*	5¾ in.	TEMMINCK'S STINT. Six outer tail feathers white ; legs brown.
319.	*minutilla,*	6 in.	AMERICAN STINT. Six outer tail feathers grey ; legs and feet pale brown.
320.	*subarquata,*	7¼ in.	CURLEW SANDPIPER. White ring barred with black round base of tail ; bill decurved.
316.	*alpina,*	7½ in.	DUNLIN. Black and chestnut above ; chin white ; breast greyish white ; lower breast black ; axillaries white ; wings not reaching to tail ; legs black.
315.	*fuscicollis,*	7½ in.	BONAPARTE'S SANDPIPER. Upper tail coverts white, lightly streaked with brown ; bill short ; legs and feet brown.
314.	*maculata,*	8¼ in.	PECTORAL SANDPIPER. Upper tail coverts blackish brown ; wings extending beyond tail.
321.	*striata,*	8½ in.	PURPLE SANDPIPER. Upper tail coverts blackish ; white bar on wings.
322.	*canutus,*	9½ in.	KNOT. Back black with chestnut spots ; upper tail coverts white with black bands ; axillaries white with brown bars.

The Little Stint—Dimensions, Ck ; Eggs, Gj—comes in spring and autumn on its migrations to and from the north. The flight is a rapid, unsteady one, with bent wings. The call is "stint," a sort of grasshopper's chirp.

Temminck's Stint—Dimensions, Dd ; Eggs, Gp—also visits us twice a year in its journeyings north and south. Like the Little Stint it is greyish brown above in the winter. It has a quick, vigorous flight, and a call of "tirrr."

The American Stint—Dimensions, Dn ; Eggs, Gi—is very rare, in fact it has only been shot twice in this country.

The Curlew Sandpiper—Dimensions, Fr—visits us on migration in the spring and autumn on its way to and from its breeding haunts in the north. Its eggs are unknown. In flight it is distinguishable by its curved beak and sharply pointed wings.

The Dunlin—Dimensions, Gg; Eggs, Iᴅ—is the commonest Sandpiper, and is found on our coast in all months of the year. The flight is swift, with occasional "sprints," and on alighting the wings are held up during the run. During the breeding season the Dunlin soars. The call is a "twee wee wee." In the winter the plumage is white below and grey above. The nest is a slight hollow, lined with rootlets, and containing four eggs.

Bonaparte's Sandpiper—Dimensions, Gi; Eggs, Iᴋ—is an occasional straggler from across the Atlantic.

The Pectoral Sandpiper—Dimensions, Hf; Eggs, Jǫ—is another American species, but a far commoner one.

The Purple Sandpiper—Dimensions, Hj; Eggs, Jʜ—appears on our rocky coasts in September, and stays with us all through the winter. It has a swift, dipping flight, and swims well. Its call has been syllabised as "ince" and "weet, weet."

The Knot—Dimensions, Ij—is really the Knut, from the king whose courtiers forgot the double tide in Southampton Water; the Latinisation of his name gives the specific Canutus. It is a winter visitor like the Purple Sandpiper; and in the winter months it is a greyish bird, with white under parts. Its flight is strong and straight, and it always alights head to wind.

Troglodytes. Plate iv. *TROGLODYTINÆ* (Passeridæ).

59. *parvulus*, 3¾ in. WREN. Brown above, barred with darker brown; greyish brown below; wing with two faint white bars; remiges 18; the secondaries and tertials equal to primaries; tail barred with black and held nearly upright.

The Wren—Dimensions, Ab; Eggs, Bi—is one of our commonest residents, but is not so common as it gets credit for. It has a short, straight, whirring flight, with no dips in it; but it is generally noticed skulking among the hedgerows. It often sings on the wing, and it sings all the year round; its call is a clicking as of winding up a clock. The female has paler legs than the male. Its nest is a large one, built with a dome, and it has the entrance at the side, generally with woven straws round the doorway. The materials are moss, leaves, hair, grass, and feathers. There are from four to nine eggs.

Tryngites. Plate xxviii. *SCOLOPACIDÆ.*

325. *rufescens*, 8 in. BUFF-BREASTED SANDPIPER. Buffish brown, mottled with black above; primaries and secondaries marbled with black on undersides.

The Buff-breasted Sandpiper—Dimensions, Hc; Eggs, Jᴇ—is an American straggler recorded here about half-a-dozen times.

Turdus. Plate i. *TURDINÆ* (Passeridæ).

3. *iliacus*, 8 in. REDWING. Spotted olive brown above; broad white stripe over eye; spotted buffish below; axillaries and flanks red.

2. *musicus*, 8½ in. THRUSH. Olive brown above, whitish below; crown very flat; plumage spotted and streaked with dark brown; axillaries pale yellow.

6. *atrigularis*, 9½ in. BLACK-THROATED THRUSH. Throat and breast black.

5. *migratorius*, 10 in. AMERICAN ROBIN. Plumage black, with reddish breast.

4. *pilaris*, 10¼ in. FIELDFARE. Greyish brown above; wings and tail dark brown; axillaries white; bluish rump; legs dark brown.

1. *viscivorus*, 11 in. MISSEL THRUSH. Brown above, buff below spotted with dark brown; axillaries white; rump brown; legs pale brown.

The Redwing—Dimensions, Gq; Eggs, Fj—comes from its northern haunts in September and leaves us in May. It appears in loose flocks. Its flight is rapid and straight, with the wings motionless in gliding down to settle. Its call is a shrill "yelp," and its song a rich, wild, flute-like trill. The female is not so bright in colour as the male.

The Thrush—Dimensions, Hi ; Eggs, Gg—is a resident, migrating a good deal about the country. It has an undulating flight, with much rapid wing work and occasional clips and glides. On the ground the wings are frequently drooped and the tail stuck out straight. The well-known song has been syllabised as " judy, judy, judy ! bopeep, bopeep, bopeep, bopeep, how d'ye do ? how d'ye do ? " but Macgillivray's more elaborate version seems nearer the truth, " qui, qui, qui ; kweéu, quip ; tiurru, tiurru, chiprivi ; tootee, tootee ; chiu, choc ; chirri, chirri, chooee ; quiu, qui, qui." The female is rather smaller than the male, and is paler on the breast. The nest is often amongst evergreens ; it has been found on the ground, but is generally about six feet up a tree ; it is built of grass, rootlets, twigs, and moss, and is plastered with cowdung, mud, and decayed wood, so that its inside resembles that of a cocoa nut. It contains four, five, or six eggs.

A Black-throated Thrush—Dimensions, Ih ; Eggs, Gs—arrived at Lewes, probably from Turkestan, in 1868, and another was shot in Scotland, in 1879.

An American Robin—Dimensions, Io—was once heard singing near Dover, "probably escaped from some ship passing through the narrow seas."

The Fieldfare—Dimensions, Jc ; Eggs, Hn—comes from the north to winter here, and has been noticed from September to the beginning of June. It flies in loose flocks, starting with much noise, progressing by flaps and pauses, a pause to about every dozen flaps, and then sweeping round and settling with head up and tail down. It sings on the wing a soft "fu-igh, fu-igh," and its call is " yack, yack." The female is duller in colour than the male. It is said to have bred here occasionally, but the statement is not generally accepted. The nest is not unlike that of the Missel Thrush.

The Missel Thrush—Dimensions, Jj ; Eggs, Hj—is with us all the months of the year. It is greyer on the wing than the other Thrushes, and has a heavier and more jerky flight, with pauses at regular intervals and no undulations. The song is a rich mellow " churrr, wheep, wheep, whirrow, whirrow, wheep," with often a low scream when on the wing. It is the earliest songster of the year, and is called the Storm Cock from its singing its cheeriest in the roughest weather. The female is paler than the male. The nest is a mass of twigs and lichens, lined with a deep bowl of mud ; but unlike the Song Thrush, the Missel lines the bowl with fine grass. There are four, five, or six eggs.

Turnix.   Plate xxiv.   *TURNICIDÆ.*

277.   *sylvatica,*   8 in.   ANDALUSIAN HEMIPODE. Crown black and brown ; sandy brown above ; buff below ; sides with black spots ; bill yellowish ; legs yellowish.

The Andalusian Hemipode—Dimensions, Go ; Eggs, Gb—otherwise Bush Quail, has been shot three times in this country.

Turtur.   Plate xxiii.   *COLUMBIDÆ.*

266.   *communis,*   11½ in.   TURTLE DOVE. Bill brown ; plumage ashy grey ; white and black chequered patch on neck ; mantle brown ; lower breast white ; tail tipped with white at sides ; legs crimson.

The Turtle Dove—Dimensions, Jt ; Eggs, Gr—is a summer migrant, arriving in April and leaving sometimes as late as November. It has a rapid and peculiarly crooked flight. Its call is " coor-r-r, coor-r-r." The female is browner than the male. It builds a slight flat nest of slender twigs, generally rather near the ground, and so open that the two eggs can often be seen by looking up through it.

Upupa.   Plate xii.   *UPUPIDÆ.*

156.   *epops,*   12 in.   Hoopoe. Crest buff, tipped with black ; warm buff above ; spotted below ; rump white ; remiges 20 ; first primary small, second equal to seventh, and third, fourth, and fifth longest ; tail black with a broad white bar.

The Hoopoe—Dimensions, Kc, Eggs, Gd—is a somewhat rare visitor, arriving in the spring and autumn, and occasionally breeding here. It has an easy, dipping flight, and the call of " hoopoe " or rather " hoop, hoop, ho ! " which has given it its name. The nest is a strongly smelling one of straws and cowdung, and contains from five to seven eggs.

Uria. Plate xxxii.   *ALCIDÆ.*

377. *grylle,* 13 in. BLACK GUILLEMOT. Breast black or speckled.;
remiges 30.

375. *troile,* 17½ in. GUILLEMOT. Breast white ; bill long and pointed.,
remiges 26.

376. *bruennichi,* 18 in. BRÜNNICH'S GUILLEMOT. Breast white ; bill short
and thick ; remiges 26.

The Black Guillemot—Dimensions, Kn ; Eggs, Pe—has a whitish head and white under-parts in the winter. His flight is low, rapid, and straight, and he dives almost as fast as he flies. The call is a scream. The nest is a mere hole, containing two or three eggs.

The Guillemot—Dimensions, Gb ; Eggs, Se—has the throat and cheeks white in the winter. He flies dartingly like a Kingfisher, and in diving he uses only his wings, while in swimming he uses only his legs. The call is a murmuring "gurr" ; the cry of the young being the "willock," from which the French made "guillemot." The female is smaller than the male. On high cliffs, where many birds breed, the Guillemots occupy the zone below the Razorbills and above the Kittiwakes. There is no nest, the one egg being laid on the bare ledge of rock. Guillemot's eggs vary more in colour than those of any other British bird.

Brünnich's Guillemot—Dimensions, Of ; Eggs, Se—is an Arctic straggler recorded here once or twice.

Vanellus. Plate xxvi.   *CHARADRIIDÆ.*

301. *cristatus,* 13 in. LAPWING. Crown and crest greenish black ; sides of throat and lower breast white : upper parts blackish green ; outer primaries tipped with white ; secondaries almost wholly black ; tail coverts pale chestnut ; tail white tipped with black, except the two outer feathers ; legs brown ; hind toe small ; two toes cleft to base, two united nearly to first joint.

The Lapwing—Dimensions, Lb ; Eggs, Mb—otherwise the Peewit, is the bird that lays the Plover's eggs for the London market. It has long been held in esteem. There is an old Scottish Act of Parliament, of the time of Edward the First, ordering all its eggs to be broken when found "in order that Peesweeps may not go south and become a delicious repast to our unnatural enemies, the English !" "Peewit," "Peesweep," "Weet a weet," "pee ween," "dix-huit," all do duty as syllabisations of its plaintive cry. The flight is a regular lap, lap, lap, of the wings, which are kept open for a little after the birds alight. The nest is a hollow, lined with grass and moss, and where there is one there are generally more. The eggs are four or five in number. Another *Vanellus*, the Sociable Plover, *gregarius*, seems to have been shot in Lancashire, in 1860, but our list is already so long that the mere mention of the fact is enough.

Xema. Plate xxxi.   *LARIDÆ.*

354. *sabinii,* 13½ in. SABINE'S GULL. Head dark grey with narrow black collar ; beak red at tip ; back and wings grey ; primaries black ; white below ; tail forked.

Sabine's Gull—Dimensions, Lk ; Eggs, Lr—was first found by Sir Edward Sabine in Greenland, and has been met with as far south as Callao. It has been recorded several times since it was first shot at Belfast, in 1822, but it can only be looked upon as a very occasional guest.

CHAPTER XII.

DIMENSIONS.

IN this list the birds are for the first time arranged in the order of their average size, with their chief dimensions reduced to decimals of their length. Though birds vary much in stature, they vary very little in their proportions, and thus their measurement put in this way is an important aid in their identification.

The double letters have been adopted to avoid any confusion that might arise from having two series of numbers running through the book. The length is taken from the tip of the beak to the tip of the tail. The wing measurement is that of the one wing, not of the wing-spread, which is a most difficult thing to measure accurately. The tail is measured from the pygostyle, which is perhaps more generally known as the "ploughshare bone." The body is measured from the base of the beak to the pygostyle. The beak is measured along its culmen, or upper edge; and the tarsus, which, as we have said, is really the tarso-metatarsus, is measured from the ankle joint, popularly and erroneously called the "knee," to the junction with the toes, which is, quite as erroneously and popularly, known as the "heel."

It is hardly necessary to point out that the measurement in inches should be divided by the length in inches to obtain these figures, and that consequently these decimals have merely to be multiplied by the length to obtain the actual dimensions. If, for instance, a Lesser Whitethroat should be found only 5 inches long, the figures in the list should be multiplied by five, and its wing should be 2·6 in.; its tail 2·3 in.; its body 2·4 in.; its beak ·3 in.; and its tarsus ·8 in.; which are in the same proportion as if the bird had been of the average size of $5\frac{1}{4}$ inches.

	Length.	Wing.	Tail.	Body.	Beak.	Tarsus.	
Aa.	$3\frac{1}{2}$	·61	·41	·5	.09	·2	Gold-crested Wren.
Ab.	$3\frac{3}{4}$	·5	·33	·57	·1	·15	Wren.
Ac.	$3\frac{3}{4}$	·6	·41	·49	·1	·21	Fire-crested Wren.
Ad.	4	·56	·46	·45	·09	·17	Yellow-browed Warbler.
Ae.	$4\frac{1}{4}$	·58	·47	·46	·07	·15	Continental Coal Tit.

Proportions.

	Length.	Proportions.					
		Wing.	Tail.	Body.	Beak.	Tarsus.	
Af.	$4\frac{1}{4}$	·58	·47	·46	·07	·15	British Coal Tit.
Ag.	$4\frac{1}{2}$	·5	·43	·5	·07	·15	Crested Tit.
Ah.	$4\frac{1}{2}$	·53	·43	·48	·09	·18	Aquatic Warbler.
Ai.	$4\frac{1}{2}$	·55	·47	·47	·06	·14	Blue Tit.
Aj.	$4\frac{1}{2}$	·55	·5	·43	·07	·12	Marsh Tit.
Ak.	$4\frac{1}{2}$	·57	·46	·47	·07	·1	Lesser Redpoll.
Al.	$4\frac{1}{2}$	·6	·3	·63	·07	·11	Wild Canary.
Am.	$4\frac{1}{2}$	·61	·39	·54	·07	·11	Serin.
An.	$4\frac{1}{2}$	·62	·42	·49	·09	·11	Siskin.
Ao.	$4\frac{3}{4}$	·5	·4	·54	·06	·12	Chiffchaff.
Ap.	$4\frac{3}{4}$	·53	·4	·52	·08	·17	Sedge Warbler.
Aq.	$4\frac{3}{4}$	·56	·46	·47	·07	·15	Little Bunting.
Ar.	$4\frac{3}{4}$	·6	·44	·49	·07	·14	Red-breasted Flycatcher.
As.	5	·4	·54	·39	·07	·15	Dartford Warbler.
At.	5	·54	·4	·53	·07	·16	Willow Wren.
Ba.	5	·55	·33	·6	·07	·13	Tree Sparrow.
Bb.	5	·6	·4	·52	·08	·17	Whinchat.
Bc.	5	·6	·44	·49	·07	·14	Pied Flycatcher.
Bd.	5	·6	·46	·48	·06	·1	Mealy Redpoll.
Be.	5	·62	·45	·45	·1	·16	Icterine Warbler.
Bf.	5	·64	·4	·51	·09	·12	Goldfinch.
Bg.	5	·85	·45	·51	·04	·1	Sand Martin.
Bh.	$5\frac{1}{4}$	·52	·46	·48	·06	·16	Lesser Whitethroat.
Bi.	$5\frac{1}{4}$	·53	·41	·5	·09	·17	Stonechat.
Bj.	$5\frac{1}{4}$	·6	·4	·54	·06	·14	Wood Wren.
Bk.	$5\frac{1}{4}$	·62	·46	·48	·06	·1	Greenland Redpoll.
Bl.	$5\frac{1}{4}$	·63	·46	·44	·1	·1	Spotted Flycatcher.
Bm.	$5\frac{1}{2}$	·42	·43	·53	·04	·1	Great Tit.
Bn.	$5\frac{1}{2}$	·42	·58	·38	·04	·1	British Long-tailed Tit.
Bo.	$5\frac{1}{2}$	·42	·58	·38	·04	·1	White-headed Long-tailed Tit.
Bp.	$5\frac{1}{2}$	·45	·36	·53	·11	·16	Reed Warbler.
Bq.	$5\frac{1}{2}$	·47	·5	·39	·11	·17	Marsh Warbler.
Br.	$5\frac{1}{2}$	·5	·41	·52	·07	·14	Hedge Sparrow.
Bs.	$5\frac{1}{2}$	·5	·44	·5	·06	·14	Whitethroat.
Bt.	$5\frac{1}{2}$	·5	·45	·45	·1	·16	Savi's Warbler.
Ca.	$5\frac{1}{2}$	·5	·5	·44	·06	·14	Garden Warbler.
Cb.	$5\frac{1}{2}$	·5	·51	·36	·13	·1	Tree Creeper.
Cc.	$5\frac{1}{2}$	·53	·4	·54	·06	·19	Red-spotted Bluethroat.
Cd.	$5\frac{1}{2}$	·53	·4	·54	·06	·19	White-spotted Bluethroat.
Ce.	$5\frac{1}{2}$	·54	·44	·51	·05	·12	Twite.
Cf.	$5\frac{1}{2}$	·58	·44	·5	·06	·14	Rustic Bunting.
Cg.	$5\frac{1}{2}$	·58	·46	·46	·08	·17	Redstart.
Ch.	$5\frac{1}{2}$	·6	·3	·58	·12	·13	Nuthatch.
Ci.	$5\frac{1}{2}$	·6	·44	·49	·07	·13	Scarlet Grosbeak.
Cj.	$5\frac{1}{2}$	·6	·45	·44	·11	·16	Black-throated Wheatear.
Ck.	$5\frac{1}{2}$	·62	·25	·64	·11	·13	Little Stint.
Cl.	$5\frac{1}{2}$	·63	·41	·52	·07	·14	Short-toed Lark.
Cm.	$5\frac{1}{2}$	·8	·47	·48	·05	·1	Martin.
Cn.	$5\frac{1}{2}$	·84	·4	·51	·09	·14	Stormy Petrel.

	Length.	Wing.	Tail.	Body.	Beak.	Tarsus.	
		Proportions.					
Co.	5¾	·44	·4	·54	·06	·13	Grasshopper Warbler.
Cp.	5¾	·5	·4	·54	·06	·16	Robin.
Cq.	5¾	·51	·41	·52	·07	·15	Blackcap.
Cr.	5¾	·53	·46	·48	·06	·12	Reed Bunting.
Cs.	5¾	·56	·42	·49	·09	·15	Black Redstart.
Ct.	5¾	·57	·45	·47	·08	·12	Chaffinch.
Da.	5¾	·58	·38	·53	·09	·13	Meadow Pipit.
Db.	5¾	·6	·42	·52	·06	·11	Linnet.
Dc.	5¾	·65	·4	·5	·1	·09	Lesser Spotted Woodpecker.
Dd.	5¾	·68	·34	·54	·12	·13	Temminck's Stint.
De.	6	·37	·54	·41	·05	·11	Bearded Tit.
Df.	6	·5	·4	·51	·09	·11	House Sparrow.
Dg.	6	·5	·43	·48	·09	·15	Orphean Warbler.
Dh.	6	·52	·47	·47	·06	·12	Cirl Bunting.
Di.	6	·53	·4	·55	·05	·11	Bullfinch.
Dj.	6	·54	·5	·43	·07	·14	Blue-headed Wagtail.
Dk.	6	·57	·43	·48	·09	·13	Tree Pipit.
Dl.	6	·58	·39	·51	·1	·16	Desert Wheatear.
Dm.	6	·58	·42	·49	·09	·14	Greenfinch.
Dn.	6	·6	·31	·59	·1	·1	American Stint.
Do.	6	·6	·44	·45	·11	·1	Two-barred Crossbill.
Dp.	6	·61	·4	·51	·09	·11	Brambling.
Dq.	6	·66	·41	·51	·08	·14	Wood Lark.
Dr.	6	·7	·26	·53	·21	·13	Broad-billed Sandpiper.
Ds.	6	·75	·37	·56	·07	·15	Little Ringed Plover.
Dt.	6¼	·47	·46	·47	·07	·14	Grey-headed Yellow Wagtail.
Ea.	6¼	·51	·41	·53	·06	·16	Nightingale.
Eb.	6¼	·55	·44	·48	·08	·15	Barred Warbler.
Ec.	6¼	·55	·46	·48	·06	·12	Ortolan Bunting.
Ed.	6¼	·58	·43	·5	·07	·12	Lapland Bunting.
Ee.	6¼	·58	·44	·47	·09	·15	Rock Pipit.
Ef.	6¼	·6	·41	·5	·09	·16	Wheatear.
Eg.	6¼	·67	·43	·45	·12	·11	Crossbill.
Eh.	6½	·47	·36	·58	·06	·11	Wryneck.
Ei.	6½	·5	·46	·46	·08	·14	Yellow Wagtail.
Ej.	6½	·52	·46	·48	·06	·11	Yellow Bunting.
Ek.	6½	·55	·45	·47	·08	·15	Water Pipit.
El.	6½	·56	·4	·53	·07	·13	Alpine Accentor.
Em.	6½	·6	·34	·46	·2	·14	Wall Creeper.
En.	6½	·62	·43	·46	·11	·1	White-winged Crossbill.
Eo.	6½	·66	·29	·6	·11	·21	Kentish Plover.
Ep.	6¾	·52	·44	·47	·09	·16	Rufous Warbler.
Eq.	6¾	·55	·46	·47	·07	·12	Black-headed Bunting.
Er.	6¾	·65	·42	·47	·11	·1	Downy Woodpecker.
Es.	6¾	·8	·6	·35	·05	·07	Purple Martin.
Et.	7	·43	·21	·59	·2	·06	Kingfisher.
Fa.	7	·5	·3	·62	·08	·14	Baillon's Crake.
Fb.	7	·5	·31	·6	·09	·14	Dipper.
Fc.	7	·5	·31	·6	·09	·14	Black-bellied Dipper.

Length.	Wing.	Tail.	Body.	Beak.	Tarsus.	
		Proportions.				
Fd.	7	·53	·4	·53	·07	·13	Corn Bunting.
Fe.	7	·54	·32	·58	·1	·11	Hawfinch.
Ff.	7	·54	·46	·46	·08	·13	Tawny Pipit.
Fg.	7	·57	·46	·47	·07	·15	Woodchat.
Fh.	7	·6	·3	·59	·11	·1	Red-necked Phalarope.
Fi.	7	·6	·35	·54	·11	·14	Crested Lark.
Fj.	7	·6	·4	·47	·13	·11	Parrot Crossbill.
Fk.	7	·61	·4	·54	·06	·11	Shore Lark.
Fl.	7	·64	·21	·72	·07	·14	Quail.
Fm.	7	·65	·38	·56	·06	·12	Snow Bunting.
Fn.	7	·71	·34	·58	·08	·14	Ringed Plover.
Fo.	7	·85	·48	·43	·09	·13	Fork-tailed Petrel.
Fp.	7	·97	·45	·5	·05	·07	Swift.
Fq.	7¼	·45	·5	·43	·07	·12	White Wagtail.
Fr.	7¼	·6	·24	·58	·18	·14	Curlew Sandpiper.
Fs.	7¼	·6	·29	·57	·14	·13	Common Sandpiper.
Ft.	7¼	·61	·43	·51	·06	·13	Sky Lark.
Ga.	7½	·48	·5	·44	·06	·11	Pied Wagtail.
Gb.	7½	·49	·43	·49	·08	·12	Red-backed Shrike.
Gc.	7½	·5	·43	·49	·08	·16	Richard's Pipit.
Gd.	7½	·51	·22	·58	·2	·1	Jack Snipe.
Ge.	7½	·52	·2	·6	·2	·2	Spotted Sandpiper.
Gf.	7½	·6	·53	·43	·04	·06	Swallow.
Gg.	7½	·61	·13	·67	·2	·14	Dunlin.
Gh.	7½	·61	.34	·6	·06	·1	Waxwing.
Gi.	7½	·64	·12	75	·13	·1	Bonaparte's Sandpiper.
Gj.	7½	·66	·4	·54	·06	·13	White-winged Lark.
Gk.	7½	·76	·37	·54	·09	·14	Scops Owl.
Gl.	7½	·86	·39	·55	·06	·16	Wilson's Petrel.
Gm.	8	·4	·5	·44	·06	·1	Grey Wagtail.
Gn.	8	·43	·4	·5	·1	·15	Great Reed Warbler.
Go.	8	·46	·21	74	·05	·12	Andalusian Hemipode.
Gp.	8	·5	·27	·64	·09	·12	Little Crake.
Gq.	8	·59	·45	·48	·07	·14	Redwing.
Gr.	8	·6	·25	·63	·12	·11	Sanderling.
Gs.	8	·6	·34	·57	·09	·14	Rock Thrush.
Gt.	8	·62	·32	·58	·1	·09	Grey Phalarope.
Ha.	8	·64	·23	·62	·15	·19	Wood Sandpiper.
Hb.	8	·64	·34	·54	·12	·14	Starling.
Hc.	8	·7	·14	·76	·1	·12	Buff-breasted Sandpiper.
Hd.	8	75	·4	·53	·07	·15	Little Owl.
He.	8	1·1	·47	·48	·05	·07	Alpine Swift.
Hf.	8¼	·6	·12	75	·13	·11	Pectoral Sandpiper.
Hg.	8½	·5	·42	·52	·06	·1	Pine Grosbeak.
Hh.	8½	·56	·45	·47	·08	·12	Lesser Grey Shrike.
Hi.	8½	·55	·4	·53	·07	·14	Thrush
Hj.	8½	·58	·12	73	·15	·11	Purple Sandpiper.
Hk.	8½	·59	·32	·58	·1	·14	Rose-coloured Starling.
Hl.	8½	·6	·0	·93	·07	·1	Little Auk.

	Length.	Wing.	Tail.	Body.	Beak.	Tarsus.	
			Proportions.				
Hm.	8½	·64	·26	·59	·15	·15	Green Sandpiper.
Hn.	8¾	·64	·41	·49	·1	.09	Hairy Woodpecker.
Ho.	8¾	1·1	·25	·7	·05	·08	Needle-tailed Swift.
Hp.	9	·44	·0	·91	·09	·15	Little Grebe.
Hq.	9	·5	·38	·52	·1	·13	Siberian Thrush.
Hr.	9	·52	·22	·69	·09	·14	Spotted Crake.
Hs.	9	·65	·24	·59	·17	·17	Solitary Sandpiper.
Ht.	9	·65	·27	·64	·09	·11	Turnstone.
Ia.	9	·66	·33	·54	·13	·15	Red-winged Starling.
Ib.	9	·66	·39	·5	·11	·09	Golden Oriole.
Ic.	9	·7	·3	·6	·1	·16	Eastern Golden Plover.
Id.	9	·7	·5	·39	·11	·11	Tengmalm's Owl.
Ie.	9	·74	·3	·64	·06	·15	Dotterel.
If.	9	·77	·33	·54	·13	·07	Little Tern.
Ig.	9½	·5	·53	·39	·08	·1	Great Grey Shrike.
Ih.	9½	·57	·46	·46	·08	·14	Black-throated Thrush.
Ii.	9½	·6	·43	·45	·12	·1	Great Spotted Woodpecker
Ij.	9½	·66	·27	·6	·13	·12	Knot.
Ik.	9½	·75	·47	·48	·05	·12	Pratincole.
Il.	9½	·86	·32	·59	·09	·09	White-winged Black Tern.
Im.	10	·47	·4	·51	·09	·13	Blackbird.
In.	10	·5	·24	·49	·27	·12	Snipe.
Io.	10	·53	·45	·48	·07	·15	American Robin.
Ip.	10	·6	·26	·64	·1	·2	Cream-coloured Courser.
Iq.	10	·62	·26	·62	·12	·17	Killdeer Plover.
Ir.	10	·7	·3	·6	·1	·16	Golden Plover.
Is.	10	·76	·2	·73	·07	·1	Bulwer's Petrel.
It.	10	·76	·53	·44	·03	·07	Nightjar.
Ja.	10	·8	·5	·44	·06	·12	Merlin.
Jb.	10	·85	·32	·56	·12	·06	Black Tern.
Jc.	10¼	·57	·4	·53	·07	·12	Fieldfare.
Jd.	10½	·47	·2	·65	·15	·15	Water Rail.
Je.	10½	·5	·2	·6	·2	·15	Red-breasted Snipe.
Jf.	10½	·56	·25	·59	·16	·16	Redshank.
Jg.	10½	·57	·35	·51	·14	·04	Bee-eater.
Jh.	10½	·58	·2	·7	·1	·2	Corn Crake.
Ji.	10¾	·59	·2	·67	·13	·2	Yellowshank.
Jj.	11	·55	·4	·53	·07	·11	Missel Thrush.
Jk.	11	·55	·44	·49	·07	·12	Ring Ouzel.
Jl.	11	·64	·24	·63	·13	·09	Ruff.
Jm.	11	·7	·27	·62	·11	·16	Grey Plover.
Jn.	11	·7	·47	·5	·03	·06	Egyptian Nightjar.
Jo.	11	·77	·18	·7	·12	·14	Dusky Shearwater.
Jp.	11	·8	·4	·54	·06	·09	Rock Dove.
Jq.	11	·88	·36	·55	·09	·09	Little Gull.
Jr.	11	·9	·45	·49	·06	·09	Red-footed Falcon.
Js.	11½	·5	·2	·6	·2	·13	Great Snipe.
Jt.	11½	·6	·37	·57	·06	·07	Turtle Dove.
Ka.	11½	·8	·3	·57	·13	·08	Whiskered Tern.

	Length.	Wing.	Tail.	Body.	Beak.	Tarsus.	
		Proportions.					
Kb.	12	·43	·0	·93	·07	·15	Eared Grebe.
Kc.	12	·48	·33	·48	·19	·06	Hoopoe.
Kd.	12	·5	·0	·86	·14	·11	Puffin.
Ke.	12	·52	·21	·6	·19	·18	Spotted Redshank.
Kf.	12	·56	·19	·69	·12	·2	Bartram's Sandpiper.
Kg.	12	·6	·58	·28	·14	·04	Blue-tailed Bee-eater.
Kh.	12	·66	·5	·39	·11	·17	Sparrow Hawk.
Ki.	12	·8	·5	·45	·05	·09	Lesser Kestrel.
Kj.	12½	·44	·28	·68	·04	·13	Partridge.
Kk.	12½	·54	·38	·52	·1	·11	White's Thrush.
Kl.	13	·43	·0	·93	·07	·15	Sclavonian Grebe.
Km.	13	·49	·17	·66	·17	·14	Little Bittern.
Kn.	13	·5	·0	·9	·1	·09	Black Guillemot.
Ko.	13	·5	·23	·67	·1	·15	Moorhen.
Kp.	13	·5	·61	·33	·06	·08	Black-billed Cuckoo.
Kq.	13	·5	·62	·31	·07	·08	Yellow-billed Cuckoo.
Kr.	13	·6	·3	·65	·05	·07	Stock Dove.
Ks.	13	·6	·4	·5	·1	·06	Roller.
Kt.	13	·6	·41	·57	·02	·07	Red-necked Nightjar.
La.	13	·6	·44	·39	·17	·15	Nutcracker.
Lb.	13	·7	·36	·55	·09	·14	Lapwing.
Lc.	13	·73	·23	·57	·2	·34	Black-winged Stilt.
Ld.	13	·75	·25	·51	·24	·04	Belted Kingfisher.
Le.	13	·85	·37	·53	·1	·2	Barn Owl.
Lf.	13	1	·5	·43	·07	·1	Black-winged Kite.
Lg.	13	1	·5	·44	·06	·11	Hobby.
Lh.	13½	·46	·28	·67	·05	·13	Red-legged Partridge.
Li.	13½	·53	·35	·53	·12	·08	Green Woodpecker.
Lj.	13½	·55	·22	·62	·16	·17	Greenshank.
Lk.	13½	·77	·33	·58	·09	·17	Sabine's Gull.
Ll.	13½	·77	·4	·5	·1	·05	Tern.
Lm.	14	·45	·19	·71	·1	·07	American Blue-winged Teal.
Ln.	14	·52	·19	·7	·11	·07	Teal.
Lo.	14	·52	·41	·5	·09	·11	Jay.
Lp.	14	·54	·24	·58	·18	·1	Woodcock.
Lq.	14	·58	·2	·64	·16	·14	Eskimo Curlew.
Lr.	14	·6	·53	·41	·06	·06	Hawk Owl.
Ls.	14	·62	·5	·45	·05	·11	Kestrel.
Lt.	14	·67	·37	·53	·1	·1	Lesser Sooty Tern.
Ma.	14	·66	·23	·67	·1	·12	Manx Shearwater.
Mb.	14	·7	·3	·59	·11	·05	Noddy.
Mc.	14	·7	·42	·48	·1	·12	Jackdaw.
Md.	14	·7	·54	·4	·06	·06	Cuckoo.
Me.	14	·72	·4	·51	·09	·17	Wedge-tailed Gull.
Mf.	14	·82	·41	·52	·07	·08	Long-eared Owl.
Mg.	14½	·87	·33	·57	·1	·08	Gull-billed Tern.
Mh.	15	·45	·14	·79	·07	·08	Buffel-headed Duck.
Mi.	15	·5	·2	·7	·1	·09	Garganey.
Mj.	15	·5	·28	·67	·05	·09	Ptarmigan.

	Length.	Wing.	Tail.	Body.	Beak.	Tarsus.	
Mk.	15	·55	·17	·67	·16	·15	Coot.
Ml.	15	·66	·39	·54	·07	·11	Alpine Chough.
Mm.	15	·7	·3	·61	·09	·18	Bonaparte's Gull.
Mn.	15	·7	·32	·58	·1	·2	Stone Curlew.
Mo.	15	·74	·28	·64	·08	·03	Arctic Tern.
Mp.	15	·78	·34	·57	·09	·08	Kittiwake.
Mq.	15	·8	·38	·55	·07	·13	Short-eared Owl.
Mr.	15½	·52	·17	·64	·19	·13	Bar-tailed Godwit.
Ms.	15½	·7	·45	·42	·13	·07	Sandwich Tern.
Mt.	16	·41	·0	·91	·09	·12	Red-necked Grebe.
Na.	16	·44	·14	·76	·1	·06	White-eyed Duck.
Nb.	16	·5	·6	·34	·06	·08	Great Spotted Cuckoo.
Nc.	16	·51	·27	.69	·04	·11	Red Grouse.
Nd.	16	·55	·45	·51	·04	·05	Passenger Pigeon.
Ne.	16	·59	·28	·67	·05	·14	Little Bustard.
Nf.	16	·6	·25	·58	·17	·11	Oystercatcher.
Ng.	16	·6	·4	·55	·05	·08	Ring Dove.
Nh.	16	·66	·5	·47	·03	·07	Pallas's Sand Grouse.
Ni.	16	·7	·34	·55	·11	·13	Chough.
Nj.	16	·7	·4	·51	·09	·1	Sooty Tern.
Nk.	16	·75	·31	·64	·05	·11	Black-headed Gull.
Nl.	16	·76	·18	·77	·05	·09	Capped Petrel.
Nm.	16½	·58	·56	·34	·1	·05	Roseate Tern.
Nn.	17	·41	·09	·83	·08	·07	Razorbill.
No.	17	·44	·22	·71	·07	·07	Smew.
Np.	17	·45	·25	·69	·06	·07	Harlequin Duck.
Nq.	17	·48	·14	·77	·09	·07	Tufted Duck.
Nr.	17	·7	·3	·61	·09	·11	Mediterranean Blk.-head.Gull.
Ns.	17	·78	·35	·57	·08	·08	Ivory Gull.
Nt.	17	·8	·43	·48	·09	·14	Peregrine Falcon.
Oa.	17	·8	·54	·4	·06	·14	Montagu's Harrier.
Ob.	17½	·44	·0	·9	·1	·08	Guillemot.
Oc.	18	·44	·7	·22	·08	·12	Magpie.
Od.	18	·47	·15	·73	·12	·08	Pochard.
Oe.	18	·47	·16	·74	·1	·17	Avocet.
Of.	18	·5	·0	·92	·08	·09	Brünnich's Guillemot.
Og.	18	·5	·13	·69	·18	·13	Whimbrel.
Oh.	18	·5	·19	·67	·14	·12	Squacco Heron.
Oi.	18	·5	·21	·67	·12	·08	Goldeneye.
Oj.	18	·51	·23	·7	·07	·07	Wigeon.
Ok.	18	·5	·4	·47	·13	·07	Great Black Woodpecker.
Ol.	18	·6	·21	·71	·08	·11	Sooty Shearwater.
Om.	18	·66	·44	·44	·12	·13	Carrion Crow.
On.	18	·7	·4	·53	·07	·12	Tawny Owl.
Oo.	18	·75	·5	·44	·06	·15	Hen Harrier.
Op.	18	·8	·31	·61	·08	·11	Gull.
Oq.	19	·4	·2	·72	·08	·05	Hooded Merganser.
Or.	19	·43	·18	·62	·2	·14	Black-tailed Godwit.
Os.	19	·55	·22	·65	·13	·13	American Wigeon.

K

	Length.	Wing.	Tail.	Body.	Beak.	Tarsus.	
Ot.	19	·6	·15	·76	·09	·1	Fulmar.
Pa.	19	·66	·25	·66	·09	·12	Great Shearwater.
Pb.	19	·67	·4	·48	·12	·12	Hooded Crow.
Pc.	20	·42	·12	·79	·09	·07	Scaup.
Pd.	20	·45	·17	·75	·08	·07	Steller's Eider.
Pe.	20	·47	·19	·69	·12	·16	Buff-backed Heron.
Pf.	20	·47	·2	·7	·1	·08	Scoter.
Pg.	20	·48	·14	·73	·13	·06	Shoveller.
Ph.	20	·55	·21	·7	·09	·07	Gadwall.
Pi.	20	·63	·32	·58	·1	·1	Rook.
Pj.	20	·68	·44	·49	·07	·08	Richardson's Skua.
Pk.	20	·77	·25	·68	·07	·12	Lesser White-fronted Goose.
Pl.	20	·82	·3	·56	·14	·07	Caspian Tern.
Pm.	21	·48	·17	·76	·07	·08	Surf Scoter.
Pn.	21	·5	·15	·74	·11	·07	Red-crested Pochard.
Po.	21	·62	·4	·54	·06	·1	Gyr Falcon.
Pp.	21	·7	·41	·52	·07	·1	Pomatorhine Skua.
Pq.	21	·75	·28	·63	·09	·11	Lesser Black-backed Gull.
Pr.	22	·34	·0	·91	·09	·1	Great Crested Grebe.
Ps.	22	·48	·16	·78	·06	·08	Velvet Scoter.
Pt.	22	·48	·34	·61	·05	·08	Black Grouse.
Qa.	22	·49	·21	·55	·24	·18	Glossy Ibis.
Qb.	22	·5	·21	·64	·15	·2	Little Egret.
Qc.	22	·54	·6	·35	·05	·07	Long-tailed Skua.
Qd.	22	·6	·5	·44	·06	·12	American Gos Hawk.
Qe.	22	·6	·39	·54	·07	·12	Greenland Falcon.
Qf.	22	·7	·3	·65	·05	·1	Red-breasted Goose.
Qg.	22	·73	·46	·48	·06	·15	Marsh Harrier.
Qh.	22	·78	·35	·54	·11	·11	Iceland Gull.
Qi.	23	·6	·19	·74	·07	·09	Brent Goose.
Qj.	23	·67	·48	·46	·06	·13	Gos Hawk.
Qk.	23	·69	·4	·54	·06	·11	Iceland Falcon.
Ql.	23	·7	·4	·54	·06	·13	Buzzard.
Qm.	23	·75	·29	·61	·1	·11	Herring Gull.
Qn.	23	·8	·37	·56	·07	·09	Osprey.
Qo.	23	·8	·46	·48	·06	·07	Black Kite.
Qp.	24	·44	·15	·76	·09	·08	Mallard.
Qq.	24	·48	·14	·76	·1	·09	Red-breasted Merganser
Qr.	24	·48	·2	·68	·12	·13	Night Heron.
Qs.	24	·5	·1	·81	·09	·12	Red-throated Diver.
Qt.	24	·5	·18	·77	·05	·07	King Eider.
Ra.	24	·55	·16	·61	·23	·15	Curlew.
Rb.	24	·56	·21	·72	·07	·09	Ruddy Sheld Duck.
Rc.	24	·69	·41	·47	·12	·1	Raven.
Rd.	24	·7	·3	·62	·08	·11	Great Skua.
Re.	24	·7	·45	·49	·06	·07	Honey Buzzard.
Rf.	24	·8	·48	·46	·06	·11	Snowy Owl.
Rg.	25	·46	·16	·75	·09	·07	Eider Duck.
Rh.	25	·63	·23	·7	·07	·13	Barnacle Goose.

	Length.	Proportions.					
		Wing.	Tail.	Body.	Beak.	Tarsus.	
Ri.	25	·76	·4	·48	·12	·13	Egyptian Vulture.
Rj.	25	·8	·48	·46	·06	·05	Swallow-tailed Kite.
Rk.	26	·4	·19	·72	·09	·07	Goosander.
Rl.	26	·4	·5	·44	·06	·06	Long-tailed Duck.
Rm.	26	·44	·05	·85	·1	·11	Black-throated Diver.
Rn,	26	·45	·31	·61	·08	·06	Pintail.
Ro,	26	·5	·19	·74	·07	·08	Sheld Duck.
Rp.	26	·63	·44	·5	·06	·12	Eagle Owl
Rq.	26	·77	·47	·44	·09	·17	Spotted Eagle.
Rr,	26	·8	·45	·49	·06	·12	Rough-legged Buzzard.
Rs,	26	·8	·56	·37	·07	·09	Kite.
Rt,	27	·4	·21	·69	·1	·09	Shag.
Sa,	27	·42	·15	·73	·12	·17	American Bittern.
Sb,	27	·7	·24	·63	·13	·1	Great Black-headed Gull.
Sc,	28	·59	·21	·71	·08	·09	White-fronted Goose.
Sd,	28	·67	·3	·61	·09	·1	Great Black-backed Gull.
Se.	29	·6	·2	·74	·06	·09	Pink-footed Goose.
Sf.	29	·6	·33	·6	·07	·15	Macqueen's Bustard.
Sg.	30	·5	·17	·72	·11	·15	Bittern.
Sh.	30	·58	·19	·73	·08	·1	Grey Lag Goose.
Si.	30	·6	·2	·72	·08	·1	Snow Goose.
Sj.	31	·63	·27	·57	·16	·09	Gannet.
Sk.	32	·23	·1	·78	·12	·07	Great Auk.
Sl.	32	·6	·27	·65	·08	·09	Glaucous Gull.
Sm.	33	·41	·1	·81	·09	·11	Great Northern Diver.
Sn.	33	·48	·17	·66	·17	·15	Purple Heron.
So.	34	·26	·66	·31	·03	·06	Pheasant.
Sp.	34	·5	·16	·62	·22	·15	Spoonbill.
Sq.	34	·6	·18	·75	·07	·09	Bean Goose.
Sr.	34	·86	·38	·5	·12	·14	Sea Eagle.
Ss.	36	·41	·1	·81	·09	·11	Yellow-billed Diver.
St.	36	·4	·2	·7	·1	·08	Cormorant.
Ta	36	·4	·31	·61	·08	·09	Capercaillie.
Tb.	36	·5	·19	·67	·14	·15	Heron.
Tc.	36	·57	·25	·7	·05	·14	Great Bustard.
Td.	36	·6	·18	·75	·07	·19	Demoiselle Crane.
Te.	36	·65	·38	·54	·08	·11	Golden Eagle.
Tf.	39	·5	·24	·58	·18	·18	Black Stork.
Tg.	41	·46	·3	·64	·06	·09	Canada Goose.
Th.	42	·4	·16	·72	·12	·18	Great White Heron.
Ti.	42	·6	·22	·6	·18	·22	White Stork.
Tj.	42	·65	·36	·57	·07	·1	Griffon Vulture.
Tk.	48	·53	·18	·72	·1	·22	Crane.
Tl.	50	·4	·14	·79	·07	·07	Bewick's Swan.
Tm.	55	·44	·12	·81	·07	·09	American Swan.
Tn.	56	·36	·16	·71	·13	·27	Flamingo.
To.	60	·38	·11	·83	·06	·06	Polish Swan.
Tp.	60	·4	·14	·8	·06	·07	Trumpeter Swan.
Tq.	60	·41	·15	·79	·06	·07	Hooper Swan.
Tr.	60	·45	·16	·78	·06	·07	Mute Swan.

CHAPTER XIII.

EGGS.

—◆—

THE Eggs are given in this chapter by themselves, owing to their taking up less space in this way than they would do if sorted out among the species.

The list may also serve as a rough guide to identification, for although eggs vary much, even when laid by the same hen, they yet vary within certain limits, and the system of average is not so very far out as far as size is concerned. But with regard to colour and grain the difficulties are greater. At the outset, it is almost impossible to describe colour accurately, even if the colour of eggs were invariable, which it is not, and even if it were, we should have the four stages that puzzle the collector still to deal with : the first, the colour of the eggs in the nest ; the second, the colour after they are blown ; the third, the colour after they have faded in a collection ; and the fourth, their colour as rendered by the chromo-lithographer ; which are four very different things. And with grain the difficulties are almost as great. At the same time, though we may not attain accuracy, we may approach it sufficiently near to enable us to distinguish one egg from another ; and to aid in this the eggs have here been classified into types.

We have thus three clues to guide us, all three of which may be of little value separately, but which will rarely fail us when used together. It must be clearly borne in mind that the sizes given are average sizes ; they have not been taken from any one book, but have been worked out from actual measurement and many authorities, and dealing as they do with hundredths of an inch, it is unlikely that the order given will be found to apply to any one collection. But where the size does not exactly fit in with a specimen, the colour and type lend their aid towards a correct determination ; where the type fails us, and it will often be found doubtful as to which type an egg should be assigned to, the size and colour will help ; when the colour fails the size and type will save us from error.

And with regard to colour it should be remembered that an egg is of a plain tint to begin with, and that the pigment spots are applied afterwards. These are normally circular, and as the egg is extruded they are rubbed and blotched against the walls of the duct. They are nearly always more numerous on the larger end of the egg, which is the first to be extruded and the first to harden. The

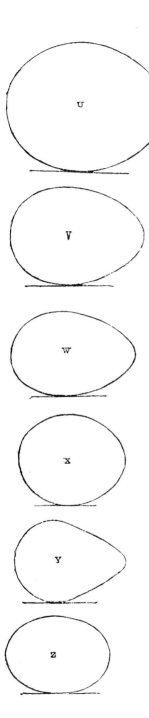

pigments are of a similar nature to the colouring matter of the blood and bile, and are richer in the case of birds in their prime and in robust health. They are generally richer in colour on the first eggs of the clutch ; for instance, in the cases in which two eggs are laid, one spotted and one unspotted, the spotted egg is laid first.

The eggs of all the birds on our opening list are given, except the nineteen which it is believed are still unknown. Some of them have been described from the only specimen that exists ; many of them have not been laid in this country, but that is no reason why they should not be found in a collection. By including them we make our book complete, and it is in that spirit we have ended it by giving a last chance to the Great Auk.

Our six types we give in the margin.

The U type is the usual one ; the V type is the longer variety, with the sharper point ; the W type is the intensified form of the V, such as we have in the eggs of the Raven ; the X type has both axes nearly equal ; the Y is the pyriform type so common among the Plovers ; and the Z is the flattened oval, such as we get among the Grebes. For the purposes of reference, the letters to the left of the page have been adopted instead of figures, in order that only one system of numbers may run through the book. The measurements are in inches, the first giving the length, the next the greatest breadth.

To take an example, let us say that we have an egg three quarters of an inch long—that is, ·75 of an inch—

and let it be a little over half an inch wide. Looking down the list
we find that there are several eggs about this measurement, all of
which are of the U type, but only one of which is of the pale
greenish blue colour of our specimen, which is thus discovered to
be the egg of the Redstart.

Aa.	·56;	·4;	U.	White, mottled with red. Gold-crested Wren.
Ab.	·56;	·45;	U.	Greyish white, dotted reddish brown. Fire-crested Wren.
Ac.	·57;	·44;	X.	White, freckled pale pink. British Long-tailed Tit.
Ad.	·6;	·45;	U.	Cream, spotted purplish brown. Chiffchaff.
Ae.	·6;	·45;	U.	Greyish, freckled light brown. Blue Tit.
Af.	·6;	·45;	U.	Pearly white, lightly spotted with red. White-headed Long-tailed Tit.
Ag.	·6;	·45;	U.	White, spotted reddish brown. Yellow-browed Warbler.
Ah.	·6;	·46;	U.	White, marbled light red. Willow Wren.
Ai.	·6;	·5;	U.	Brownish white, blotched or streaked slaty blue. Lesser Whitethroat.
Aj.	·6;	·5;	U.	Greyish white, freckled brown. Marsh Tit.
Ak.	·62;	·45;	V.	Greenish, spotted light and dark brown. Mealy Redpoll.
Al.	·63;	·46;	V.	Greenish, spotted light brown. Lesser Redpoll.
Am.	·65;	·45;	V.	Greenish, spotted and streaked with brown. Greenland Redpoll.
An.	·65;	·5;	U.	Greenish grey, freckled with brown. Red-breasted Flycatcher.
Ao.	·65;	·5;	U.	Greenish grey, capped and spotted brown. Serin.
Ap.	·65;	·5;	U.	Greenish grey, spotted reddish brown. Siskin.
Aq.	·65;	·5;	X.	Greyish white, blotched light brown. Crested Tit.
Ar.	·65;	·51;	U.	Pearl grey, spotted light and dark brown. Goldfinch.
As.	·65;	·52;	U.	White, freckled light and dark brown. Tree Creeper.
At.	·65;	·55;	U.	Greyish, thickly spotted with browns. Wood Wren.
Ba.	·65;	·55;	X.	Light brown, speckled red. Sedge Warbler.
Bb.	·7;	·47;	X.	Greyish, freckled brown. British Coal Tit.
Bc.	·7;	·48;	X.	Greyish, freckled brown. Continental Coal Tit.
Bd.	·7;	·5;	U.	Greenish, blotched olive and dark brown. Reed Warbler.
Be.	·7;	·5;	U.	Greenish, marbled brown and olive. Dartford Warbler.
Bf.	·7;	·5;	U.	Greenish blue, streaked and spotted brown. Twite.
Bg.	·7;	·5;	U.	Yellowish white, speckled red. Aquatic Warbler.
Bh.	·7;	·5;	U.	White. Sand Martin.
Bi.	·7;	·5;	U.	White, spotted light brown. Wren.

BJ.	·7 ;	·5 ;	V. Greyish, spotted lightly with brown. Linnet.
BK.	·7 ;	·5 ;	X. Yellowish white, blotched light brown. Great Tit.
BL.	·7 ;	·55 ;	U. Cream, freckled greyish brown. Bearded Tit.
BM.	·7 ;	·55 ;	U. Greenish blue, marbled with brown. Bluethroat.
BN.	·7 ;	·55 ;	U. Pale grey, with dark curving spots and blotches. Little Bunting.
BO.	·73 ;	·55 ;	U. White, freckled evenly with pink. Grasshopper Warbler.
BP.	·75 ;	·52 ;	W. White. Martin.
BQ.	·75 ;	·55 ;	U. Bluish green, spotted light brown. Whinchat.
BR.	·75 ;	·55 ;	U. Greenish, with brownish purple spots. Desert Wheatear.
BS.	·75 ;	·55 ;	U. Pale greenish blue. Redstart.
BT.	·75 ;	·55 ;	U. Pale olive, spotted yellowish brown. Spotted Flycatcher.
CA.	·75 ;	·55 ;	U. Whitish grey, marbled purplish brown. Marsh Warbler.
CB.	·75 ;	·56 ;	U. Cream, streaked and spotted purplish brown. Reed Bunting.
CC.	·75 ;	·56 ;	U. Pale blue. Pied Flycatcher.
CD.	·75 ;	·56 ;	U. Rose pink, blotched purplish brown. Icterine Warbler.
CE.	·75 ;	·56 ;	U. Greenish white, spotted green and brown. Whitethroat.
CF.	·75 ;	·56 ;	Z. Greyish, marbled yellowish brown. Grey Wagtail.
CG.	·75 ;	·6 ;	U. Greenish blue, clouded brown. Chaffinch.
CH.	·75 ;	·6 ;	U. Greyish green, freckled brown. Stonechat.
CI.	·75 ;	·61 ;	U. Grey, marbled yellowish brown. Yellow Wagtails.
CJ.	·77 ;	·55 ;	U. White, freckled brown. Wall Creeper.
CK.	·78 ;	·55 ;	X. White. Lesser Spotted Woodpecker.
CL.	·8 ;	·55 ;	U. Bluish green, speckled reddish brown. Wild Canary.
CM.	·8 ;	·55 ;	U. Dark green, spotted brown. White-spotted Bluethroat.
CN.	·8 ;	·55 ;	U. Greyish, marbled yellowish brown. Blueheaded Wagtail.
CO.	·8 ;	·55 ;	U. White, spotted brown. Nuthatch.
CP.	·8 ;	·55 ;	W. White, spotted yellowish brown. Swallow.
CQ.	·8 ;	·55 ;	X. Buff, freckled ashy brown. Savi's Warbler.
CR.	·8 ;	·56 ;	U. Bluish green, spotted ashy brown. Two-barred Crossbill.
CS.	·8 ;	·56 ;	U. Bluish green, spotted ashy brown. Whitewinged Crossbill.
CT.	·8 ;	·57 ;	U. Bluish green, dotted brown. Brambling.
DA.	·8 ;	·6 ;	U. Pale greenish blue. Hedge Sparrow.
DB.	·8 ;	·6 ;	U. Greenish blue, blotched and streaked brown. Bullfinch.
DC.	·8 ;	·6 ;	U. Greenish blue, spotted dark brown. Scarlet Grosbeak.

DD.	·8 ;	·6 ;	U. Greyish white, spotted brown. Pied Wagtail.
DE.	·8 ;	·6 ;	U. Greyish white, blotched brown at large end. Orphean Warbler.
DF.	·8 ;	·6 ;	U. Greyish white, spotted brown. Greenfinch.
DG.	·8 ;	·6 ;	U. Yellowish white, spotted brown. Robin.
DH.	·8 ;	·61 ;	U. Greyish white, spotted light and dark brown. White Wagtail.
DI.	·8 ;	·62 ;	U. Greyish white. Black Redstart.
DJ.	·8 ;	·62 ;	U. Light brown, spotted brown and blue. Blackcap.
DK.	·8 ;	·62 ;	U. Pale greenish blue. Wheatear.
DL.	·8 ;	·63 ;	U. Pale green, spotted brownish red. Black-throated Wheatear.
DM.	·8 ;	·63 ;	U. Pale purple, mottled brown. Meadow Pipit.
DN.	·8 ;	·63 ;	U. Reddish white, spotted pale brown. Garden Warbler.
DO.	·8 ;	·63 ;	U. White. Wryneck.
DP.	·8 ;	·65 ;	U. White, spotted browns and greys. Lapland Bunting.
DQ.	·82 ;	·75 ;	X. Pinkish white. Kingfisher.
DR.	·83 ;	·6 ;	V. Pale blue, streaked and blotched brown. Ortolan.
DS.	·84 ;	·6 ;	U. Cream, streaked and spotted brown. Rustic Bunting.
DT.	·85 ;	·55 ;	U. White, mottled with grey. Short-toed Lark.
EA.	·85 ;	·6 ;	U. Grey, mottled with greenish brown. Tree Sparrow.
EB.	·85 ;	·6 ;	U. Greyish purple, mottled with brown. Tree Pipit.
EC.	·85 ;	·61 ;	U. Olive. Nightingale.
ED.	·85 ;	·65 ;	U. Buff, spotted brown and grey. Wood Lark.
EE.	·85 ;	·65 ;	U. Purplish green, mottled brown. Water Pipit.
EF.	·85 ;	·66 ;	U. Greyish, freckled brown. Rock Pipit.
EG.	·85 ;	·67 ;	X. Greenish white, blotched dark brown. Cirl Bunting.
EH.	·85 ;	·7 ;	X. Light brown, mottled with browns. Richard's Pipit.
EI.	·85 ;	·72 ;	V. Greenish blue, spotted brown, often with letters on it. Blackheaded Bunting.
EJ.	·9 ;	·6 ;	U. Pale blue, blotched brown and lilac. House Sparrow.
EK.	·9 ;	·61 ;	U. Buff, spotted light grey. Barred Warbler.
EL.	·9 ;	·61 ;	V. Greenish blue, spotted dark brown. Parrot Crossbill.
EM.	·9 ;	·65 ;	U. Greenish blue, spotted dark brown. Crossbill.
EN.	·9 ;	·65 ;	U. Greenish white, mottled dark brown. Tawny Pipit.
EO.	·9 ;	·66 ;	U. Cream, spotted light brown. Red-backed Shrike.
EP.	·9 ;	·66 ;	U. Pale green, blotched greens and browns. Great Reed Warbler.
EQ.	·9 ;	·66 ;	V. White, streaked and spotted purplish brown. Yellow Bunting.

ER.	·9 ;	·66 ; X.	Pale green, speckled brown and slate. Rufous Warbler.
ES.	·9 ;	·66 ; Z.	White, spotted olive brown. Skylark.
ET.	·9 ;	·7 ; U.	Cream, blotched with browns. Woodchat.
FA.	·9 ;	·71 ; U.	Various colours, spotted and unspotted. Cuckoo.
FB.	·9 ;	·72 ; X.	Greenish blue, streaked olive brown. Hawfinch.
FC.	·95 ;	·62 ; U.	White, spotted and streaked brown. Snow Bunting.
FD.	·95 ;	·64 ; U.	Pale grey, spotted with greys. White-winged Lark.
FE.	·95 ;	·65 ; W.	Pale green. Alpine Accentor.
FF.	·95 ;	·65 ; Z.	Pale green, spotted grey. Shore Lark.
FG.	·95 ;	·65 ; Z.	White, thickly spotted grey. Crested Lark.
FH.	·95 ;	·75 ; U.	Grey, blotched with dark brown. Redwinged Starling.
FI.	·95 ,	·75 ; U.	White. Purple Martin.
FJ.	·98 ;	·75 ; U.	Pale green, spotted and. streaked reddish brown. Redwing.
FK.	1 ;	·65 ; W.	White. Swift.
FL.	1 ;	·7 ; U.	Pale olive, spotted brown. Waxwing.
FM.	1 ;	·71 ; U.	Greenish, clouded with brown. Lesser Grey Shrike.
FN.	1 ;	·71 ; U.	Pale slate, blotched purplish brown. Corn Bunting.
FO.	1 ;	·71 ; U.	White, coarse-grained shell. Dipper.
FP.	1 ;	·71 ; U.	White. Black-bellied Dipper.
FQ.	1 ;	·71 ; V.	Greenish blue, spotted dark brown. Pine Grosbeak.
FR.	1 ;	·75 ; X.	White. Great Spotted Woodpecker.
FS.	1 ;	·75 ; X.	White. Hairy Woodpecker.
FT.	1 ;	·75 ; X.	White. Downy Woodpecker.
GA.	1 ;	·8 ; X.	Pale green. Rock Thrush.
GB.	1 ;	·85 ; X.	Buff, spotted brown and grey. Andalusian Hemipode or Bush Quail.
GC.	1 ;	·9 ; X.	White. Bee-eater.
GD.	1·1 ;	·7 ; V.	Bluish green. Hoopoe.
GE.	1·1 ;	·8 ; U.	Buff, blotched with browns. Quail.
GF.	1·1 ;	·8 ; U.	Pale grey. Rose-coloured Starling.
GG.	1·1 ;	·8 ; U.	Greenish blue, spotted dark brown. Song Thrush.
GH.	1·1 ;	·8 ; U.	Greenish grey, blotched with browns. Great Grey Shrike.
GI.	1·1 ;	·8 ; Y.	Greenish grey, spotted reddish brown. American Stint.
GJ.	1·1 ;	·8 ; Y.	Greenish grey, spotted grey and brown. Little Stint.
GK.	1·1 ;	·8 ; Z.	Buff, spotted brown. Baillon's Crake.
GL.	1·1 ;	·85 ; U.	Greenish grey, freckled light brown. Black-bird.
GM.	1·1 ;	·85 ; U.	Pale green. Black-billed Cuckoo.
GN.	1·1 ;	·85 ; X.	White, with a ring of red specks. Stormy Petrel.

GO. 1.15 ; ·85 ; U. Rough-grained, greenish blue. Starling.
GP. 1·15 ; ·85 ; Y. Greenish, spotted red, brown, and grey. Temminck's Stint.
GQ. 1·15 ; ·86 ; Y. Olive, spotted red and brown, Red-necked Phalarope.
GR. 1·17 ; ·9 ; X. White. Turtle Dove.
GS. 1·2 ; ·8 ; U. Greyish green, freckled light brown. Black-throated Thrush.
GT. 1·2 ; ·85 ; U. Greenish, blotched reddish brown. Ring Ouzel.
HA. 1·2 ; ·9 ; U. White. Green Woodpecker.
HB. 1·2 ; ·9 ; U. Whitish green, spotted reddish brown. White's Thrush.
HC. 1·2 ; ·9 ; W. White, lightly spotted with purplish brown. Golden Oriole.
HD. 1·2 ; ·9 ; Y. Pale brown, speckled brown, red, and grey. Little Ringed Plover.
HE. 1·2 ; ·9 ; Y. Pale olive, spotted and streaked grey and brown. Kentish Plover.
HF. 1·2 ; ·9 ; Y. Pale olive, blotched and marbled with greys and browns. Grey Phalarope.
HG. 1·2 ; ·91 ; V. Buffish olive, blotched with greys and browns. Spotted Sandpiper.
HH. 1·2 ; 1 ; X. White. Scops Owl.
HI. 1·2 ; 1 ; X. Buff, with purplish brown markings. Pratin-cole.
HJ. 1·25 ; ·9 ; U. Greyish, lightly spotted brown and purple. Missel Thrush.
HK. 1·25 ; ·92 ; U. Greenish blue, speckled olive. Jay.
HL. 1·25 ; 1 ; U. Buff, marked brown and grey. Little Tern.
HM. 1·25 ; 1 ; Z. Buffish brown. Little Crake.
HN. 1·3 ; ·8 ; V. Greenish, mottled reddish brown. Fieldfare.
HO. 1·3 ; ·8 ; Z. White. Alpine Swift.
HP. 1·3 ; ·9 ; U. Pea green. Yellow-billed Cuckoo.
HQ. 1·3 ; ·9 ; U. White. Wilson's Petrel.
HR. 1·3 ; ·9 ; Y. Chocolate brown, with grey and brown freckles. Broad-billed Sandpiper.
HS. 1·3 ; ·9 ; Y. Chocolate brown, with grey and brown blotches. White-winged Black Tern.
HT. 1·3 ; ·9 ; Z. White, marbled and clouded greys and browns. Nightjars.
IA. 1·3 ; ·95 ; U. Bluish green, spotted with browns. Great Spotted Cuckoo.
IB. 1·3 ; ·95 ; U. White, ringed with fine red spots. Forktailed Petrel.
IC. 1·3 : ·95 ; W. Buff, spotted grey, brown, and lilac. Spotted Crake.
ID. 1·3 ; ·95 ; Y. Greenish buff, marked with browns. Dunlin.
IE. 1·3 ; ·97 ; U. White. Great Black Woodpecker.
IF. 1·3 ; 1 ; U. Buff, spotted reddish brown and lilac. Water Rail.
IG. 1·3 ; 1 ; W. White. Little Bittern.
IH. 1·3 ; 1 ; X. Pale olive, speckled brown and grey. Cream-coloured Courser.

II. 1·3 ; 1·1 ; X. White. Tengmalm's Owl.

IJ. 1·35 ; ·95 ; U. Greenish, freckled light brown. Magpie.

IK. 1·35 ; ·95 ; Y. Buff, freckled red and grey. Bonaparte's Sandpiper.

IL. 1·35 ; 1·05 ; X. White. Belted Kingfisher.

IM. 1·4 ; ·95 ; Y. Olive, spotted brown and red. Sanderling.

IN. 1·4 ; ·95 ; Z. Bluish white, freckled grey and brown. Nutcracker.

IO. 1·4 ; 1 ; U. Greyish brown, blotched with browns and greys. Black Tern.

IP. 1·4 ; 1 ; Y. Buff, spotted with greys and browns. Common Sandpiper.

IQ. 1·4 ; 1 ; Y. Greenish buff, spotted with browns and lilac. Killdeer Plover.

IR. 1·4 ; 1 ; Y. Olive, clouded with reds, browns, and greys. Ringed Plover.

IS. 1·4 ; 1 ; Z. Pale green. Little Grebe.

IT. 1·4 ; 1·1 ; U. Yellowish brown. Partridge.

JA. 1·4 ; 1·1 ; W. Greyish, spotted with browns and lilac. Corn Crake.

JB. 1·4 ; 1·1 ; X. White. Little Owl.

JC. 1·4 ; 1·15 ; X. White. Roller.

JD. 1·44 ; 1·15 ; X. White. Rock Dove.

JE. 1·45 ; 1 ; Y. Pale olive, spotted brown and grey. Buff-breasted Sandpiper.

JF. 1·45 ; 1·15 ; X. Pale red, with darker spots. Lesser Kestrel.

JG. 1·45 ; 1·15 ; X. White. Stock Dove.

JH. 1·5 ; 1 ; V. Buff, spotted light and dark brown. Purple Sandpiper.

JI. 1·5 ; 1 ; V. Whitish green, with darker green spots Jackdaw.

JJ. 1·5 ; 1 ; W. White. Passenger Pigeon.

JK. 1·5 ; 1·1 ; V. Olive, spotted reddish brown. Jack Snipe.

JL. 1·5 ; 1·1 ; Y. Buffish green, spotted browns and greys. Green Sandpiper.

JM. 1·5 ; 1·1 ; Y. Olive, blotched red and brown. Wood Sand-piper.

JN. 1·5 ; 1·2 ; X. Reddish brown, finely freckled. Merlin.

JO. 1·5 ; 1·3 ; U. Greenish blue. Squacco Heron.

JP. 1·5 ; 1·3 ; X. White. Short-eared Owl.

JQ. 1·55 ; 1 ; Y. Greenish grey, marbled with browns. Pectoral Sandpiper.

JR. 1·55 ; 1·05 ; V. Light brown, spotted brown. Alpine Chough.

JS. 1·55 ; 1·15 ; X. Pale red, finely freckled and blotched. Red-footed Falcon.

JT. 1·55 ; 1·2 ; X. Pearl grey, blotched reddish brown. Sparrow Hawk.

KA. 1·55 ; 1·2 ; U. Buffish brown, with light brown spots. Red-legged Partridge.

KB. 1·6 ; 1·1 ; V. Buff, spotted brown and olive. Turnstone.

KC. 1·6 ; 1·1 ; V. Greenish grey, spotted reddish brown. Snipe.

KD. 1·6 ; 1·1 ; V. Light brown, clouded with darker browns. Arctic Tern.

KE.	1·6 ; 1·1 ;	V.	Malachite green, with darker spots. Rook.
KF.	1·6 ; 1·1 ;	Y.	Greenish grey, mottled with browns. Whiskered Tern.
KG.	1·6 ; 1·15 ;	V.	Brownish green, clouded brown. Hooded Crow.
KH.	1·6 ; 1·15 ;	U.	Creamy white, lightly spotted. Chough.
KI.	1·6 ; 1·2 ;	U.	Buff, spotted with browns. Little Gull.
KJ.	1·6 ; 1·2 ;	U.	White. Bulwer's Petrel.
KK.	1·6 ; 1·2 ;	X.	Grey, freckled and spotted reddish brown. Kestrel.
KL.	1·6 ; 1·2 ;	X.	White. Hawk Owl.
KM.	1·6 ; 1·25 ;	X.	Greenish white. Montagu's Harrier.
KN.	1·6 ; 1.25 ;	X.	White. Ring Dove.
KO.	1·6 ; 1·3 ;	X.	Cream coloured. American Blue-winged Teal
KP.	1·6 ; 1·3 ;	X.	White. Long-eared Owl.
KQ.	1·6 ; 1·3 ;	X.	White, thickly freckled reddish brown. Hobby.
KR.	1·65 ; 1·2 ;	W.	Greenish, spotted with browns. Carrion Crow.
KS.	1·7 ; 1·1 ;	Y.	Light brown, spotted reddish brown. Yellow-shank.
KT.	1·7 ; 1·1 ;	Y.	Olive, marbled browns and greys. Dotterel.
LA.	1·7 ; 1·15 ;	U.	Pale olive, spotted with brown. Pallas's Sand Grouse.
LB.	1·7 ; 1·15 ;	Y.	Buff, lightly speckled brown and grey. Red-breasted Snipe.
LC.	1·7 ; 1·2 ;	U.	Buff, blotched and clouded brown and grey. Roseate Tern.
LD.	1·7 ; 1·25 ;	U.	White. Barn Owl.
LE.	1·7 ; 1·3 ;	U.	Greenish blue. Little Egret.
LF.	1·7 ; 1·3 ;	V.	Buff. Teal.
LG.	1·75 ; 1·15 ;	Z.	Greenish white. Sclavonian Grebe.
LH.	1·75 ; 1·2 ;	U.	Olive, blotched purplish brown and grey. Tern.
LI.	1·75 ; 1·2 ;	V.	Buff, blotched with chocolate. Ptarmigan.
LJ.	1·75 ; 1·2 ;	X.	Light brown, spotted light red. Moorhen.
LK.	1·75 ; 1·2 ;	Y.	Olive, spotted red and brown. Ruff.
LL.	1·75 ; 1·25 ;	Y.	Olive, blotched and clouded with brown. Great Snipe.
LM.	1·75 ; 1·3 ;	U.	Green, darker when held up to light. Buff-backed Heron.
LN.	1·75 ; 1·3 ;	V.	Buff, speckled grey and brown. Bartram's Sandpiper.
LO.	1·75 ; 1·32 ;	U.	Buff, spotted purplish brown. Red Grouse.
LP.	1·75 ; 1·35 ;	U.	Buff, spotted light red and pale brown. Wood-cock.
LQ.	1·75 ; 1·45 ;	U.	Whitish blue, green when held up to light. Hen Harrier.
LR.	1·8 ; 1·2 ;	V.	Light brown, with grey spots. Sabine's Gull.
LS.	1·8 ; 1·2 ;	W.	Buff, marked brown and grey. Black-winged Stilt.
LT.	1·8 ; 1·25 ;	Y.	Buff, spotted and blotched rich dark brown. Redshank.
MA.	1·8 ; 1·3 ;	X.	Buff. Garganey.
MB.	1·8 ; 1·3 ;	Y.	Olive, thickly blotched dark brown and grey. Lapwing.

MC. 1·8 ; 1·4 ; U. Greenish blue. Night Heron.
MD. 1·8 ; 1·4 ; U. Olive green. Pheasant.
ME. 1·8 ; 1·5 ; X. White. Tawny Owl.
MF. 1·85 ; 1·25 ; U. Greenish blue. Little Auk.
MG. 1·9 ; 1·1 ; Z. Green. Eared Grebe.
MH. 1·9 ; 1·3 ; W. Pale buff, blotched brown and grey. Lesser Sooty Tern.
MI. 1·9 ; 1·3 ; Y. Buff, blotched with reddish brown. Lesser Golden Plover.
MJ. 1·9 ; 1·3 ; Y. Greenish, spotted sepia and lilac. Spotted Redshank.
MK. 1·9 ; 1·4 ; U. Buff, spotted brown and grey. Mediterranean Black-headed Gull.
ML. 1·95 ; 1·5 ; X. Pale blue, spotted reddish brown. Swallow-tailed Kite.
MM. 2 ; 1·3 ; W. Greenish, lightly spotted olive brown. Raven.
MN. 2 ; 1·3 ; Z. Pale green. Red-necked Grebe.
MO. 2 ; 1·35 ; Y. Light brown, spotted browns and greys. Greenshank.
MP. 2 ; 1·4 ; U. Buff, spotted with reddish brown. Black Grouse.
MQ. 2 ; 1·4 ; U. Buff, marked with reddish and grey. Gull-billed Tern.
MR. 2 ; 1·4 ; U. Greenish grey. Buffel-headed Duck.
MS. 2 ; 1·4 ; U. Light brown, spotted brown, red, and grey. Bonaparte's Gull.
MT. 2 ; 1·4 ; U. Olive green, blotched brown and grey. Black-headed Gull.
NA. 2 ; 1·4 ; V. Buff, blotched purplish brown and grey. Avocet.
NB. 2 ; 1·4 ; Y. Greenish grey, spotted purplish brown. Grey Plover.
NC. 2 ; 1·45 ; U. Buff. Wigeon.
ND. 2 ; 1·45 ; U. Cream, spotted with browns. Sooty Tern.
NE. 2 ; 1·5 ; U. Sandy brown. Bittern.
NF. 2 ; 1·5 ; U. Pale olive. American Bittern.
NG. 2 ; 1·5 ; W. Buff. White-eyed Duck.
NH. 2 ; 1·5 ; X. Greenish buff. Shoveller.
NI. 2 ; 1·51 ; X. Creamy buff. Smew.
NJ. 2 ; 1·6 ; X. Cream, spotted and capped reddish brown. Honey Buzzard.
NK. 2 ; 1·7 ; X. White. Hooded Merganser.
NL. 2·05 ; 1·5 ; U. Greenish white. Marsh Harrier.
NM. 2·1 ; 1·4 ; U. Buff, spotted dark brown. Coot.
NN. 2·1 ; 1·4 ; U. Buffish white, marked with browns. Sandwich Tern.
NO. 2·1 ; 1·4 ; U. Greenish blue. Glossy Ibis.
NP. 2·1 ; 1·4 ; W. Cream, spotted lightly with brown. Noddy.
NQ. 2·1 ; 1·4 ; Y. Buff, spotted with browns and grey. Eskimo Curlew.
NR. 2·1 ; 1·4 ; Y. Light brown, spotted with purples and greys. Golden Plover.
NS. 2·1 ; 1·5 ; U. Greenish buff. Pintail.

NT.	2·1 ;	1·5 ; U.	Olive, clouded with browns. Long-tailed Skua.
OA.	2·1 ;	1·5 ; V.	Pale buff, spotted and streaked brown and grey. Stone Curlew.
OB.	2·1 ;	1·5 ; W.	Pale olive. Long-tailed Duck.
OC.	2·1 ;	1·5 ; W.	Light brown. Gadwall.
OD.	2·1 ;	1·5 ; Y.	Olive, spotted brown and grey. Black-tailed Godwit.
OE.	2·1 ;	1·55 ; U.	Brownish red, freckled darker red. Peregrine Falcon.
OF.	2·1 ;	1·7 ; X.	Grey, clouded with brown, green when held to light. Buzzard.
OG.	2·15 ;	1·6 ; U.	Light brown, spotted reddish brown. Caper-caillie.
OH.	2·15 ;	1·65 ; U.	Pale buff, freckled and spotted with browns. Black Kite.
OI.	2·2 ;	1·4 ; Z.	Green. Great Crested Grebe.
OJ.	2·2 ;	1·4 ; Z.	White. Dusky Shearwater.
OK.	2·2 ;	1·45 ; Y.	Olive, lightly spotted with brown and grey. Bar-tailed Godwit.
OL.	2·2 ;	1·5 ; U.	Pale buff. American Wigeon.
OM.	2·2 ;	1·5 ; U.	Buff, streaked with purplish brown. Oyster-catcher.
ON.	2·2 ;	1·5 ; W.	Greenish blue. Purple Heron.
OO.	2·2 ;	1·6 ; U.	Buff. Harlequin Duck.
OP.	2·2 ;	1·6 ; U.	Greenish brown, spotted red, brown, and black. Kittiwake.
OQ.	2·2 ;	1·6 ; U.	Olive green, mottled and speckled brown and grey. Little Bustard.
OR.	2·2 ;	1·7 ; V.	Olive brown, spotted dark brown and grey. Gull.
OS.	2·2 ;	1·75 ; U.	Greyish, clouded with brown. Rough-legged Buzzard.
OT.	2·25 ;	1·8 ; U.	Light red, spotted dark red. Gyr, Iceland and Greenland Falcons.
PA.	2·3 ;	1·5 ; W.	Pale grey. Steller's Eider.
PB.	2·3 ;	1·6 ; U.	Buff. Mallard.
PC.	2·3 ;	1·6 ; U.	Brownish green. Red-crested Pochard.
PD.	2·3 ;	1·6 ; U.	Pale green. Goldeneye.
PE.	2·3 ;	1·6 ; U.	Greenish, clouded and spotted brown. Black Guillemot.
PF.	2·3 ;	1·6 ; W.	Pale buff. Tufted Duck.
PG.	2·3 ;	1·65 ; V.	Olive, spotted dark brown. Pomatorhine Skua.
PH.	2·3 ;	1·7 ; U.	Pale green, with faint red spots. American Gos Hawk.
PI.	2·3 ;	1·7 ; W.	Greenish buff. Pochard.
PJ.	2·3 ;	1·7 ; Y.	Olive green, spotted reddish brown and grey. Whimbrel.
PK.	2·3 ;	1·75 ; U.	Greenish white, blotched with browns. Kite.
PL.	2·3 ;	1·8 ; Z.	White. Snowy Owl.
PM.	2·4 ;	1·6 ; Y.	Olive, spotted brown and grey. Richardson's Skua.
PN.	2·4 ;	1·7 ; U.	Buff, spotted grey and brown. Puffin.

PO.	2·4 ;	1·7 ;	V.	White. Manx Shearwater.
PP.	2·4 ;	1·8 ;	U.	Greenish white. Gos Hawk.
PQ.	2·45 ;	1·7 ;	U.	Buff, spotted with browns. Ivory Gull.
PR.	2.45 ;	1·8 ;	U.	White, blotched with browns and greys. Osprey.
PS.	2·5 ;	1·5 ;	W.	White, emerald green when held to light. Shag.
PT.	2·5 ;	1·6 ;	W.	Greenish blue. Heron.
QA.	2·5 ;	1·7 ;	U.	Pale buff. Scaup.
QB.	2·5 ;	1·7 ;	U.	White, spotted reddish brown. Spoonbill.
QC.	2·5 ;	1·7 ;	V.	Buff. Surf Scoter.
QD.	2·5 ;	1·7 ;	W.	Greenish blue. Great White Heron.
QE.	2·5 ;	1·75 ;	V.	Buff, spotted brown and grey. Caspian Tern.
QF.	2·5 ;	1·8 ;	V.	Pale greenish yellow. King Eider.
QG.	2·5 ;	1·85 ;	U.	White. Eagle Owl.
QH.	2·5 ;	2·1 ;	X.	Greyish, streaked and spotted reddish brown. Lesser Spotted Eagle.
QI.	2·55 ;	1·85 ;	U.	Pale buff, spotted browns and greys. Macqueen's Bustard.
QJ.	2·55 ;	2 ;	X.	Cream and brownish red. Egyptian Vulture.
QK.	2·6 ;	1·7 ;	U.	Sandy buff. Scoter.
QL.	2·6 ;	1·7 ;	U.	White. Sooty Shearwater.
QM.	2·6 ;	1·7 ;	W.	Pale buff. Red-breasted Merganser.
QN.	2·6 ;	1·8 ;	U.	Greenish, blotched brown and grey. Lesser Black-backed Gull.
QO.	2·6 ;	1·8 ;	U.	Pale olive, blotched light brown and grey. Curlew.
QP.	2·6 ;	1·9 ;	U.	Pale buff. Sheld Duck.
QQ.	2·6 ;	1·9 ;	U.	White, green when held to light. Black Stork.
QR.	2·6 ;	2 ;	V.	Pale buff. Ruddy Sheld Duck.
QS.	2·7 ;	1·7 ;	W.	White, green when held to light. Cormorant.
QT.	2·7 ;	1·8 ;	U.	Greenish white. Red-breasted Goose.
RA.	2·7 ;	1·85 ;	X.	White. Goosander.
RB.	2·7 ;	1·9 ;	U.	White. Brent Goose.
RC.	2·75 ;	1·8 ;	U.	Coffee brown, blotched purplish brown. Iceland Gull.
RD.	2·8 ;	1·8 ;	W.	Buff, marbled and spotted purplish brown. Razorbill.
RE.	2·8 ;	1·9 ;	U.	White. Great Shearwater.
RF.	2·8 ;	1·9 ;	V.	Pale buff. Velvet Scoter.
RG.	2·8 ;	2 ;	U.	Olive green, spotted grey and brown. Herring Gull.
RH.	2·8 ;	2 ;	V.	Olive brown, spotted brown and grey. Great Skua.
RI.	2·8 ;	2·2 ;	U.	White, green when held to light. Sea Eagle.
RJ.	2·9 ;	2 ;	U.	Chalky white. Fulmar.
RK.	2·9 ;	2 ;	U.	Creamy white. White-fronted Goose.
RL.	2·9 ;	2 ;	U.	White. Barnacle Goose.
RM.	2·9 ;	2 ;	V.	White. Lesser White-fronted Goose.
RN.	2·9 ;	2 ;	W.	White, yellow when held to light. White Stork.
RO.	3 ;	1·8 ;	W.	Olive, spotted green and brown. Red-throated Diver.
RP.	3 ;	2 ;	V.	Buff, spotted light and dark brown. Great Black-backed Gull.

RQ.   3 ;   2 ; Z.   Pale bluish green. Gannet.

RR.   3 ; 2·1 ; U.   Buff, streaked purple and brown. Great Black-headed Gull.

RS.   3 ; 2·3 ; V.   Olive, clouded with light brown. Great Bustard.

RT.   3 ; 2·5 ; X.   White, or white freckled reddish brown, green when held to light. Golden Eagle.

SA.   3·1 ;   2 ; V.   Cream, spotted brown and grey. Glaucous Gull.

SB.   3·1 ;   2 ; V.   Greenish buff. Eider Duck.

SC.   3·1 ; 2·1 ; V.   Creamy white. Pink-footed Goose.

SD.   3·1 ; 2·1 ; V.   Chalky white. Snow Goose.

SE.   3·2 ;   2 ; W.   Green or buff, plain or blotched with browns. Guillemot.

SF.   3·2 ; 2·1 ; W.   Creamy white. Bean Goose.

SG.   3·3 ;   2 ; W.   Chocolate, with blackish spots. Black-throated Diver.

SH.   3·3 ; 2·1 ; W.   Buff, mottled with greys and light browns. Demoiselle Crane.

SI.   3·5 ; 2·4 ; W.   Chalky white. Grey Lag Goose.

SJ.   3·5 ; 2·4 ; W.   Pinkish white. Canada Goose.

SK.   3·5 ; 2·5 ; W.   Olive brown, spotted brown. Yellow-billed Diver.

SL.   3·6 ; 2·2 ; W.   White. Flamingo.

SM.   3·6 ; 2·3 ; W.   Olive, spotted dark brown. Great Northern Diver.

SN.   3·7 ; 2·5 ; W.   Buff, mottled grey and light brown. Crane.

SO.   3·8 ; 2·9 ; U.   White, spotted brown at one end. Griffon Vulture.

SP.   4 ; 2·6 ; W.   Creamy white. Bewick's Swan.

SQ.   4·5 ; 2·8 ; W.   Creamy white. Hooper Swan.

SR.   4·5 ; 2·9 ; W.   Pale green. Mute Swan.

SS.   4·9 ;   3 ; W.   White or buff, blotched and clouded brown. Great Auk.

First published as *Our Country's Birds* by Simpkin, Marshall, Hamilton, Kent & Co. Ltd.

This edition published 1988 by Omega Books Ltd, 14 Greville Street, Hatton Garden, London EC1.

ISBN 1-85007-024 5

Printed and bound in Spain by Gráficas Estella, Navarra.